Practice*Planners*®

Arthur E. Jongsma, Jr., Series Editor

Helping therapists help their clients...

Over 250,000 Practice*Planners*® sold...

WILEY

Treatment Planners cover all the necessary elements for developing formal treatment plans, including detailed problem definitions, long-term goals, short-term objectives, therapeutic interventions, and DSM-IV™ diagnoses.

❏ **The Complete Adult Psychotherapy Treatment Planner,** Third Edition
  0-471-27113-6 / $49.95

❏ **The Child Psychotherapy Treatment Planner,** Third Edition
  0-471-27050-4 / $49.95

❏ **The Adolescent Psychotherapy Treatment Planner,** Third Edition
  0-471-27049-0 / $49.95

❏ **The Addiction Treatment Planner,** Second Edition
  0-471-41814-5 / $49.95

❏ **The Couples Psychotherapy Treatment Planner**
  0-471-24711-1 / $49.95

❏ **The Group Therapy Treatment Planner**
  0-471-37449-0 / $49.95

❏ **The Family Therapy Treatment Planner**
  0-471-34768-X / $49.95

❏ **The Older Adult Psychotherapy Treatment Planner**
  0-471-29574-4 / $49.95

❏ **The Employee Assistance (EAP) Treatment Planner**
  0-471-24709-X / $49.95

❏ **The Gay and Lesbian Psychotherapy Treatment Planner**
  0-471-35080-X / $49.95

❏ **The Crisis Counseling and Traumatic Events Treatment Planner**
  0-471-39587-0 / $49.95

❏ **The Social Work and Human Services Treatment Planner**
  0-471-37741-4 / $49.95

❏ **The Continuum of Care Treatment Planner**
  0-471-19568-5 / $49.95

❏ **The Behavioral Medicine Treatment Planner**
  0-471-31923-6 / $49.95

❏ **The Mental Retardation and Developmental Disability Treatment Planner**
  0-471-38253-1 / $49.95

❏ **The Special Education Treatment Planner**
  0-471-38872-6 / $49.95

❏ **The Severe and Persistent Mental Illness Treatment Planner**
  0-471-35945-9 / $49.95

❏ **The Personality Disorders Treatment Planner**
  0-471-39403-3 / $49.95

❏ **The Rehabilitation Psychology Treatment Planner**
  0-471-35178-4 / $49.95

❏ **The Pastoral Counseling Treatment Planner**
  0-471-25416-9 / $49.95

❏ **The Juvenile Justice and Residential Care Treatment Planner**
  0-471-43320-9 / $49.95

❏ **The Psychiatric Evaluation & Psychopharmacology Treatment Planner**
  0-471-43322-5 / $49.95 (available 8/03)

❏ **The Probation and Parole Treatment Planner**
  0-471-20244-4 / $49.95 (available 3/03)

❏ **The School Counseling and School Social Work Treatment Planner**
  0-471-08496-4 / $49.95

❏ **The Sexual Abuse Victim and Sexual Offender Treatment Planner**
  0-471-21979-7 / $49.95

Progress Notes Planners contain complete prewritten progress notes for each presenting problem in the companion Treatment Planners.

❏ **The Adult Psychotherapy Progress Notes Planner**
  0-471-34763-9 / $49.95

❏ **The Adolescent Psychotherapy Progress Notes Planner**
  0-471-38104-7 / $49.95

❏ **The Child Psychotherapy Progress Notes Planner**
  0-471-38102-0 / $49.95

❏ **The Addiction Progress Notes Planner**
  0-471-10330-6 / $49.95

❏ **The Severe and Persistent Mental Illness Progress Notes Planner**
  0-471-21986-X / $49.95

Name_____

Affiliation_____

Address_____

City/State/Zip_____

Phone/Fax_____

E-mail_____

On the web: practiceplanners.wiley.com

*Prices subject to change without notice.

To order, call 1-800-225-5945
(Please refer to promo #1-4019 when ordering.)

Or send this page with payment* to:
John Wiley & Sons, Inc., Attn: J. Knott
111 River Street, Hoboken, NJ 07030

❏ Check enclosed   ❏ Visa   ❏ MasterCard   ❏ American Express
Card #_____

Expiration Date_____

Signature_____

*Please add your local sales tax to all orders.

The Complete Adult
Psychotherapy Treatment Planner

Practice*Planners*® Series

Treatment Planners

The Complete Adult Psychotherapy Treatment Planner, 3e
The Child Psychotherapy Treatment Planner, 3e
The Adolescent Psychotherapy Treatment Planner, 3e
The Continuum of Care Treatment Planner
The Couples Psychotherapy Treatment Planner
The Employee Assistance Treatment Planner
The Pastoral Counseling Treatment Planner
The Older Adult Psychotherapy Treatment Planner
The Behavioral Medicine Treatment Planner
The Group Therapy Treatment Planner
The Gay and Lesbian Psychotherapy Treatment Planner
The Family Therapy Treatment Planner
The Severe and Persistent Mental Illness Treatment Planner
The Mental Retardation and Developmental Disability Treatment Planner
The Social Work and Human Services Treatment Planner
The Crisis Counseling and Traumatic Events Treatment Planner
The Personality Disorders Treatment Planner
The Rehabilitation Psychology Treatment Planner
The Addiction Treatment Planner, 2e
The Special Education Treatment Planner
The Juvenile Justice and Residential Care Treatment Planner
The School Counseling and School Social Work Treatment Planner
The Sexual Abuse Victim and Sexual Offender Treatment Planner
The Probation and Parole Treatment Planner

Progress Notes Planners

The Child Psychotherapy Progress Notes Planner
The Adolescent Psychotherapy Progress Notes Planner
The Adult Psychotherapy Progress Notes Planner
The Addiction Progress Notes Planner
The Severe and Persistent Mental Illness Progress Notes Planner

Homework Planners

Brief Therapy Homework Planner
Brief Couples Therapy Homework Planner
Chemical Dependence Treatment Homework Planner
Brief Child Therapy Homework Planner
Brief Adolescent Therapy Homework Planner
Brief Employee Assistance Homework Planner
Brief Family Therapy Homework Planner
Grief Counseling Homework Planner
Group Therapy Homework Planner
Divorce Counseling Homework Planner
School Counseling and School Social Work Homework Planner
Child Therapy Activity and Homework Planner
Addiction Treatment Homework Planner, Second Edition

Client Education Handout Planners

Adult Client Education Handout Planner
Child and Adolescent Client Education Handout Planner
Couples and Family Client Education Handout Planner

Documentation Sourcebooks

The Clinical Documentation Sourcebook
The Forensic Documentation Sourcebook
The Psychotherapy Documentation Primer
The Chemical Dependence Treatment Documentation Sourcebook
The Clinical Child Documentation Sourcebook
The Couple and Family Clinical Documentation Sourcebook
The Clinical Documentation Sourcebook, 2e
The Continuum of Care Clinical Documentation Sourcebook

PracticePlanners®

Arthur E. Jongsma, Jr., Series Editor

The Complete Adult Psychotherapy Treatment Planner

Third Edition

Arthur E. Jongsma, Jr.

L. Mark Peterson

JOHN WILEY & SONS, INC.

Copyright © 2003 by Arthur E. Jongsma, Jr. and L. Mark Peterson. All rights reserved.

Published by John Wiley & Sons, Inc., Hoboken, New Jersey.
Published simultaneously in Canada.

Library of Congress Cataloging-in-Publication Data:

Jongsma, Arthur E., 1943–
  The complete adult psychotherapy treatment planner / Arthur E. Jongsma, Jr.,
L. Mark Peterson.
      p. cm. — (Practice planners)
Includes bibliographical references and index.
    ISBN 0-471-27113-6 (pbk. : alk. paper)
      1. Mental illness—Treatment—Planning—Handbooks, manuals, etc. 2. Psychiatric
records—Handbooks, manuals, etc. I. Peterson, L. Mark. II. Title. III. Series.
    RC480.5 .J664 2002
    616.89'1—dc21   2002151336

Printed in the United States of America

10 9 8 7 6 5 4 3

We dedicate this book to our most influential
teachers and mentors early in our professional journey:

Dr. Solomon E. Feldman
Dr. Richard A. Westmaas
Dr. Richard Brown
Dr. Jack Carr

CONTENTS

PRACTICE*PLANNERS*® SERIES PREFACE

The practice of psychotherapy has a dimension that did not exist 30, 20, or even 15 years ago—accountability. Treatment programs, public agencies, clinics, and even group and solo practitioners must now justify the treatment of patients to outside review entities that control the payment of fees. This development has resulted in an explosion of paperwork.

Clinicians must now document what has been done in treatment, what is planned for the future, and what the anticipated outcomes of the interventions are. The books and software in this Practice*Planners* series are designed to help practitioners fulfill these documentation requirements efficiently and professionally.

The Practice*Planners* series is growing rapidly. It now includes not only the original *Complete Adult Psychotherapy Treatment Planner,* third edition; *The Child Psychotherapy Treatment Planner,* third edition, and *The Adolescent Psychotherapy Treatment Planner,* third edition, but also Treatment Planners targeted to specialty areas of practice, including: addictions, juvenile justice/residential care, couples therapy, employee assistance, behavioral medicine, therapy with older adults, pastoral counseling, family therapy, group therapy, neuropsychology, therapy with gays and lesbians, special education, school counseling, and more.

Several of the Treatment Planner books now have companion Progress Notes Planners (e.g., Adult, Adolescent, Child, Addictions, Severe and Persistent Mental Illness, and Couples). More of these planners that provide a menu of progress statements that elaborate on the client's symptom presentation and the provider's therapeutic intervention are in production. Each Progress Notes Planner statement is directly integrated with "Behavioral Definitions" and "Therapeutic Interventions" items from the companion Treatment Planner.

The list of therapeutic Homework Planners is also growing from the original Brief Therapy Homework for adults to Adolescent, Child, Couples, Group, Family, Addiction, Divorce, Grief, Employee Assistance, and School Counseling/School Social Work Homework Planners. Each of these books can be used alone or in conjunction with their companion Treatment Planner. Homework assignments are designed around each presenting problem (e.g., Anxiety, Depression, Chemical Dependence, Anger Management, Panic, Eating Disorders) that is the focus of a chapter in its corresponding Treatment Planner.

Client Education Handout Planners, a new branch in the series, provides brochures and handouts to help educate and inform adult, child, adolescent, couples, and family clients on a myriad of mental health issues, as well as life skills techniques. Handouts are included on CD-ROMs and are ideal for use in waiting rooms, at presentations, or as newsletters.

In addition, the series also includes Thera*Scribe*®, the latest version of the popular treatment planning, clinical record-keeping software. Thera*Scribe* allows the user to import the data from any of the Treatment Planner, Progress Notes Planner, or Homework Planner books into the software's expandable database. Then the point-and-click method can create a detailed, neatly organized, individualized, and customized treatment plan along with optional integrated progress notes and homework assignments.

Adjunctive books, such as *The Psychotherapy Documentation Primer* and *Clinical, Forensic, Child, Couples* and *Family, Continuum of Care,* and *Chemical Dependence Documentation Sourcebook* contain forms and resources to aid the mental health practice management. The goal of the series is to provide practitioners with the resources they need in order to provide high-quality care in the era of accountability—or, to put it simply, we seek to help you spend more time on patients, and less time on paperwork.

ARTHUR E. JONGSMA, JR.
Grand Rapids, Michigan

INTRODUCTION

Since the early 1960s, formalized treatment planning has gradually become a vital aspect of the health care delivery system, whether it is treatment related to physical health, mental health, child welfare, or substance abuse. What started in the medical sector in the 1960s spread into the mental health sector in the 1970s as clinics, psychiatric hospitals, agencies, and so on began to seek accreditation from bodies such as the Joint Commission on Accreditation of Healthcare Organizations (JCAHO) to qualify for third-party reimbursements. With the advent of managed care in the 1980s, treatment planning took on even greater importance. Managed care systems required clinicians to move rapidly from problem assessment to the formulation and implementation of the treatment plan. The goal of most managed care companies is to expedite the treatment process by encouraging the client and treatment provider to focus on identifying and changing behavioral problems as quickly as possible. Treatment plans must be specific as to the presenting problems, behaviorally defined symptoms, treatment goals and objectives, and interventions. Treatment plans must be individualized to meet the client's needs and goals, and the observable objectives must allow for setting milestones that can be used to chart the client's progress. Pressure from third-party payers, accrediting agencies, and other outside parties has increased the need for clinicians to produce effective, high-quality treatment plans in a short time frame. However, many mental health providers have little experience in treatment plan development. Our purpose in writing this book is to clarify, simplify, and accelerate the treatment planning process.

PLANNER FOCUS

The Complete Adult Psychotherapy Treatment Planner offers a menu of statements that can be included in outpatient and inpatient treatment plans for adults over age 18. The objectives and interventions suggested are not focused on any one treatment modality. Instead, the items reflect an eclectic approach of family therapy, individual therapy, pharmacotherapy, insight orientation, cognitive and behavioral techniques, and others. The clinician may select items from the menu that best fit their therapeutic approach and the client's individual strengths and needs.

This third edition of *The Complete Adult Psychotherapy Treatment Planner* contains several content changes compared to the second edition including:

- Three new presenting chapters have been included: Parenting, Phase of Life Problems, and Sexual Identity Confusion.
- Refinements to previous treatment plan statements—each item from the second edition was carefully reviewed to clarify the language, reduce redundancies, and sharpen the focus of interventions coordinated with objectives.
- An additional sample treatment plan revised into more measurable terms illustrates how to modify a treatment plan to include more quantifiable language.
- An appendix with a chapter revised into measurable, quantifiable language.

The new Appendix A contains the Borderline Personality chapter, which has been revised into more measurable, quantifiable language than in previous editions. In today's clinical-economic marketplaces of both managed care/third-party payors and accrediting bodies—JCAHO, NCQA, and CARF—there is an increased emphasis on behaviorally observable and/or quantifiable aspects of treatment plans. Among the reasons for this is a general and national movement toward even shorter stays in inpatient facilities (public and private hospitals, and residential facilities) and briefer managed outpatient treatment, with the focus on very specific symptom resolution. If you are experiencing such pressure, you may need to alter our Treatment Planner observable behavioral criteria into language that is more measurable and quantifiable.

Clinicians may want to look for the opportunity to craft measurable/quantifiable aspects of the patient's behaviors into their treatment plans. You may introduce measurability at the symptomatic level (e.g., Behavioral Definitions) and/or at the treatment outcome level (e.g., Short-Term Objectives). Behavioral Definition terms such as *repeated, frequent, tendency, pattern, consistent, excessive, high-level, persistent, displays, heightened, recurrent,* and the like, and even words like *verbalizes, displays, demonstrates, refuses, unable, avoids, seeks, difficulty, increasing,* or *declining* can all have frequencies or circumstances added to quantify the item. For example, the Definition item "Verbalizes having suicidal ideation" can be made more quantifiably measurable by changing it to "Verbalizes having suicidal ideation once to twice daily for the last two weeks."

Clinicians may add aspects of severity to symptom Definition statements, in addition to frequency, to introduce greater measurability. For example, "Verbalizes having sad thoughts four to five times daily for the last two weeks, and on a scale from 1 to 10 (10 being the worst), were judged to be at an 8." Or, alternatively, the clinician may list quantified psychometric data as a criterion measure, such as scores from symptom screening instruments such as the BPRS, BDI, Ham-D, BSI, SCL-90-R, or GAF. This helps in reducing subjectivity.

The Short-Term Objective language found in the Treatment Planner can also be modified to follow the more quantified approach; thus "Engage in physical and recreational activities that reflect increased energy and interest" becomes "Engage in physical and recreational activities that reflect increased energy and interest, at least five times per shift within one week's time (by 1/20/2004)." Also, "Verbally express an understanding of the relationship between depressed mood and repression of sadness and anger" becomes "Verbally express an understanding of the relationship between depressed mood and repression of sadness and anger (by 1/18/2004)."

HOW TO DEVELOP A TREATMENT PLAN

The process of developing a treatment plan involves a logical series of steps that build on each other much like constructing a house. The foundation of any effective treatment plan is the data gathered in a thorough biopsychosocial assessment. As the client presents himself or herself for treatment, the clinician must sensitively listen to and understand what the client struggles with in terms of family-of-origin issues, current stressors, emotional status, social network, physical health, coping skills, interpersonal conflicts, self-esteem, and so on. Assessment data may be gathered from a social history, physical exam, clinical interview, psychological testing, or contact with a client's significant others. The integration of the data by the clinician or the multidisciplinary treatment team members is critical for understanding the client, as is an awareness of the basis of the client's struggle. We have identified six specific steps for developing an effective treatment plan based on the assessment data.

STEP ONE: PROBLEM SELECTION

Although the client may discuss a variety of issues during the assessment, the clinician must ferret out the most significant problems on which to focus the treatment process. Usually a *primary* problem will surface, and *secondary* problems may also be evident. Some *other* problems may have to be set aside as not urgent enough to require treatment at this time. An effective treatment plan can only deal with a few selected problems or treatment will lose its direction. This Planner offers 42 problems from which to select those that most accurately represent your client's presenting issues.

As the problems to be selected become clear to the clinician or the treatment team, it is important to include opinions from the client as to his or her prioritization of issues for which help is being sought. A client's motivation to participate in and cooperate with the treatment process depends, to some extent, on the degree to which treatment addresses his or her greatest needs.

STEP TWO: PROBLEM DEFINITION

Each individual client presents with unique nuances as to how a problem behaviorally reveals itself in his or her life. Therefore, each problem that is selected for treatment focus requires a specific definition about how it is evidenced in the particular client. The symptom pattern should be associated with diagnostic criteria and codes such as those found in the *Diagnostic and Statistical Manual (DSM-IV-TR)* or the *International Classification of Diseases*. This Planner, following the pattern established by *DSM-IV-TR*, offers such behaviorally specific definition statements to choose from or to serve as a model for your own personally crafted statements. You will find several behavior symptoms or syndromes listed that may characterize one of the 42 presenting problems.

STEP THREE: GOAL DEVELOPMENT

The next step in treatment plan development is to set broad goals for the resolution of the target problem. These statements need not be crafted in measurable terms but can be global, long-term goals that indicate a desired positive outcome to the treatment procedures. The Planner suggests several possible goal statements for each problem, but one statement is all that is required in a treatment plan.

STEP FOUR: OBJECTIVE CONSTRUCTION

In contrast to long-term goals, objectives must be stated in behaviorally measurable language. It must be clear when the client has achieved the established objectives; therefore, vague, subjective objectives are not acceptable. Review agencies (e.g., JCAHO), health maintenance organizations (HMOs), and managed care organizations insist that psychological treatment outcomes be measurable. The objectives presented in this Planner are designed to meet this demand for accountability. Numerous alternatives are presented to allow construction of a variety of treatment plan possibilities for the same presenting problem. The clinician must exercise professional judgment as to which objectives are most appropriate for a given client.

Each objective should be developed as a step toward attaining the broad treatment goal. In essence, objectives can be thought of as a series of steps that, when completed, will result in the achievement of the long-term goal. There should be at least two objectives for each problem, but the clinician may construct as many as are necessary for goal achievement. Target attainment dates may be listed for each objective. New objectives should be added to the plan as the individual's treatment progresses. When all of the necessary objectives have been achieved, the client should have resolved the target problem successfully.

STEP FIVE: INTERVENTION CREATION

Interventions are the actions of the clinician designed to help the client complete the objectives. There should be at least one intervention for every objective. If the client does not accomplish the objective after the initial intervention, new interventions should be added to the plan.

Interventions should be selected on the basis of the client's needs and the treatment provider's full therapeutic repertoire. This Planner contains interventions from a broad range of therapeutic approaches, including cognitive, dynamic, behavioral, pharmacologic, family-oriented, and solution-focused brief therapy. Other interventions may be written by the provider to reflect his or her own training and experience. The addition of new problems, definitions, goals, objectives, and interventions to those found in the Planner is encouraged because doing so adds to the database for future reference and use.

Some suggested interventions listed in the Planner refer to specific books that can be assigned to the client for adjunctive bibliotherapy. Appendix B contains a full bibliographic reference list of these materials. The books are arranged under each problem for which they are appropriate as assigned reading for clients. When a book is used as part of an intervention plan, it should be reviewed with the client after it is read, enhancing the application of the content of the book to the specific client's circumstances. For further information about self-help books, mental health professionals may wish to consult *The Authoritative Guide to Self-Help Books* (1994) by Santrock, Minnett, and Campbell (available from The Guilford Press, New York).

Assigning an intervention to a specific provider is most relevant if the client is being treated by a team in an inpatient, residential, or intensive outpatient setting. Within these settings, personnel other than the primary clinician may be responsible for implementing a specific intervention. Review agencies require that the responsible provider's name be stipulated for every intervention.

STEP SIX: DIAGNOSIS DETERMINATION

The determination of an appropriate diagnosis is based on an evaluation of the client's complete clinical presentation. The clinician must compare the behavioral, cognitive, emotional, and interpersonal symptoms that the client presents with the criteria for diagnosis of a mental illness condition as described in *DSM-IV-TR*. The issue of differential diagnosis is admittedly a difficult one that research has shown to have rather low interrater reliability. Psychologists have also been trained to think more in terms of maladaptive behavior than in disease labels. In spite of these factors, diagnosis is a reality that exists in the world of mental health care, and it is a necessity for third-party reimbursement. (Recently, however, managed care agencies have become more interested in behavioral indices that are exhibited by the client than in the actual diagnosis.) It is the clinician's thorough knowledge of *DSM-IV-TR* criteria and a complete understanding of the client assessment data that contribute to the most reliable, valid diagnosis. An accurate assessment of behavioral indicators will also contribute to more effective treatment planning.

HOW TO USE THIS PLANNER

Our experience has taught us that learning the skills of effective treatment plan writing can be a tedious and difficult process for many clinicians. It is even more stressful to try to develop this expertise when under the pressure of increased client load and short time frames placed on clinicians today by managed care systems. The documentation demands can be overwhelming when we must move quickly from assessment to treatment plan to progress notes. In the process, we must be very specific about how and when objectives can be achieved, and how progress is exhibited in each client. *The Complete Adult Psychotherapy Treatment Planner* was developed as a tool to aid clinicians in writing a treatment plan in a rapid manner that is clear, specific, and highly individualized, according to the following progression:

1. Choose one presenting problem (Step One) you have identified through your assessment process. Locate the corresponding page number for that problem in the Planner's table of contents.
2. Select two or three of the listed behavioral definitions (Step Two) and record them in the appropriate section on your treatment plan form. Feel free to add your own defining statement if you determine that your client's behavioral manifestation of the identified problem is not listed. (Note that while our design for treatment planning is vertical, it will work equally well on plan forms formatted horizontally.)
3. Select a single long-term goal (Step Three) and again write the selection, exactly as it is written in the Planner or in some appropriately modified form, in the corresponding area of your own form.
4. Review the listed objectives for this problem and select the ones that you judge to be clinically indicated for your client (Step Four). Remember, it is recommended that you select at least two objectives for each problem. Add a target date or the number of sessions allocated for the attainment of each objective.
5. Choose relevant interventions (Step Five). The Planner offers suggested interventions related to each objective in the parentheses following the objective statement. But do not limit yourself to those interventions. The entire list is eclectic and may offer options that are more tailored to your theoretical approach or preferred way of working with clients. Also, just as with definitions,

goals, and objectives, there is space allowed for you to enter your own interventions into the Planner. This allows you to refer to these entries when you create a plan around this problem in the future. You will have to assign responsibility to a specific person for implementation of each intervention if the treatment is being carried out by a multidisciplinary team.

6. Several *DSM-IV-TR* diagnoses that are commonly associated with a client who has this problem are listed at the end of each chapter. These diagnoses are meant to be suggestions for clinical consideration. Select a diagnosis listed or assign a more appropriate choice from the *DSM-IV-TR* (Step Six).

Note: To accommodate those practitioners who tend to plan treatment in terms of diagnostic labels rather than presenting problems, Appendix C lists all of the *DSM-IV-TR* diagnoses that have been presented in the various presenting problem chapters as suggestions for consideration. Each diagnosis is followed by the presenting problem that has been associated with that diagnosis. The provider may look up the presenting problems for a selected diagnosis to review definitions, goals, objectives, and interventions that may be appropriate for their clients with that diagnosis.

Congratulations! You should now have a complete, individualized treatment plan that is ready for immediate implementation and presentation to the client. It should resemble the format of the first example, the Sample Standard Treatment Plan. The second example, the Sample Quantitative Treatment Plan, may serve as a better example for you to follow if you choose to revise the standard language of our treatment plan suggestions into more quantifiable terms.

A FINAL NOTE

One important aspect of effective treatment planning is that each plan should be tailored to the individual client's problems and needs. Treatment plans should not be mass-produced, even if clients have similar problems. The individual's strengths and weaknesses, unique stressors, social network, family circumstances, and symptom patterns *must* be considered in developing a treatment strategy. Drawing upon our own years of clinical experience, we have put together a variety of treatment choices. These statements can be combined in thousands of permutations to develop detailed treatment plans. Relying on their own good judgment, clinicians can easily select the statements that are appropriate for the individuals whom they are treating. In addition, we encourage readers to add their own definitions, goals, objectives, and interventions to the existing samples. It is our hope that *The Complete Adult Psychotherapy Treatment Planner,* third edition, will promote effective, creative treatment planning—a process that will ultimately benefit the client, clinician, and mental health community.

SAMPLE STANDARD TREATMENT PLAN

PROBLEM: BORDERLINE PERSONALITY

Definitions: A minor stress leads to extreme emotional reactivity (anger, anxiety, or depression) that usually lasts from a few hours to a few days.

A pattern of intense, chaotic interpersonal relationships.

Recurrent suicidal gestures, threats, or self-mutilating behavior.

Chronic feelings of emptiness and boredom.

Frequent eruptions of intense, inappropriate anger.

Goals: Develop and demonstrate coping skills to deal with mood swings.

Develop and demonstrate anger management skills.

Learn and practice interpersonal relationship skills.

Terminate self-damaging behaviors (such as substance abuse, reckless driving, sexual acting out, binge eating, or suicidal behaviors).

OBJECTIVES

1. Verbalize the situations that can easily trigger feelings of fear, depression, and anger.

2. Identify the negative, distorted cognitions that mediate intense negative emotions.

INTERVENTIONS

1. Explore the client's situations that trigger feelings of fear, depression, and anger.

2. Assign the client to record a daily journal of feelings along with the circumstances that he/she was reacting to; process the journal material to identify triggers for emotional reactivity.

1. Assist the client in identifying the distorted schemas and related automatic thoughts that mediate his/her anxiety response.

2. Require the client to keep a daily record of self-defeating thoughts (e.g., regarding hopelessness, helplessness, worthlessness,

catastrophizing, negatively predicting the future); challenge each thought for accuracy, then replace each dysfunctional thought with one that is positive and self-enhancing.

3. Verbalize realistic, positive self-talk to replace distorted negative messages.

1. Train the client in revising core schema using cognitive restructuring techniques.

2. Reinforce the client's positive, realistic cognitive self-talk that mediates a sense of peace.

3. Assign the client to record instances of successfully using revised, constructive cognitive patterns; process and reinforce positive consequences.

4. Utilize cognitive methods to control impulsive behavior.

1. Teach the client cognitive methods (e.g., thought stoppage, thought substitution, reframing) for gaining and improving control over impulsive actions; encourage implementation in daily life.

5. Verbalize the impact that childhood experiences of abuse, neglect, or abandonment have upon current feelings and relationships.

1. Explore instances of abuse, neglect, or emotional/physical abandonment in the client's childhood; process the feelings associated with these experiences.

2. Reinforce the client's insight into the effect of childhood experiences of neglect or abuse on current urges to react with rage or possessiveness.

6. Verbalize the intense feelings that motivate self-mutilating behavior and

1. Probe the nature and history of the client's self-mutilating behavior.

how those feelings are relieved by such behavior.

2. Interpret the client's self-
   mutilation as an expression
   of the rage and helplessness
   that could not be expressed
   as a child victim of emotional
   abandonment or abuse.

Diagnosis: 301.83   Borderline Personality Disorder

SAMPLE QUANTITATIVE TREATMENT PLAN

PROBLEM: BORDERLINE PERSONALITY

Definitions: The client (MJ) reports that minor stressors lead to extreme emotional reactivity, including becoming angry 2 to 4 times daily, feeling anxious once or twice per week, and feelings of depression at a rate of 3 to 4 times weekly.

MJ reports a pattern of intense, chaotic interpersonal relationships that occurs with 75 percent of her personal and professional relationships, and focally with her mother.

MJ has a history of making suicidal gestures and self-mutilating behavior (superficial cuts on her forearm) that occur once or twice per month, usually occurring after an argument with her mother.

MJ complains of feelings of emptiness and boredom that occur 3 to 7 times per week.

MJ notes having eruptions of intense, inappropriate anger that occur 3 to 4 times per week. The focus of these feelings tends to be directed toward her mother.

Goals: Develop and demonstrate coping skills to deal with mood swings.

Develop and demonstrate anger management skills.

Learn and practice interpersonal relationship skills, especially with her mother.

Terminate self-damaging behaviors of cutting.

OBJECTIVES

1. By 10/05/05 MJ is to identify and verbalize the situations that trigger her feelings of fear, depression, and anger, noting which emotions and the associated

INTERVENTIONS

1. Explore the client's situations that trigger feelings of fear, depression, and anger.

2. Assign the client to record a daily journal of feelings along with the

frequency of occurrence 75 percent of the time for each emotional state experienced.

circumstances that he/she was reacting to; process the journal material to identify triggers for emotional reactivity.

2. By 10/05/05 MJ is to identify and verbalize her negative, distorted cognitions that mediate intense negative emotions, noting which emotions and the associated frequency of occurrence 75 percent of the time.

1. Assist the client in identifying the distorted schemas and related automatic thoughts that mediate his/her anxiety response.

2. Require the client to keep a daily record of self-defeating thoughts (e.g., regarding hopelessness, helplessness, worthlessness, catastrophizing, negatively predicting the future); challenge each thought for accuracy, then replace each dysfunctional thought with one that is positive and self-enhancing.

3. By 10/12/05 MJ is to identify and utilize realistic, positive self-talk to replace distorted negative messages, noting which negative messages and the associated frequency of occurrence 50 percent of the time.

1. Train the client in revising core schema using cognitive restructuring techniques.

2. Reinforce the client's positive, realistic cognitive self-talk that mediates a sense of peace.

3. Assign the client to record instances of successfully using revised, constructive cognitive patterns; process and reinforce positive consequences.

4. By 10/12/05 MJ is to start utilizing cognitive methods to control impulsive behavior 50 percent of the time.

1. Teach the client mediational and self-control strategies (e.g., "stop, look, listen, and think") to delay gratification and inhibit impulses.

2. Assign the client to record instances of successfully implementing "stop, look, listen, and think" to control reactive impulses; process and reinforce the successes.

3. Teach the client cognitive methods (e.g., thought stoppage, thought substitution, reframing) for gaining and improving control over impulsive actions; encourage implementation in daily life.

5. By 10/20/05 MJ is to identify and start to verbalize the impact that childhood experiences of abuse, neglect, or abandonment have upon current feelings and relationships—especially with her mother.

1. Explore instances of abuse, neglect, or emotional/physical abandonment in the client's childhood; process the feelings associated with these experiences.

2. Point out to the client the destructive effect of overcontrol of others and angry resentment when others pull back from relationships. Encourage separation of helpless, desperate feelings of the past from current relationships.

3. Reinforce the client's insight into the effect of childhood experiences of neglect or abuse on current urges to react with rage or possessiveness.

6. By 11/05/05 MJ is to start to verbalize the intense feelings that motivate self-mutilating behavior and how those feelings are relieved by such behavior.

1. Explore instances of abuse, neglect, or emotional/physical abandonment in the client's childhood; process the feelings associated with these experiences.

2. Reinforce the client's insight into the effect of childhood experiences of neglect or abuse on current urges to react with rage or possessiveness.

3. Probe the nature and history of the client's self-mutilating behavior.

4. Interpret the client's self-mutilation as an expression of the rage and helplessness that could not be expressed as a child victim of emotional abandonment or abuse.

Diagnosis: 301.83   Borderline Personality Disorder

ANGER MANAGEMENT

BEHAVIORAL DEFINITIONS

1. History of explosive aggressive outbursts out of proportion to any precipitating stressors, leading to assaultive acts or destruction of property.
2. Overreactive hostility to insignificant irritants.
3. Swift and harsh judgment statements made to or about others.
4. Body language of tense muscles (e.g., clenched fist or jaw), glaring looks, or refusal to make eye contact.
5. Use of passive-aggressive patterns (e.g., social withdrawal, lack of complete or timely compliance in following directions or rules, complaining about authority figures behind their backs, nonparticipation in meeting expected behavioral norms) due to anger.
6. Consistent pattern of challenging or disrespectful attitudes toward authority figures.
7. Use of abusive language.

—. _____
   _____
—. _____
   _____
—. _____
   _____

LONG-TERM GOALS

1. Decrease overall intensity and frequency of angry feelings, and increase ability to recognize and appropriately express angry feelings as they occur.

2. Develop an awareness of current angry behaviors, clarifying origins of and alternatives to aggressive anger.
3. Come to an awareness and acceptance of angry feelings while developing better control and more serenity.
4. Become capable of handling angry feelings in constructive ways that enhance daily functioning.

__. _____
   _____
__. _____
   _____
__. _____
   _____

SHORT-TERM OBJECTIVES

1. Verbally acknowledge frequently feeling angry. (1)

2. Identify targets of and causes for anger. (2, 3, 4)

3. Verbalize increased awareness of anger expression patterns. (5, 6)

THERAPEUTIC INTERVENTIONS

1. Assist the client in coming to the realization that he/she is angry, by reviewing triggers and frequency of angry outbursts.

2. Assign the client to read the book *Of Course You're Angry* (Rosellini and Worden) or *The Angry Book* (Rubin).

3. Ask the client to keep a daily journal in which he/she documents persons, situations, and so on that cause anger, irritation, or disappointment.

4. Assign and process a list of all the client's targets of and causes for anger.

5. Confront/reflect the client's angry behaviors that occur within sessions.

6. Refer the client to an anger management class or group.

4. Verbalize how people influential in your upbringing have modeled anger expressions. (7)

7. Assist the client in identifying ways that key life figures (e.g., father, mother, teachers) have expressed angry feelings and how these experiences have positively or negatively influenced the way he/she handles anger.

5. Identify pain and hurt of past or current life that fuels anger. (8, 9)

8. Assign the client to list the experiences of life that have hurt him/her and led to anger.

9. Empathize with and clarify the client's feelings of hurt and anger tied to traumas of the past.

6. Verbalize feelings of anger in a controlled, assertive way. (10, 11, 12)

10. Assign the client to attend assertiveness training classes.

11. Process the client's angry feelings or angry outbursts that have recently occurred and review alternative behaviors available.

12. Using role-playing techniques, assist the client in developing non-self-defeating ways (e.g., assertive use of "I messages") of handling angry feelings.

7. Decrease the number and duration of angry outbursts. (11, 13)

11. Process the client's angry feelings or angry outbursts that have recently occurred and review alternative behaviors available.

13. Assign a specific exercise from the *Anger Work Out Book* (Weisinger) or similar workbook and process the exercise with the client.

8. Utilize relaxation techniques to cope with angry feelings. (14)

9. Verbalize increased awareness of how past ways of handling angry feelings have had a negative impact. (15, 16)

10. Decrease verbal and physical manifestations of anger, aggression, or violence while increasing awareness and acceptance of feelings. (17, 18)

11. Verbalize increased awareness of and ability to react to hot buttons or anger triggers in a nonaggressive manner. (19)

12. Write an angry letter to target of anger and process this letter with the therapist. (20, 21)

14. Teach the client relaxation techniques (e.g., deep breathing, positive imagery, deep muscle relaxation) to help him/her to respond appropriately to angry feelings when they occur.

15. Ask the client to list ways anger has negatively impacted his/her daily life; process this list.

16. Expand the client's awareness of the negative affects that anger has on his/her body.

17. Use the empty chair technique to coach the client in expressing his/her angry feelings in a constructive, non-self-defeating manner.

18. Train the client in Rational Emotive Therapy (RET) techniques for coping with feelings of anger, frustration, and rage.

19. Assist the client in developing the ability to recognize his/her hot buttons/triggers that lead to angry explosions.

20. Ask the client to write an angry letter to parents, spouse, or whomever, focusing on the reasons for his/her anger toward that person; process this letter in session.

21. While in session, encourage the client to express and release feelings of anger or

13. Verbalize recognition of how holding on to angry feelings freezes you and hands control over to others, and cite the advantages of forgiveness. (22, 23)

14. Write a letter of forgiveness to the perpetrator of past or present pain and process this letter with the therapist. (24)

—. _____
    _____
—. _____
    _____
—. _____
    _____

rage, violent fantasies, or plots for revenge.

22. Discuss with the client forgiveness of the perpetrators of pain as a process of letting go of his/her anger.

23. Assign the client to read *Forgive and Forget* (Smedes).

24. Ask the client to write a forgiving letter to the target of anger as a step toward letting go of anger; process this letter in session.

—. _____
    _____
—. _____
    _____
—. _____
    _____

DIAGNOSTIC SUGGESTIONS

Axis I:	312.43	Intermittent Explosive Disorder
	296.xx	Bipolar I Disorder
	296.89	Bipolar II Disorder
	312.8	Conduct Disorder
	310.1	Personality Change Due to (Axis III Disorder)
	309.81	Posttraumatic Stress Disorder
	_____	_____
	_____	_____
Axis II:	301.83	Borderline Personality Disorder
	301.7	Antisocial Personality Disorder
	301.0	Paranoid Personality Disorder
	301.81	Narcissistic Personality Disorder
	301.9	Personality Disorder NOS
	_____	_____
	_____	_____

ANTISOCIAL BEHAVIOR

BEHAVIORAL DEFINITIONS

1. An adolescent history of consistent rule-breaking, lying, stealing, physical aggression, disrespect for others and their property, and/or substance abuse resulting in frequent confrontation with authority.
2. Failure to conform with social norms with respect to the law, as shown by repeatedly performed antisocial acts (e.g., destroying property, stealing, or pursuing an illegal job) for which he/she may or may not have been arrested.
3. Pattern of interacting in a confrontive, aggressive, and/or argumentative way with authority figures.
4. Little or no remorse for causing pain to others.
5. Consistent pattern of blaming others for what happens to him/her.
6. Little regard for truth as reflected in a pattern of consistently lying to and/or conning others.
7. Frequent initiation of verbal or physical fighting.
8. History of reckless behaviors that reflect a lack of regard for self or others and show a high need for excitement, fun, and living on the edge.
9. Pattern of sexual promiscuity; has never been totally monogamous in any relationship for a year and does not take responsibility for children resulting from relationships.
10. Pattern of impulsive behaviors, such as moving often, traveling with no goal, or quitting a job without having secured another one.
11. Inability to sustain behavior that would maintain consistent employment.
12. Failure to function as a consistently concerned and responsible parent.

—. _____

_____

—. _____
    _____
—. _____
    _____

LONG-TERM GOALS

1. Accept responsibility for own behavior and keep behavior within the acceptable limits of the rules of society.
2. Develop and demonstrate a healthy sense of respect for social norms, the rights of others, and the need for honesty.
3. Improve method of relating to the world, especially authority figures; be more realistic, less defiant, and more socially sensitive.
4. Come to an understanding and acceptance of the need for conforming to prevailing social limits and boundaries on behavior.
5. Maintain consistent employment and demonstrate financial and emotional responsibility for children.

—. _____
    _____
—. _____
    _____
—. _____
    _____

SHORT-TERM OBJECTIVES

1. Admit to illegal and/or unethical behavior that has trampled on the law and/or the rights and feelings of others. (1, 2)

THERAPEUTIC INTERVENTIONS

1. Explore the history of the client's pattern of illegal and/or unethical behavior and confront his/her attempts at minimization, denial, or projection of blame.

2. Review the consequences for the client and others of his/her antisocial behavior.

2. Verbalize an understanding of the benefits for self and others of living within the laws and rules of society. (3, 4)

3. Teach the client that the basis for all relationships is trust that the other person will treat one with respect and kindness.

4. Teach the client the need for lawfulness as the basis for trust that forestalls anarchy in society as a whole.

3. Make a commitment to live within the rules and laws of society. (5, 6)

5. Solicit a commitment from the client to conform to a pro-social, law-abiding lifestyle.

6. Emphasize the reality of negative consequences for the client if he/she continues to practice lawlessness.

4. List relationships that have been broken because of disrespect, disloyalty, aggression, or dishonesty. (7, 8)

7. Review relationships that have been lost due to the client's antisocial attitudes and practices (e.g., disloyalty, dishonesty, aggression).

8. Confront the client's lack of sensitivity to the needs and feelings of others.

5. Acknowledge a pattern of selfcenteredness in virtually all relationships. (8, 9)

8. Confront the client's lack of sensitivity to the needs and feelings of others.

9. Point out the self-focused, me-first, look-out-for-number-one attitude that is reflected in the client's antisocial behavior.

6. Make a commitment to be honest and reliable. (10, 11, 12)

10. Teach the client the value for self of honesty and reliability in all relationships, since he/she benefits from social approval as well as increased trust and respect.

	11. Teach the client the positive effect that honesty and reliability have for others, since they are not disappointed or hurt by lies and broken promises.
	12. Ask the client to make a commitment to be honest and reliable.
7. Verbalize an understanding of the benefits to self and others of being empathetic and sensitive to the needs of others. (3, 13, 14)	3. Teach the client that the basis for all relationships is trust that the other person will treat one with respect and kindness.
	13. Attempt to sensitize the client to his/her lack of empathy for others, by revisiting the consequences of his/her behavior on others. Use role-reversal techniques.
	14. Confront the client when he/she is rude or not being respectful of others and their boundaries.
8. List three actions that will be performed that will be acts of kindness and thoughtfulness toward others. (15)	15. Assist the client in listing three actions that he/she will perform as acts of service or kindness for others.
9. Indicate the steps that will be taken to make amends or restitution for hurt caused to others. (16, 17, 18)	16. Assist the client in identifying those who have been hurt by his/her antisocial behavior.
	17. Teach the client the value of apologizing for hurt caused as a means of accepting responsibility for behavior and of developing sensitivity to the feelings of others.

10. Verbally demonstrate an understanding of the rules and duties related to employment. (19)

11. Attend work reliably and treat supervisors and coworkers with respect. (20, 21)

12. Verbalize the obligations of parenthood that have been ignored. (22, 23)

13. State a plan to meet responsibilities of parenthood. (24)

14. Increase statements of accepting responsibility for own behavior. (25, 26, 27)

18. Encourage the client's commitment to specific steps that will be taken to apologize and make restitution to those who have suffered from his/her hurtful behaviors.

19. Review the rules and expectations that must govern the client's behavior in the work environment.

20. Monitor the client's attendance at work and reinforce reliability as well as respect for authority.

21. Ask the client to make a list of behaviors and attitudes that must be modified in order to decrease his/her conflict with authorities; process the list.

22. Confront the client's avoidance of responsibilities toward his/her children.

23. Assist the client in listing the behaviors that are required to be a responsible, nurturing, consistently reliable parent.

24. Develop a plan with the client that will begin to implement the behaviors of a responsible parent.

25. Confront the client when he/she makes blaming statements or fails to take responsibility for own actions, thoughts, or feelings.

26. Explore the client's reasons for blaming others for

his/her own actions (e.g., history of physically abusive punishment, parental modeling, fear of rejection, shame, low self-esteem, avoidance of facing consequences).

27. Give verbal positive feedback to the client when he/she takes responsibility for his/her own behavior.

15. Verbalize an understanding of how childhood experiences of pain have led to an imitative pattern of self-focused protection and aggression toward others. (28, 29)

28. Explore the client's history of abuse, neglect, or abandonment in childhood; explain how the cycle of abuse or neglect is repeating itself in the client's behavior.

29. Point out that the client's pattern of emotional detachment in relationships and self-focused behavior is related to a dysfunctional attempt to protect self from pain.

16. Verbalize a desire to forgive perpetrators of childhood abuse. (30)

30. Teach the client the value of forgiving the perpetrators of hurt versus holding on to hurt and rage and using the hurt as an excuse to continue antisocial practices.

17. Practice trusting a significant other with disclosure of personal feelings. (31, 32, 33)

31. Explore the client's fears associated with placing trust in others.

32. Identify some personal thoughts and feelings that the client could share with a significant other as a means of beginning to demonstrate trust in someone.

33. Process the experience of the client making self vulnerable by self-disclosing to someone.

___. _____   ___. _____
    _____   _____
___. _____   ___. _____
    _____   _____
___. _____   ___. _____
    _____   _____

DIAGNOSTIC SUGGESTIONS

Axis I:	303.90	Alcohol Dependence
	304.20	Cocaine Dependence
	304.89	Polysubstance Dependence
	309.3	Adjustment Disorder With Disturbance of Conduct
	312.8	Conduct Disorder
	312.34	Intermittent Explosive Disorder
	_____	_____
	_____	_____
Axis II:	301.7	Antisocial Personality Disorder
	301.81	Narcissistic Personality Disorder
	799.9	Diagnosis Deferred
	V71.09	No Diagnosis
	_____	_____
	_____	_____

ANXIETY

BEHAVIORAL DEFINITIONS

1. Excessive and persistent daily worry about several life circumstances that has no factual or logical basis.
2. Motor tension such as restlessness, tiredness, shakiness, or muscle tension.
3. Autonomic hyperactivity such as palpitations, shortness of breath, dry mouth, trouble swallowing, nausea, or diarrhea.
4. Hypervigilance such as feeling constantly on edge, experiencing concentration difficulties, having trouble falling or staying asleep, and exhibiting a general state of irritability.

__. _____
   _____

__. _____
   _____

__. _____
   _____

LONG-TERM GOALS

1. Reduce overall level, frequency, and intensity of the anxiety so that daily functioning is not impaired.
2. Stabilize anxiety level while increasing ability to function on a daily basis.
3. Resolve the core conflict that is the source of anxiety.
4. Enhance ability to handle effectively the full variety of life's anxieties.

—. _____

_____

—. _____

_____

—. _____

_____

SHORT-TERM OBJECTIVES

1. Tell the story of the anxiety complete with attempts to resolve it and the suggestions others have given. (1, 2)

2. Identify the major life conflicts from the past and present that form the basis for present anxiety. (3, 4, 5)

3. Complete anxiety homework exercises that identify cognitive distortions that generate anxious feelings. (6)

THERAPEUTIC INTERVENTIONS

1. Build a level of trust with the client and create a supportive environment that will facilitate a description of his/her fears.

2. Probe with questions (see *Anxiety Disorders and Phobias* by Beck and Emery) that require the client to produce evidence of the anxiety and logical reasons for it being present.

3. Ask the client to develop and process a list of key past and present life conflicts that continue to cause worry.

4. Assist the client in becoming aware of key unresolved life conflicts and in starting to work toward their resolution.

5. Reinforce the client's insights into the role of his/her past emotional pain and present anxiety.

6. Assign the client to complete the anxiety section exercises in *Ten Days to Self-Esteem!* (Burns) that

reveal cognitive distortions; process the completed assignments.

4. Complete a psychiatric evaluation for medications. (7)

5. Take medications as prescribed and report any side effects to appropriate professionals. (8)

6. Implement appropriate relaxation and diversion activities to decrease level of anxiety. (9, 10, 11)

7. Increase daily social and vocational involvement. (12)

8. Acknowledge the irrational nature of the fears. (13, 14, 15)

7. Refer the client to a physician for a psychotropic medication consultation.

8. Monitor the client's psychotropic medication compliance, side effects, and effectiveness; confer regularly with the physician.

9. Train the client in a guided imagery technique to be used for anxiety relief.

10. Utilize biofeedback techniques to facilitate the client's relaxation skills.

11. Assign or allow the client to choose a chapter in *Relaxation and Stress Reduction Workbook* (Davis, Eshelman, and McKay); encourage implementation of the chosen stress reduction technique.

12. Assist the client in developing behavioral coping and distraction strategies (e.g., increased social involvement, obtaining employment, physical exercise) for his/her anxiety.

13. Assist the client in developing an awareness of the irrational nature of his/her fears.

14. Analyze the client's fear by examining the probability of the negative expectation occurring, the real

consequences of it occurring, his/her ability to control the outcome, the worst possible outcome, and his/her ability to accept it. (See *Anxiety Disorders and Phobias* by Beck and Emery).

15. Explore the irrational cognitive messages that mediate the client's anxiety response and retrain him/her in adaptive cognitions.

9. Report a decreased daily level of anxiety due to the use of positive self-talk. (16)

16. Help the client develop reality-based, positive cognitive messages that will increase his/her self-confidence in coping with irrational fears.

10. Implement a thought-stopping technique to interrupt anxiety-producing thoughts. (17)

17. Teach the client to implement a thought-stopping technique (thinking of a stop sign and then a pleasant scene) that cognitively interferes with obsessions; monitor and encourage the client's use of the technique in daily life between sessions.

11. List the advantages and disadvantages of the anxiety. (18)

18. Ask the client to complete the Cost Benefit Analysis exercise in *Ten Days to Self-Esteem!* (Burns), in which he/she lists the advantages and disadvantages of the negative thought, fear, or anxiety; process the completed assignment.

12. Verbalize alternative positive views of reality that are incompatible with anxiety-producing views. (19, 20)

19. Read and process with the client a fable from *Friedman's Fables* (Friedman) that pertains to anxiety.

13. Identify an anxiety coping mechanism that has been successful in the past and increase its use. (21)

14. Utilize a paradoxical intervention technique to reduce the anxiety response. (22)

20. Reframe the client's fear or anxiety by offering another way of looking at it, various alternatives, or by enlarging the perspective.

21. Utilize a brief solution-focused therapy approach in which the client is probed to find a time or situation in his/her life when he/she handled the specific anxiety or an anxiety in general. Clearly focus the approach he/she used and then encourage the client to increase its use. Monitor, and modify the solution as required.

22. Develop a paradoxical intervention (see *Ordeal Therapy* by Haley) in which the client is encouraged to have the problem (e.g., anxiety) and then schedule that anxiety to occur at specific intervals each day in a specific way and for a defined length of time. (It is best to have it happen at a time of day/night when the client would be clearly wanting to do something else.)

__. _____

_____

__. _____

_____

__. _____

_____

__. _____

_____

__. _____

_____

__. _____

_____

DIAGNOSTIC SUGGESTIONS

Axis I: 300.02   Generalized Anxiety Disorder
300.0   Anxiety Disorder NOS
309.24   Adjustment Disorder With Anxiety
_____   _____
_____   _____

ATTENTION DEFICIT DISORDER (ADD)—ADULT

BEHAVIORAL DEFINITIONS

1. Childhood history of Attention Deficit Disorder (ADD) that was either diagnosed or later concluded due to the symptoms of behavioral problems at school, impulsivity, temper outbursts, and lack of concentration.
2. Unable to concentrate or pay attention to things of low interest, even when those things are important to his/her life.
3. Easily distracted and drawn from task at hand.
4. Restless and fidgety; unable to be sedentary for more than a short time.
5. Impulsive; has an easily observable pattern of acting first and thinking later.
6. Rapid mood swings and mood liability within short spans of time.
7. Disorganized in most areas of his/her life.
8. Starts many projects but rarely finished any.
9. Has a "low boiling point and a short fuse."
10. Exhibits low stress tolerance; is easily frustrated, hassled, or upset.
11. Chronic low self-esteem.
12. Tendency toward addictive behaviors.

—. _____
   _____
—. _____
   _____
—. _____
   _____

LONG-TERM GOALS

1. Reduce impulsive actions while increasing concentration and focus on low-interest activities.
2. Minimize ADD behavioral interference in daily life.
3. Accept ADD as a chronic issue and need for continuing medication treatment.
4. Sustain attention and concentration for consistently longer periods of time.
5. Achieve a satisfactory level of balance, structure, and intimacy in personal life.

—. _____
   _____

—. _____
   _____

—. _____
   _____

SHORT-TERM OBJECTIVES

1. Cooperate with and complete psychological testing. (1)

2. Cooperate with and complete a psychiatric evaluation. (2)

3. Comply with all recommendations based on the psychiatric and/or psychological evaluations. (3, 4)

THERAPEUTIC INTERVENTIONS

1. Arrange for the administration of psychological testing to the client to establish or rule out Attention-Deficit/ Hyperactivity Disorder (ADHD); provide feedback as to testing results.

2. Arrange for a psychiatric evaluation of the client to assess his/her need for psychotropic medication.

3. Process the results of the psychiatric evaluation and/or psychological testing with the client and answer any questions that may arise.

4. Conduct a conjoint session with significant others and

the client to present the results of the psychological
and psychiatric evaluations.
Answer any questions they
may have and solicit their
support in dealing with the
client's condition.

4. Take medication as prescribed, on a regular, consistent basis. (5, 6)

5. Monitor and evaluate the
client's psychotropic medication prescription compliance and the effectiveness
of the medications on his/
her level of functioning.

6. Confer with the client's psychiatrist on a regular basis
regarding the effectiveness
of the medication regime.

5. Identify specific benefits of
taking prescribed medica-
tions on a long-term basis.
(7, 8, 9)

7. Ask the client to make a
"pros and cons" spreadsheet
regarding staying on medications after doing well;
process the results.

8. Encourage and support the
client in remaining on medications and warmly but
firmly confront thoughts of
discontinuing when they
surface.

9. Assign the client to list the
positive effects that have occurred for him/her since
starting on medication.

6. Read material that is infor-
mative regarding ADD to
gain knowledge about the
condition. (10)

10. Ask the client to read material on ADD (e.g., *Driven to
Distraction* by Hallowell
and Raty, *The Hyperactive
Child, Adolescent and Adult*
by Wender, *Putting on the
Brakes* by Quinn and Stern;
or *You Mean I'm Not Lazy,
Stupid or Crazy* by Kelly

7. Identify the specific ADD behaviors that cause the most difficulty. (11, 12, 13)

8. List the negative consequences of the ADD problematic behavior. (14)

9. Apply problem-solving skills to specific ADD behaviors that are interfering with daily functioning. (15, 16)

and Ramundo); process the material read.

11. Assist the client in identifying the specific behaviors that cause him/her the most difficulty.

12. Review the results of psychological testing and/or psychiatric evaluation again with the client assisting in identifying or in affirming his/her choice of the most problematic behavior(s) to address.

13. Ask the client to have extended family members and close collaterals complete a ranking of the three behaviors they see as interfering the most with his/her daily functioning (e.g., mood swings, temper outbursts, easily stressed, short attention span, never completes projects).

14. Assign the client to make a list of negative consequences that he/she has experienced or that could result from a continuation of the problematic behavior; process the list.

15. Teach the client problem-solving skills (i.e., identify problem, brainstorm all possible options, evaluate each option, select best option, implement course of action, and evaluate results) that can be applied to his/her ADD behaviors.

16. Assign problem-solving homework to the client specific to the identified behavior (i.e., impulse control, anger outbursts, mood swings, staying on task, attentiveness); process the completed assignment and give appropriate feedback to the client.

10. Utilize cognitive strategies to curb impulsive behavior. (17)

17. Teach the client the self-control strategies of "stop, listen, think, act" and "problem-solving self-talk." Role-play these techniques to improve his/her skill level.

11. Implement a specific, time-limited period if indulging impulses that are not self-destructive. (18)

18. Structure a "blowout" time each week when the client can do whatever he/she likes to do that is not self-destructive (e.g., blast themselves with music, gorge on ice cream).

12. Use "time out" to remove self from situations and think about behavioral reaction alternatives and their consequences. (19)

19. Train the client to use a "time-out" intervention in which he/she settles down by going away from the situation and calming down to think about behavioral alternatives and their consequences.

13. Implement relaxation procedures to reduce tension and physical restlessness. (20)

20. Instruct the client in various relaxation techniques (e.g., deep breathing, meditation, guided imagery) and encourage him/her to use them daily or when stress increases.

14. Reward self when impulsivity, inattention, or forgetfulness are replaced by positive alternatives. (21, 22)

21. Design and implement a self-administered reward system to reinforce and encourage the client's

15. Cooperate with brainwave biofeedback to improve impulse control and reduce distractibility. (23, 24)

16. Report a decrease in statements and feelings of negativity regarding self and life. (25)

17. Introduce behaviors into life that improve health and/or serve others. (26, 27)

18. Attend an ADD support group. (28)

decreased impulsiveness, loss of temper, inattentiveness, etc.

22. Teach the client to utilize external structure (e.g., lists, reminders, files, daily rituals) to reduce the effects of his/her inattention and forgetfulness; encourage the client to reward himself/ herself for successful recall and follow-through.

23. Refer for or administer brainwave biofeedback to improve attention span, impulse control, and mood regulation.

24. Encourage the client to transfer the biofeedback training skills of relaxation and cognitive focusing to everyday situations (e.g., home, work, social).

25. Conduct conjoint sessions in which positive aspects of the relationship, the client, and significant other are identified and affirmed.

26. Direct the client toward healthy addictions (e.g., exercise, volunteer work, community service).

27. After clearance from the client's personal physician, refer client to a physician fitness trainer who can design an aerobic exercise routine for him/her.

28. Refer the client to a specific group therapy for adults with ADD to increase the

19. Use a "coach" who has been trained by therapist to increase organization and task focus. (29, 30)

client's understanding of ADD, to boost his/her self-esteem, and to obtain feedback from others.

29. Direct the client to pick a "coach" who is a friend or colleague to assist him/her in getting organized and staying on task and to provide encouragement support (see *Driven to Distraction* by Hallowell and Raty).

30. Instruct the coach in HOPE technique (i.e., Help, Obligations, Plans, and Encouragement) as described in *Driven to Distraction* by Hallowell and Raty).

20. Report improved listening skills without defensiveness. (31)

31. Use role-playing and modeling to teach the client how to listen and accept feedback from others regarding his/her behavior.

21. Have significant other attend an ADD support group to increase his/her understanding of the condition. (32)

32. Educate the client's significant other on ADD and encourage him/her to attend a support group.

22. Report improved communication, understanding, and feelings of trust between self and significant other. (33, 34, 35, 36)

33. Ask the client and significant other to list the expectations they have for the relationship and each other. Process the list in conjoint session with a focus on identifying how the expectations can be met and how realistic they are.

34. Assist the client and his/her significant other in removing blocks in their commu-

nication and in developing new communication skills.

35. Refer the client and significant other to a skill-based marriage/relationship seminar (e.g., PREP, Marriage Encounter, Engaged Encounter) to improve communication and conflict resolution skills.

36. Assign the client and significant other to schedule a specific time each day to devote to communicating together, expressing affection, having fun, or talking through problems. Move assignment toward becoming a daily ritual.

23. Develop a signal to act as a warning system to indicate when anger levels are escalating with the partner. (37)

37. Assist the client and significant other in developing a signal system as a means of giving feedback when conflict behaviors and anger begin to escalate.

DIAGNOSTIC SUGGESTIONS

Axis I: 314.00   Attention-Deficit/Hyperactivity Disorder, Predominantly Inattentive Type
314.01   Attention-Deficit/Hyperactivity Disorder, Predominantly Hyperactive-Impulsive Type
314.9   Attention-Deficit/Hyperactivity Disorder NOS

296.xx	Bipolar I Disorder
301.13	Cyclothymic Disorder
296.90	Mood Disorder NOS
312.30	Impulse-Control Disorder NOS
303.90	Alcohol Dependence
305.0	Alcohol Abuse
304.30	Cannabis Dependence
305.20	Cannabis Abuse
_____	_____
_____	_____

BORDERLINE PERSONALITY

BEHAVIORAL DEFINITIONS

1. A minor stress leads to extreme emotional reactivity (anger, anxiety, or depression) that usually lasts from a few hours to a few days.
2. A pattern of intense, chaotic interpersonal relationships.
3. Marked identity disturbance.
4. Impulsive behaviors that are potentially self-damaging.
5. Recurrent suicidal gestures, threats, or self-mutilating behavior.
6. Chronic feelings of emptiness and boredom.
7. Frequent eruptions of intense, inappropriate anger.
8. Easily feels unfairly treated and believes that others can't be trusted.
9. Analyzes most issues in simple terms (e.g., right/wrong, black/white, trustworthy/deceitful) without regard for extenuating circumstances or complex situations.
10. Becomes very anxious with any hint of perceived abandonment in a relationship.

—. _____
   _____

—. _____
   _____

—. _____
   _____

LONG-TERM GOALS

1. Develop and demonstrate coping skills to deal with mood swings.
2. Develop the ability to control impulsive behavior.

3. Replace dichotomous thinking with the ability to tolerate ambiguity and complexity in people and issues.
4. Develop and demonstrate anger management skills.
5. Learn and practice interpersonal relationship skills.
6. Terminate self-damaging behaviors (such as substance abuse, reckless driving, sexual acting out, binge eating, or suicidal behaviors).

—. _____
   _____
   _____

—. _____
   _____
   _____

—. _____
   _____

SHORT-TERM OBJECTIVES

1. Verbalize the situations that can easily trigger feelings of fear, depression, and anger. (1, 2)

2. Identify the negative, distorted cognitions that mediate intense negative emotions. (3, 4)

THERAPEUTIC INTERVENTIONS

1. Explore the client's situations that trigger feelings of fear, depression, and anger.

2. Assign the client to record a daily journal of feelings along with the circumstances that he/she was reacting to; process the journal material to identify triggers for emotional reactivity.

3. Assist the client in identifying the distorted schemas and related automatic thoughts that mediate his/her anxiety response.

4. Require the client to keep a daily record of self-defeating thoughts (e.g., regarding hopelessness, helplessness, worthlessness, catastrophizing, negatively predicting the future); challenge each thought for

3. Verbalize realistic, positive self-talk to replace distorted negative messages. (5, 6, 7)

4. List some negative consequences to self and others of self-defeating, impulsive behaviors. (8)

5. Utilize cognitive methods to control impulsive behavior. (9, 10, 11)

accuracy, then replace each dysfunctional thought with one that is positive and self-enhancing.

5. Train the client in revising core schema using cognitive restructuring techniques.

6. Reinforce the client's positive, realistic cognitive self-talk that mediates a sense of peace.

7. Assign the client to record instances of successfully using revised, constructive cognitive patterns; process and reinforce positive consequences.

8. Assign the client to list the destructive consequences of his/her impulsive behavior to self and others.

9. Teach the client mediational and self-control strategies (e.g., "stop, look, listen, and think") to delay gratification and inhibit impulses.

10. Assign the client to record instances of successfully implementing "stop, look, listen, and think" to control reactive impulses; process and reinforce the successes.

11. Teach the client cognitive methods (e.g., thought stoppage, thought substitution, reframing) for gaining and improving control over impulsive actions; encourage implementation in daily life.

6. Record and report instances of using relaxation techniques to manage intense feelings and control impulsive reactive behavior. (12, 13)

12. Using techniques such as progressive relaxation, self-hypnosis, or biofeedback, teach the client how to relax completely; then encourage the client to relax whenever he/she feels uncomfortable.

13. Ask the client to record instances of using relaxation techniques to cope with stress rather than reacting with anger; reinforce successful implementation of this coping skill.

7. Implement assertiveness and describe the consequences. (14, 15, 16)

14. Use role-playing, modeling, and behavioral rehearsal to teach the client assertiveness (versus passivity and aggressiveness).

15. Refer the client to an assertiveness training group.

16. Review the client's implementation of assertiveness and his/her feelings about it as well as the consequences of it; reinforce success and redirect for failure.

8. Implement the use of "I messages" to communicate feelings without aggression. (17, 18)

17. Use modeling, role-playing, and behavioral rehearsal to teach the client the use of "I messages" to communicate feelings directly (i.e., I feel . . . When you . . . I would prefer it if you . . .).

18. Reinforce the client's reported use of "I messages" in place of aggressiveness or possessiveness when feeling threatened.

9. Verbalize the impact that childhood experiences of abuse, neglect, or abandonment have upon current feelings and relationships. (19, 20, 21)

19. Explore instances of abuse, neglect, or emotional/physical abandonment in the client's childhood; process the feelings associated with these experiences.

20. Point out to the client the destructive effect of overcontrol of others and angry resentment when others pull back from relationships. Encourage separation of helpless, desperate feelings of the past from current relationships.

21. Reinforce the client's insight into the effect of childhood experiences of neglect or abuse on current urges to react with rage or possessiveness.

10. List and implement coping strategies to deal with fear of abandonment. (22)

22. Teach the client to use coping strategies (e.g., delay of reaction, "stop, look, listen, and plan," relaxation and deep breathing techniques, "I messages," expanded social network versus few intense relationships) to deal with fear of abandonment; process his/her implementation of these strategies in daily life.

11. Initiate enjoyable activities that can be done alone. (4, 23, 24)

4. Require the client to keep a daily record of self-defeating thoughts (e.g., regarding hopelessness, helplessness, worthlessness, catastrophizing, negatively predicting the future); challenge each thought for accuracy, then replace each

dysfunctional thought with one that is positive and self-enhancing.

23. Explore the client's automatic thoughts associated with being alone.

24. Encourage the client to break his/her pattern of avoiding being alone by initiating activities without a companion (e.g., starting a hobby; exercising; attending lectures, concerts, movies; reading a book; taking a class).

12. Cooperate with a referral to a physician to evaluate the need for psychotropic medication. (25)

25. Refer the client to a physician to evaluate his/her need for a psychotropic medication to stabilize mood.

13. Take medication as prescribed and report as to effectiveness and side effects. (26)

26. Monitor and evaluate the client's psychotropic medication prescription compliance, effectiveness, and side effects.

14. Verbalize the intense feelings that motivate self-mutilating behavior and how those feelings are relieved by such behavior. (19, 21, 27, 28)

19. Explore instances of abuse, neglect, or emotional/physical abandonment in the client's childhood; process the feelings associated with these experiences.

21. Reinforce the client's insight into the effect of childhood experiences of neglect or abuse on current urges to react with rage or possessiveness.

27. Probe the nature and history of the client's self-mutilating behavior.

15. Verbalize a promise to contact the therapist or some other emergency helpline if a serious urge toward self-harm arises. (29, 30, 31, 32)

28. Interpret the client's self-mutilation as an expression of the rage and helplessness that could not be expressed as a child victim of emotional abandonment or abuse.

29. Assess the client's suicidal gestures as to triggers, frequency, seriousness, secondary gain, and onset.

30. Elicit a promise (as part of a self-mutilation and suicide prevention contract) from the client that he/she will initiate contact with the therapist or a helpline if a suicidal urge becomes strong and before any self-injurious behavior occurs.

31. Provide the client with an emergency helpline telephone number that is available 24 hours a day.

32. Encourage the client to express his/her feelings directly using assertive "I messages" rather than indirectly through self-mutilating behavior.

16. List negative consequences of judging people rigidly and harshly. (33, 34)

33. Assist the client in examining his/her style of evaluating people, especially with regard to his/her dichotomous thinking.

34. Teach the client the alienating consequences of judging people harshly and impulsively.

17. Verbalize weaknesses or faults of those who have been judged to be perfect, and strengths or assets of those people who have been judged to be evil, worthless, and deceitful. (35, 36)

35. Challenge the client in understanding how dichotomous thinking leads to feelings of interpersonal mistrust.

36. Use role reversal and modeling to assist the client in seeing positive and negative qualities in all people.

__. _____   __. _____
    _____   _____

__. _____   __. _____
    _____   _____

__. _____   __. _____
    _____   _____

DIAGNOSTIC SUGGESTIONS

Axis I: 300.4   Dysthymic Disorder
              296.3x   Major Depressive Disorder, Recurrent

              _____   _____

Axis II: 301.83   Borderline Personality Disorder
              301.9   Personality Disorder NOS
              799.9   Diagnosis Deferred
              V71.09   No Diagnosis

              _____   _____
              _____   _____

CHEMICAL DEPENDENCE

BEHAVIORAL DEFINITIONS

1. Consistent use of alcohol or other mood-altering drugs until high, intoxicated, or passed out.
2. Inability to stop or cut down use of mood-altering drug once started, despite the verbalized desire to do so and the negative consequences continued use brings.
3. Blood work that reflects the results of a pattern of heavy substance use (e.g., elevated liver enzymes).
4. Denial that chemical dependence is a problem despite direct feedback from spouse, relatives, friends, and employers that the use of the substance is negatively affecting them and others.
5. Amnestic blackouts occur when abusing alcohol.
6. Continued drug and/or alcohol use despite experiencing persistent or recurring physical, legal, vocational, social, or relationship problems that are directly caused by the use of the substance.
7. Increased tolerance for the drug as evidenced by the need to use more to become intoxicated or to attain the desired effect.
8. Physical symptoms (i.e., shaking, seizures, nausea, headaches, sweating, anxiety, insomnia, and/or depression) when withdrawing from the substance.
9. Suspension of important social, recreational, or occupational activities because they interfere with using the mood-altering drug.
10. Large time investment in activities to obtain the substance, to use it, or to recover from its effects.
11. Consumption of a mood-altering substance in greater amounts and for longer periods than intended.
12. Continued abuse of a mood-altering chemical after being told by a physician that it is causing health problems.

—. _____

_____

—. _____
   _____
   _____
—. _____
   _____

LONG-TERM GOALS

1. Accept fact of chemical dependence and begin to actively participate in a recovery program.
2. Establish a sustained recovery, free from the use of all mood-
   altering substances.
3. Establish and maintain total abstinence while increasing knowledge of the disease and the process of recovery.
4. Acquire the necessary skills to maintain long-term sobriety from
   all mood-altering substances.
5. Improve quality of personal life by maintaining an ongoing abstinence from all mood-altering chemicals.
6. Withdraw from mood-altering substance, stabilize physically and
   emotionally, and then establish a supportive recovery plan.

—. _____
   _____
—. _____
   _____
—. _____
   _____

SHORT-TERM OBJECTIVES	THERAPEUTIC INTERVENTIONS
1. Describe the amount, frequency, and history of substance abuse. (1, 2)	1. Gather a complete drug/alcohol history from the client, including the amount and pattern of his/her use, signs and symptoms of use, and negative life consequences (e.g., social, legal, familial, vocational).

2. Obtain a medical examination to evaluate the effects of chemical dependence. (3)

3. Identify the negative consequences of drug and/or alcohol abuse. (3, 4)

4. Decrease the level of denial around using as evidenced by fewer statements about minimizing amount of use and its negative impact on life. (5, 6)

5. Make verbal "I" statements that reflect a knowledge and acceptance of chemical dependence. (7)

6. Verbalize increased knowledge of alcoholism and the process of recovery. (8, 9)

2. Administer to the client an objective test of drug and/or alcohol abuse (e.g., the Alcohol Severity Index, the MAST); process the results with the client.

3. Refer the client for thorough physical examination to determine any physical effects of chemical dependence.

3. Refer the client for thorough physical examination to determine any physical effects of chemical dependence.

4. Ask the client to make a list of the ways substance abuse has negatively impacted his/her life and process it with him/her.

5. Assign the client to ask two or three people who are close to him/her to write a letter to therapist in which they identify how they saw the client's chemical dependence negatively impacting his/her life.

6. Assign the client to complete a First Step paper and then to process it with group, sponsor, or therapist to receive feedback.

7. Model and reinforce statements that reflect the client's acceptance of his/her chemical dependence and its destructive consequences for self and others.

8. Require the client to attend didactic lectures related to chemical dependence and the process of recovery.

Then ask the client to identify in writing several key
points attained from each
lecture for further processing with therapist.

7. Verbalize a commitment to
abstain from the use of
mood-altering drugs.
(10, 11)

9. Assign the client to read an
article/pamphlet on the disease concept of alcoholism
and to select several key
ideas to discuss with therapist.

10. Develop an abstinence contract with the client regarding the termination of the
use of his/her drug of choice.

11. Direct the client to write a
good-bye letter to drug of
choice; read it and process
related feelings with therapist.

8. Attend Alcoholics Anony-
mous/Narcotics Anonymous
(AA/NA) meetings on a regular basis as frequently as
necessary to support sobriety. (12, 13)

12. Assign the client to meet
with an AA/NA member
who has been working the
Twelve-Step program for
several years and find out
specifically how the pro-
gram has helped him/her to
stay sober; afterward, process the meeting.

13. Recommend that the client
attend AA or NA meetings
and report on the impact of
the meetings.

9. Verbalize an understanding
of personality, social, and
family factors, including
childhood experiences, that
foster chemical dependence.
(14, 15, 16)

14. Assess the client's intellec-
tual, personality, and cognitive functioning as to their
contribution to his/her
chemical dependence.

15. Investigate situational
stress factors that may foster the client's chemical dependence.

10. Review extended family alcohol use history and verbalize an acceptance of a genetic component to chemical dependence. (17)

11. Identify the ways being sober could positively impact life. (18)

12. State changes that will be made in social relationships to support recovery. (19, 20)

13. Identify projects and social and recreational activities that sobriety will now afford the time and energy to do. (21, 22)

14. Verbalize how living situation contributes to chemical dependence and acts as a hindrance to recovery. (23, 24)

16. Probe the client's family history for chemical dependence patterns and relate these to his/her use.

17. Explore extended family chemical dependence and relate this to a genetic vulnerability for the client to also develop chemical dependence.

18. Ask the client to make a list of how being sober could positively impact his/her life; process the list.

19. Review the negative influence of the client continuing his/her alcohol-related friendships ("drinking buddies") and assist him/her in making a plan to develop new sober relationships.

20. Assist the client in developing insight into life changes needed in order to maintain long-term sobriety.

21. Assist the client in planning social and recreational activities that are free from association with substance abuse.

22. Plan household or work-related projects that can be accomplished to build the client's self-esteem now that sobriety affords time and energy for such constructive activity.

23. Evaluate the role of the client's living situation in fostering a pattern of chemical dependence.

15. Make arrangements to terminate current living situation and move to a place more conducive to recovery. (25, 26)

16. Identify the positive impact that sobriety will have on intimate and family relationships. (27)

17. Agree to make amends to significant others who have been hurt by the life dominated by substance abuse. (28, 29)

18. Identify sources of ongoing support in maintaining sobriety. (30)

19. Identify potential relapse triggers and develop strategies for constructively dealing with each trigger. (31, 32)

24. Assign the client to write a list of the negative influences for chemical dependence inherent in his/her living situation.

25. Encourage a plan for the client to change his/her living situation in order to foster recovery.

26. Reinforce the client's positive change in living situation.

27. Assist the client in identifying positive changes that will be made in family relationships during recovery.

28. Discuss the negative effects the client's substance abuse has had on family, friends, and work relationships and encourage a plan to make amends for such hurt.

29. Elicit from the client a verbal commitment to make initial amends now to key individuals and further amends when working steps Eight and Nine of AA program.

30. Explore with the client the positive support system personally available in sobriety and discuss ways to develop and reinforce a positive support system.

31. Help the client develop an awareness of relapse triggers and alternative ways of effectively handling them.

32. Recommend that the client read material on how to avoid relapse (e.g., *Staying Sober: A Guide to Relapse Prevention* by Gorski and Miller and *The Staying Sober Workbook* by Gorski).

20. Develop a written aftercare plan that will support the maintenance of long-term sobriety. (33)

33. Assign and review the client's written aftercare plan to ensure it is adequate to maintain sobriety.

—. _____

_____

—. _____

_____

—. _____

_____

—. _____

_____

—. _____

_____

—. _____

_____

DIAGNOSTIC SUGGESTIONS

Axis I:	303.90	Alcohol Dependence
	305.0	Alcohol Abuse
	304.30	Cannabis Dependence
	304.20	Cocaine Dependence
	305.60	Cocaine Abuse
	304.80	Polysubstance Dependence
	291.2	Alcohol-Induced Persisting Dementia
	291.1	Alcohol-Induced Persisting Amnestic Disorder
	V71.01	Adult Antisocial Behavior
	300.4	Dysthymic Disorder
	312.34	Intermittent Explosive Disorder
	309.81	Posttraumatic Stress Disorder
	304.10	Sedative, Hypnotic, or Anxiolytic Dependence
	_____	_____
	_____	_____
Axis II:	301.7	Antisocial Personality Disorder
	_____	_____
	_____	_____

CHEMICAL DEPENDENCE—RELAPSE

BEHAVIORAL DEFINITIONS

1. Inability to remain abstinent from mood-altering drugs after receiving treatment for substance abuse.
2. Inability to stay sober even though attending Alcoholics Anonymous (AA) meetings regularly.
3. Relapse into abuse of mood-altering substances after a substantial period of sobriety.
4. Chronic pattern of period of sobriety (six months plus) followed by a relapse, then reestablishing sobriety.

—. _____

_____

—. _____

_____

—. _____

_____

LONG-TERM GOALS

1. Establish a consistently alcohol/drug-free lifestyle.
2. Develop an understanding of personal pattern of relapse in order to help sustain long-term recovery.
3. Develop an increased awareness of relapse triggers and the coping strategies needed to effectively deal with them.
4. Achieve a quality of life that is substance-free on a continuing basis.

—. _____

_____

—. _____
_____
—. _____
_____

SHORT-TERM OBJECTIVES

1. Verbalize a commitment to abstinence/sobriety. (1, 2)

2. Outline and implement a daily routine that is structured and includes AA involvement. (3, 4)

3. Reestablish ongoing relationships with people who are supportive of sobriety. (5, 6)

THERAPEUTIC INTERVENTIONS

1. Discuss with the client the specific behaviors, attitudes, and feelings that led up to the last relapse, focusing on triggers for the relapse. Obtain a clear, firm commitment to renewed sobriety.

2. Assess the client for ability to reestablish total abstinence and refer to more intense level of care if he/she is not able to detox and stay sober.

3. Teach the importance of structure and routine that have either been abandoned or never been present in the client's daily life and then assist the client in developing and implementing a balanced, structured daily routine.

4. Urge the client to attend AA consistently as a part of the routine structure of his/her life.

5. Assist the client in reuniting with his/her AA sponsor.

6. Ask the client to find a second AA/NA sponsor who is an opposite of the primary

sponsor (e.g., if the primary is mainly supportive, seek another who is more confrontive) and meet regularly with both sponsors on at least a weekly basis.

4. Verbalize feelings about the loss of sobriety. (7, 8)

7. Assist the client in expanding his/her ability to identify feelings, process them, and then express them in a timely, healthy way.

8. Assign the client to read *The Golden Book of Resentment* (Father John Doe) or readings on resentment from *As Bill Sees It* (Bill Wilson); choose three key concepts that he/she feels relate to him/her; and process them together.

5. Identify people and places to be avoided to maintain recovery. (9, 10)

9. Assist the client in identifying the negative influence of people and situations that encourage relapse, and ways to avoid them.

10. Assign the client to read a book or pamphlet on recovery. Select items from it that relate to him/her and process them together.

6. Identify the specific behaviors, attitudes, and feelings that led up to the last relapse, focusing on triggers for the relapse. (11, 12, 13, 14)

11. Assign the client to complete a relapse workbook (e.g., *The Staying Sober Workbook* by Gorski), and process it with him/her.

12. Assign the client to do a focused autobiography dating from his/her first attempt to get sober to the present. Then have him/her read it aloud for feedback as to triggers for relapse.

13. Ask the client to gather from significant others an observation list of the client's behavior or attitudes prior to his/her returning to using; process the feedback in group therapy or in individual session.

14. Develop a symptom line with the client that looks at each relapse in terms of when it happened (i.e., time of year, dates, and their significance) and what was occurring in regard to self, spouse, family, work, and social activities.

7. Identify behavior patterns that will need to be changed to maintain sobriety. (15, 16)

15. Ask the client to develop a list of behaviors, attitudes, and feelings that could have been involved in the relapse, and process it with him/ her.

16. Assign the client to read *Many Roads, One Journey: Moving Beyond the 12 Steps* (Kasl-Davis) or *Stage II Recovery* (Larsen), and process the key ideas with him/her.

8. Identify positive rewards associated with abstinence. (17, 18)

17. Assist the client in identifying positive rewards of total abstinence.

18. Assign the client to complete and process with therapist a "Cost-Benefit Analysis" (see *Ten Days to Self-Esteem!* by Burns) on his/her return to substance abuse.

9. Complete medical assessment for Antabuse or antidepressant medications. (19)

19. Refer the client to physician/psychiatrist for an evaluation for Antabuse or antidepressant medication.

10. Cooperate with acupuncturist for treatment to reduce the urge to use mood-altering substances. (20)

20. Refer the client to acupuncturist for treatment on a regular basis and monitor effectiveness.

11. Comply with medication recommendations as prescribed and report any side effects to the therapist and/or physician. (21, 22)

21. Monitor the client for compliance with medication orders or other treatments and possible side effects, and answer any questions he/she may have.

22. Confer with the prescribing physician on a regular basis regarding the effectiveness of the treatment.

12. Verbalize insights learned from talking and listening to successfully recovering chemically dependent people. (23)

23. Ask the client to interview NA/AA members who have been sober for three or more years, focusing on what they have specifically done to accomplish this, and if they have relapsed, what they have done to get back on track to stay. Process the client's findings with him/her.

13. Meet with a spiritual leader to make progress on AA Steps Two, Three, and Five. (24)

24. Refer the client to a pastor, rabbi, priest, or other spiritual leader with knowledge of substance abuse and recovery to work through any blocks regarding Steps Two and Three or to complete Step Five.

14. Report increased tolerance for uncomfortable emotions. (25, 26)

25. Teach the client various methods of stress reduction (e.g., meditation, deep

breathing, positive imagery) and assist him/her in implementing them into daily life.

26. Ask the client to develop a list of ways of coping with uncomfortable feelings; process the list with him/her.

15. Implement assertiveness skills to communicate feelings directly. (27)

27. Assist the client in developing assertiveness techniques.

16. Develop in writing two possible coping strategies for each specific relapse trigger. (26, 28)

26. Ask the client to develop a list of ways of coping with uncomfortable feelings; process the list with him/her.

28. Assist the client in developing two coping strategies for each identified trigger to relapse.

17. Verbally describe the family and relationship conflicts that played a role in triggering relapse. (29)

29. Conduct conjoint and/or family sessions that identify and resolve relationship stress that has served as a trigger for relapse.

18. The spouse or significant other verbalize an understanding of constructive actions that can be taken in reaction to the client's relapse and recovery. (30)

30. Conduct sessions with spouse or significant other to educate him/her regarding relapse triggers and instruct them on how to be supportive of sobriety. Encourage him/her to attend Alanon on a regular basis.

19. Participate in rituals that support recovery. (31)

31. Assist the client in developing and establishing rituals in life that will enhance sobriety and be a deterrent to relapse (e.g., receiving AA/NA coins, regular membership in a Step Study Group, coffee with sponsor at set date and time).

20. Identify successful sober living strategies of the past. (32)

32. Utilize a brief solution-focused approach with the client to identify specific things he/she did when sobriety was going well and then select and direct the client to increase the use of the identified behaviors. Monitor and adjust direction as needed.

21. Verbalize principles to live by that will support sobriety. (33)

33. Assign the client to read a fable or story such as "The Boy Who Lost His Way," "The Prodigal Son," or "Three Little Pigs" (see *Stories For the 3rd Ear*, by Wallas), and then process it together to identify key concepts connected to staying sober.

22. Develop written continuing aftercare plan with focus on coping with family and other stressors. (34, 35)

34. Ask the client to complete and process a relapse contract with significant other that identifies previous relapse-associated behaviors, attitudes, and emotions, coupling them with agreed-upon warnings from significant other as they are observed.

35. Assign the client to develop and process a written aftercare plan that specifically addresses previously identified relapse triggers.

—. _____
_____
—. _____
_____
—. _____
_____

—. _____
_____
—. _____
_____
—. _____
_____

DIAGNOSTIC SUGGESTIONS

Axis I:

303.90	Alcohol Dependence
305.0	Alcohol Abuse
304.30	Cannabis Dependence
304.20	Cocaine Dependence
304.80	Polysubstance Dependence
291.2	Alcohol-Induced Persisting Amnestic Disorder
300.4	Dysthymic Disorder
309.81	Posttraumatic Stress Disorder
_____	_____
_____	_____

Axis II:

301.7	Antisocial Personality Disorder
_____	_____
_____	_____

CHILDHOOD TRAUMAS

BEHAVIORAL DEFINITIONS

1. Reports of childhood physical, sexual, and/or emotional abuse.
2. Description of parents as physically or emotionally neglectful as they were chemically dependent, too busy, absent, etc.
3. Description of childhood as chaotic as parent(s) was substance abuser (or mentally ill, antisocial, etc.), leading to frequent moves, multiple abusive spousal partners, frequent substitute caretakers, financial pressures, and/or many stepsiblings.
4. Reports of emotionally repressive parents who were rigid, perfectionist, threatening, demeaning, hypercritical, and/or overly religious.
5. Irrational fears, suppressed rage, low self-esteem, identity conflicts, depression, or anxious insecurity related to painful early life experiences.
6. Dissociation phenomenon (multiple personality, psychogenic fugue or amnesia, trance state, and/or depersonalization) as a maladaptive coping mechanism resulting from childhood emotional pain.

—. _____
   _____

—. _____
   _____

—. _____
   _____

LONG-TERM GOALS

1. Develop an awareness of how childhood issues have affected and continue to affect one's family life.

2. Resolve past childhood/family issues, leading to less anger and depression, greater self-esteem, security, and confidence.
3. Release the emotions associated with past childhood/family issues, resulting in less resentment and more serenity.
4. Let go of blame and begin to forgive others for pain caused in childhood.

—. _____
   _____

—. _____
   _____

—. _____
   _____

SHORT-TERM OBJECTIVES

1. Describe what it was like to grow up in the home environment. (1, 2)

2. Describe each family member and identify the role each played within the family. (2, 3)

THERAPEUTIC INTERVENTIONS

1. Actively build the level of trust with the client in individual sessions through consistent eye contact, active listening, unconditional positive regard, and warm acceptance to help increase his/her ability to identify and express feelings.

2. Develop the client's family genogram and/or symptom line and help identify patterns of dysfunction within the family.

2. Develop the client's family genogram and/or symptom line and help identify patterns of dysfunction within the family.

3. Assist the client in clarifying his/her role within the family and his/her feelings connected to that role.

3. Identify patterns of abuse, neglect, or abandonment within the family of origin, both current and historical, nuclear and extended. (4, 5)

4. Assign the client to ask parents about their family backgrounds and develop insight regarding patterns of behavior and causes for parents' dysfunction.

5. Explore the client's painful childhood experiences.

4. Identify feelings associated with major traumatic incidents in childhood and with parental child-rearing patterns. (6, 7, 8)

6. Support and encourage the client when he/she begins to express feelings of rage, sadness, fear, and rejection relating to family abuse or neglect.

7. Assign the client to record feelings in a journal that describes memories, behavior, and emotions tied to his/her traumatic childhood experiences.

8. Ask the client to read books on the emotional effects of neglect and abuse in childhood (e.g., *It Will Never Happen To Me* by Black, *Outgrowing the Pain* by Gil, *Healing the Child Within* by Whitfield, and *Why I'm Afraid to Tell You Who I Am* by Powell); process insights attained.

5. Identify how own parenting has been influenced by childhood experiences. (9)

9. Ask the client to compare his/her parenting behavior to that of parent figures of his/her childhood; encourage the client to be aware of how easily we repeat patterns that we grew up with.

6. Acknowledge any dissociative phenomena that have resulted from childhood trauma. (10, 11)

10. Assist the client in understanding the role of dissociation in protecting himself/herself from the

pain of childhood abusive betrayals. (See Dissociation chapter in this Planner).

11. Assess the severity of the client's dissociation phenomena and hospitalize as necessary for his/her protection.

7. State the role substance abuse has in dealing with emotional pain of childhood. (12)

12. Assess the client's substance abuse behavior that has developed, in part, as a means of coping with feelings of childhood trauma. If alcohol or drug abuse is found to be a problem, encourage treatment focused on this issue (see the Chemical Dependence chapter of this Planner).

8. Decrease feelings of shame by being able to verbally affirm self as not responsible for abuse. (13, 14, 15, 16)

13. Assign writing a letter to mother, father, or other abuser in which the client expresses his/her feelings regarding the abuse.

14. Hold conjoint sessions where the client confronts the perpetrator of the abuse.

15. Guide the client in an empty chair exercise with a key figure connected to the abuse—that is, perpetrator, sibling, or parent; reinforce the client for placing responsibility for the abuse or neglect on the caretaker.

16. Consistently reiterate that responsibility for the abuse falls on the abusive adults, not the surviving child (for deserving the abuse), and reinforce statements that

accurately reflect placing blame on perpetrators and on nonprotective, nonnurturant adults.

9. Identify the positive aspects for self of being able to forgive all those involved with the abuse. (17, 18, 19)

17. Assign the client to write a forgiveness letter to the perpetrator of abuse; process the letter.

18. Teach the client the benefits (i.e., release of hurt and anger, putting issue in the past, opens door for trust of others, etc.) of beginning a process of forgiveness of (not necessarily forgetting or fraternizing with) abusive adults.

19. Recommend the client read books on the topic of forgiveness (e.g., *Forgive and Forget* by Smedes, *When Bad Things Happen to Good People* by Kushner, etc.).

10. Decrease statements of being a victim while increasing statements that reflect personal empowerment. (20, 21)

20. Ask the client to complete an exercise that identifies the positives and negatives of being a victim and the positives and negatives of being a survivor; compare and process the lists.

21. Encourage and reinforce the client's statements that reflect movement away from viewing self as a victim and toward personal empowerment as a survivor.

11. Increase level of trust of others as shown by more socialization and greater intimacy tolerance. (22, 23)

22. Teach the client the share-check method of building trust in relationships (sharing a little information and checking as to the recipient's

sensitivity in reacting to that information).

23. Teach the client the advantages of treating people as trustworthy given a reasonable amount of time to assess their character.

—. ——————————————   —. ——————————————
   ——————————————   ——————————————
—. ——————————————   —. ——————————————
   ——————————————   ——————————————
—. ——————————————   —. ——————————————
   ——————————————   ——————————————

DIAGNOSTIC SUGGESTIONS

Axis I:

300.4	Dysthymic Disorder
296.xx	Major Depressive Disorder
300.3	Obsessive-Compulsive Disorder
300.02	Generalized Anxiety Disorder
309.81	Posttraumatic Stress Disorder
300.14	Dissociative Identity Disorder
995.53	Sexual Abuse of Child, Victim
995.54	Physical Abuse of Child, Victim
995.52	Neglect of Child, Victim
————	————————————

Axis II:

301.7	Antisocial Personality Disorder
301.6	Dependent Personality Disorder
301.4	Obsessive-Compulsive Personality Disorder
————	————————————
————	————————————

CHRONIC PAIN

BEHAVIORAL DEFINITIONS

1. Experiences pain beyond the normal healing process (6 months or more) that significantly limits physical activities.
2. Complains of generalized pain in many joints, muscles, and bones that debilitates normal functioning.
3. Overuse or use of increased amounts of medications with little, if any, pain relief.
4. Experiences tension, migraine, cluster, or chronic daily headaches of unknown origin.
5. Experiences back or neck pain, interstitial cystitis, or diabetic neuropathy.
6. Experiences intermittent pain such as that related to rheumatoid arthritis or irritable bowel syndrome.
7. Decreased or stopped activities such as work, household chores, socializing, exercise, sex, or other pleasurable activities because of pain.
8. Experiences an increase in general physical discomfort (e.g., fatigue, night sweats, insomnia, muscle tension, body aches).
9. Exhibits signs and symptoms of depression.
10. Makes statements like "I can't do what I used to"; "No one understands me"; "Why me?"; "When will this go away?;" "I can't take this pain anymore" and "I can't go on."

—. _____
_____

—. _____
_____

—. _____
_____

LONG-TERM GOALS

1. Acquire and utilize the necessary pain management skills.
2. Regulate pain in order to maximize daily functioning and return to productive employment.
3. Find relief from pain and build renewed contentment and joy in performing activities of everyday life.
4. Find an escape route from the pain.
5. "Make peace with the chronic pain and move on." (Hunter)
6. Lessen daily suffering from pain.
7. Gain control over own life.

—. _____
   _____

—. _____
   _____

—. _____
   _____

SHORT-TERM OBJECTIVES

1. Describe the nature of, history of, impact of, and understood causes of chronic pain. (1, 2)

2. Complete a thorough medical examination to rule out any alternative causes for the pain and reveal any new treatment possibilities. (3)

THERAPEUTIC INTERVENTIONS

1. Gather a history and current status of the client's chronic pain.

2. Explore the changes in the client's mood, attitude, social, vocational, and familial/marital roles that have occurred in accommodation to pain.

3. Refer the client to a physician or clinic to undergo a thorough examination to rule out any undiagnosed condition and to receive recommendations on any further treatment options.

3. Follow through on a referral to a pain management or rehabilitation program. (4, 5, 6)

4. Give the client information on the options of pain management specialists or rehabilitation programs that are available and help him/her make a decision on which would be the best for him/her.

5. Make a referral to a pain management specialist or clinic of the client's choice and have him/her sign appropriate releases for the therapist to have updates on progress from the program and to coordinate services.

6. Elicit from the client a verbal commitment to cooperate with pain management specialists, headache clinic, or rehabilitation program.

4. Complete a thorough medication review by a physician who is a specialist in dealing with chronic pain or headache conditions. (7)

7. Ask the client to complete a medication review with a specialist in chronic pain or headaches. Confer with the physician afterward about his/her recommendations and process them with the client.

5. Verbalize a statement of ownership of the pain. (8, 9)

8. Assist the client in working through the defenses that prevent him/her from owning the pain as his/hers.

9. Elicit from the client statements of ownership of the pain.

6. Verbalize an increased understanding of pain. (10, 11)

10. Teach the client key concepts of rehabilitation versus biological healing, conservative versus aggressive medical interventions,

acute versus chronic pain, benign versus nonbenign pain, cure versus management, appropriate use of medication, role of exercise and self-regulation techniques, and so on.

11. Assign the client to read books on the place of pain in our lives (e.g., *Pain* by Fields or *The Culture of Pain* by Morris); process key concept/insights gained from the reading.

7. Identify specific non-headache pain triggers. (12, 13)

12. Ask the client to read the chapter on "Identifying Pain Triggers" from *Making Peace with Chronic Pain* (Hunter), then ask him/her to make a list of the triggers that apply to his/her condition; process the list content.

13. Ask the client to keep a pain journal that records time of day, where and what he/she was doing, the severity, and what was done to alleviate the pain. Process the journal with the client to increase insight into nature of the pain, trigger, and what intervention seems to offer the most consistent relief.

8. Identify causes for and triggers of headache pain. (13, 14)

13. Ask the client to keep a pain journal that records time of day, where and what he/she was doing, the severity, and what was done to alleviate the pain. Process the journal with the client to increase insight into nature of the pain, trigger, and

what intervention seems to offer the most consistent relief.

14. Assign the client to read the chapter on "Causes and Triggers" in *Taking Control of Your Headaches* (Duckro, Richardson, and Marshall) or similar information obtained from the National Headache Foundation (800-255-2243).

9. Identify the steps of the "dance of pain" in his/her life. (15)

15. Develop with the client the metaphor of pain as a dance (see *Making Peace with Chronic Pain* by Hunter), working to identify the particular steps of the dance as it moves through his/her daily life. Then challenge the client either to alter the steps of his/her present dance or to design a completely new dance.

10. Verbalize an increased awareness of the mind-body connection. (16, 17)

16. Ask the client to read *Peace, Love, and Healing* (Siegel) or *The Mind/Body Effect* (Benson) or to attend a seminar related to holistic healing for insight into the body-mind connection.

17. Assist the client in beginning to see the connection between chronic pain and chronic stress.

11. Implement the use of relaxation techniques to reduce muscle tension and pain level. (18, 19, 20)

18. Teach the client relaxation techniques (e.g., breathing exercises, using a focus word or phrase, progressive muscle relaxation, creating a safe place, and positive imagery).

12. Utilize yoga and/or meditation to reduce tension and pain. (21, 22)

13. Incorporate physical exercise into daily routine. (23, 24)

14. Identify dysfunctional attitudes about pain that are a foundation for pain being the focus of life. (25, 26)

19. Encourage the client to use relaxation tapes, videos, and so forth, on a daily basis. Especially recommend "Pachelbel's Canon" by D. Kabialka.

20. Refer for or conduct biofeedback training with the client to increase relaxation skills.

21. Ask the client to read *How to Meditate* (LeShan) and then assist him/her in implementing meditation into daily life.

22. Refer the client to a beginners' yoga class.

23. Assist the client in recognizing his/her need for regular exercise. Then encourage him/her to implement exercise in daily life and monitor results, and offer ongoing encouragement to stay with the regime.

24. Refer the client to an athletic club or a physical therapist to develop an individually tailored exercise program that is approved by his/her personal physician.

25. Assign Chapter 6 ("The Power of Mind") and Chapter 7 ("Adopting Healthy Attitudes") from the book *Managing Pain Before It Manages You* (Caudill). Process key concepts gathered from the reading and exercises.

26. Ask the client to gather from several friends, relatives,

and so on feedback in terms of negative attitudes they see in the client. Process the feedback and identify possible changes he/she could make.

15. Verbalize new, healthier attitudes about pain and life in general. (27, 28)

27. Confront the client's negative attitudes about pain and assist him/her in replacing them with more positive, constructive attitudes.

28. Assist the client in becoming capable of seeing humor in more of his/her daily life. Promote this expansion with the use of humorous teaching tapes, Dr. Seuss, telling jokes, and assigning the client to watch one or two comedy movies each week.

16. Investigate the use of alternative pain remedies to reduce dependence of doctor visits and/or painkilling medication. (29)

29. Explore the client's alternatives to doctors and medications to remove his/her pain (e.g., acupuncture, hypnosis, or myotheraphy [therapeutic] massage).

17. Make changes in diet that will promote health and fitness. (30)

30. Refer the client to a dietician for consultation around eating and nutritional patterns; process the results of the consultation, identifying changes he/she can make and how he/she might start implementing these changes.

18. Increase the frequency of identified pleasurable activities. (31)

31. Ask the client to create a list of activities that are pleasurable for him/her. Then process list with therapist and develop a plan of increasing the frequency of

the selected pleasurable activities.

19. Increase the frequency of assertive behaviors in becoming more active in managing his/her life. (32)

32. Train in assertiveness or refer the client to a group that will educate and facilitate assertiveness skills via lectures and assignments.

20. Identify and replace negative self-talk that promotes helplessness, anger, and depression. (33, 34, 35)

33. Assign the chapter entitled "You Can Change the Way You Feel" in *The Feeling Good Handbook* (Burns) to assist the client in identifying his/her distorted automatic thoughts that promote depression, helplessness, and/or anger.

34. Assign the client to complete the written exercises in Step 2: "You *Feel* The Way You Think" from *Ten Days to Self Esteem!* (Burns). Process exercises when completed.

35. Assist the client in replacing negative, distorted thoughts with positive, reality-based thoughts.

21. Identify negative "tapes" and those new positive "tapes" that must replace them. (36)

36. Utilize a Transactional Analysis (TA) approach to help the client become aware of "old tapes," and using the same approach, begin to erase them or create new healthier "tapes."

22. Identify sources of and coping mechanisms for stress in daily life. (37, 38)

37. Educate the client on the various types of stressors, then ask him/her to list the stressors he/she experiences in daily life and process the list with the therapist.

38. Assist the client in identifying specific ways to cope

effectively with the major internal, external, and family stressors.

23. Write a thorough, realistic relapse prevention plan. (39, 40)

39. Assist the client in developing a written relapse prevention plan that has a special emphasis on pain- and stress-trigger identification and specific ways to handle each, strengthening areas that are weak or lack an adequate level of thought or planning.

40. Assign the client to share his/her relapse prevention plan with those who are going to be supportive so they might help with implementation, support, and feedback of the plan.

—. _____   —. _____
   _____   _____
—. _____   —. _____
   _____   _____
—. _____   —. _____
   _____   _____

DIAGNOSTIC SUGGESTIONS

Axis I: 307.89   Pain Disorder Associated With Both Psychological Factors and an Axis III Disorder
            307.80   Pain Disorder Associated With Psychological Factors
            300.81   Somatization Disorder
            300.11   Conversion Disorder
            296.3   Major Depressive Disorder, Recurrent

300.3	Obsessive-Compulsive Disorder
302.70	Sexual Dysfunction NOS
304.10	Sedative, Hypnotic, or Anxiolytic Dependence
304.80	Polysubstance Dependence
＿＿＿	＿＿＿＿＿＿＿＿＿＿＿＿＿
＿＿＿	＿＿＿＿＿＿＿＿＿＿＿＿＿

COGNITIVE DEFICITS

BEHAVIORAL DEFINITIONS

1. Concrete thinking or impaired abstract thinking.
2. Lack of insight into the consequences of behavior (i.e., impaired judgment).
3. Short-term memory deficits.
4. Long-term memory deficits.
5. Difficulty following complex or sequential directions.
6. Loss of orientation to person, place, or time,
7. Distractibility in attention.
8. Impulsive behavior that violates social mores.
9. Speech and language impairment.

—. _____
   _____
   _____

—. _____
   _____
   _____

—. _____
   _____

LONG-TERM GOALS

1. Develop an understanding and acceptance of the cognitive impairment.
2. Develop alternative coping strategies to compensate for cognitive limitations.

—. _____
   _____

___. _____

_____

___. _____

_____

SHORT-TERM OBJECTIVES

1. Describe all symptoms that may be related to neurological deficit. (1, 2)

2. Cooperate with and complete neuropsychological testing. (3, 4)

THERAPEUTIC INTERVENTIONS

1. Explore signs and symptoms of the client's possible neurological impairment (e.g., memory loss, defective coordination, flawed abstract thinking, speech and language deficits, unsound executive functions, disorientation, impaired judgment, inattention, headaches, dizziness, blurry vision, etc.).

2. Assess and monitor the client's cognitive behavior in individual sessions.

3. Arrange for the client to have psychological testing administered to determine the nature and degree of cognitive deficits.

4. Administer appropriate psychological tests (e.g., Wechsler Adult Intelligence Scale–III, Booklet Category Test, Trailmaking, Haldstead-Reitan Battery, Michigan Neurological Battery, Luria-Nebraska Battery, Wechsler Memory Scale, Memory Assessment Scales) to determine the nature, extent, and possible origin of the client's cognitive deficits.

3. Obtain a neurological examination. (5)

4. Understand and accept cognitive limitations and use alternate coping mechanisms. (6, 7)

5. Verbalize feelings associated with acceptance of cognitive impairment. (8)

6. Attempt to follow through to completion simple sequential tasks. (9)

7. Implement memory-enhancing mechanisms. (10)

8. Identify when it is appropriate to seek help with a task and when it is not. (7, 11)

5. Refer the client to a neurologist to further assess his/her organic deficits and determine possible causes.

6. Inform the client of the results of the cognitive assessment and develop appropriate objectives based on testing.

7. Assist the client in coming to an understanding and acceptance of his/her limitations.

8. Explore the client's feelings of depression and anxiety related to his/her cognitive impairment; provide encouragement and support.

9. Assign appropriate sequential tasks for the client to perform and redirect when needed so as to assess his/her cognitive abilities.

10. Assign and monitor memory-enhancing activities/exercises for the client (e.g., crossword puzzles, card games, TV game shows) and memory-loss coping strategies (e.g., lists, routines, post notes, repeating items aloud to yourself, using mnemonic strategies).

7. Assist the client in coming to an understanding and acceptance of his/her limitations.

11. Establish with the client and his/her significant other appropriate points for the client to ask for help.

9. Write a plan identifying who will provide daily supervisory contact and when they will do it. (12, 13)

12. Assist the client in identifying dependable resource people who can provide regular supervision.

13. Develop a written schedule with the client for times of supervisory contact and identify who will provide it.

—. _____

_____

—. _____

_____

—. _____

_____

—. _____

_____

—. _____

_____

—. _____

_____

DIAGNOSTIC SUGGESTIONS

Axis I:	310.1	Personality Change Due to (Axis III Disorder)
	294.8	Dementia NOS
	294.1	Dementia Due to (Axis III Disorder)
	291.2	Alcohol-Induced Persisting Dementia
	291.1	Alcohol-Induced Persisting Amnestic Disorder
	294.8	Amnestic Disorder NOS
	303.90	Alcohol Dependence
	304.30	Cannabis Dependence
	294.0	Amnestic Disorder Due to (Axis III Disorder)
	294.9	Cognitive Disorder NOS
	_____	_____
	_____	_____
Axis II:	799.9	Diagnosis Deferred
	V71.09	No Diagnosis
	_____	_____
	_____	_____

DEPENDENCY

BEHAVIORAL DEFINITIONS

1. Inability to become self-sufficient, consistently relying on parents to provide financial support, housing, or caregiving.
2. A history of many intimate relationships with little, if any, space between the ending of one and the start of the next.
3. Strong feelings of panic, fear, and helplessness when faced with being alone as a close relationship ends.
4. Feelings easily hurt by criticism and preoccupied with pleasing others.
5. Inability to make decisions or initiate actions without excessive reassurance from others.
6. Frequent preoccupation with fears of being abandoned.
7. All feelings of self-worth, happiness, and fulfillment derive from relationships.
8. Involvement in at least two relationships wherein he/she was physically abused but had difficulty leaving.
9. Avoidance of disagreeing with others for fear of being rejected.

__. _____
   _____
__. _____
   _____
__. _____
   _____

LONG-TERM GOALS

1. Develop confidence that he/she is capable of meeting own needs and of tolerating being alone.

86

2. Achieve a healthy balance between independence and dependence.
3. Decrease dependence on relationships while beginning to meet own needs, build confidence, and practice assertiveness.
4. Establish firm individual self-boundaries and improved self-worth.
5. Break away permanently from any abusive relationships.
6. Emancipate self from emotional and economic dependence on parents.

—. _____
_____
_____

—. _____
_____
_____

—. _____
_____

SHORT-TERM OBJECTIVES

1. Describe the style and pattern of emotional dependence in relationships. (1)

2. Verbalize an increased awareness of own dependency. (2, 3)

3. Verbalize insight into the automatic practice of striving to meet other people's expectations. (4, 5, 6)

THERAPEUTIC INTERVENTIONS

1. Explore the client's history of emotional dependence extending from unmet childhood needs to current relationships.

2. Develop a family genogram to increase the client's awareness of family patterns of dependence in relationships and how he/she is repeating them in the present relationship.

3. Assign the client to read *Codependent No More* (Beattie), *Women Who Love Too Much* (Norwood), or *Getting Them Sober* (Drews). Process key ideas.

4. Explore the client's family of origin for experiences of emotional abandonment.

5. Assist the client in identifying the basis for his/her fear of disappointing others.

6. Read with the client the fable entitled "The Bridge" in *Friedman's Fables* (Friedman). Process the meaning of the fable.

4. List positive things about self. (7, 8)

7. Assist the client in developing a list of his/her positive attributes and accomplishments.

8. Assign the client to institute a ritual of beginning each day with 5 to 10 minutes of solitude where the focus is personal affirmation.

9. Explore and identify the client's distorted, negative automatic thoughts associated with assertiveness, being alone, or not meeting others' needs.

5. Identify and replace distorted automatic thoughts associated with assertiveness, being alone, or keeping personal responsibility boundaries. (5, 10, 11)

5. Assist the client in identifying the basis for his/her fear of disappointing others.

10. Explore and clarify the client's fears or other negative feelings associated with being more independent.

11. Assist the client in developing positive, reality-based messages for self to replace the distorted, negative self-talk.

6. Verbalize a decreased sensitivity to criticism. (12, 13, 14)

12. Explore the client's sensitivity to criticism and help him/her develop new ways of receiving, processing, and responding to it.

	13. Assign the client to read books on assertiveness (e.g., *When I Say No I Feel Guilty* by Smith).
	14. Verbally reinforce the client for any and all signs of assertiveness and independence.
7. Increase saying no to others' requests. (15, 16)	15. Assign the client to say no without excessive explanation for a period of one week and process this with him/her.
	16. Train the client in assertiveness or refer him/her to a group that will facilitate and develop his/her assertiveness skills via lectures and assignments.
8. Report incidents of verbally stating own opinion. (16, 17)	16. Train the client in assertiveness or refer him/her to a group that will facilitate and develop his/her assertiveness skills via lectures and assignments.
	17. Assign the client to speak his/her mind for one day, and process the results with him/her.
9. Identify own emotional and social needs and ways to fulfill them. (18, 19)	18. Ask the client to compile a list of his/her emotional and social needs and ways that these could possibly be met; process the list.
	19. Ask the client to list ways that he/she could start taking care of himself/herself; then identify two to three that could be started now and elicit the client's agreement to do so. Monitor for

10. Report examples of receiving favors from others without feeling the necessity of reciprocating. (20)

11. Verbalize an increased sense of self-responsibility while decreasing sense of responsibility for others. (21, 22, 23)

12. Verbalize an increased awareness of boundaries and when they are violated. (24, 25, 26)

follow-through and feelings of change about self.

20. Assign the client to allow others to do favors for him/her and to receive without giving. Process progress and feelings related to this assignment.

21. Assist the client in identifying and implementing ways of increasing his/her level of independence in day-to-day life.

22. Assist the client in developing new boundaries for not accepting responsibility for others' actions or feelings.

23. Facilitate conjoint session with the client's significant other with focus on exploring ways to increase independence within the relationship.

24. Assign the client to keep a daily journal regarding boundaries for taking responsibility for self and others and when he/she is aware of boundaries being broken by self or others.

25. Assign the client to read the book *Boundaries: Where You End and I Begin* (Katherine) and process key ideas.

26. Ask the client to read the chapter on setting boundaries and limits in the book *A Gift To Myself* (Whitfield) and complete the accompanying survey on personal boundaries. Process the key

13. Increase the frequency of verbally clarifying boundaries with others. (27)

14. Increase the frequency of making decisions within a reasonable time and with self-assurance. (28, 29)

15. Attend an Alanon group to reinforce efforts to break dependency cycle with a chemically dependent partner. (30)

16. Develop a plan to end the relationship with abusive partner, and implement the plan with therapist's guidance. (31, 32, 33)

ideas and results of the survey.

27. Reinforce the client for implementing boundaries and limits for self.

28. Confront the client's tendency toward decision avoidance and encourage his/her efforts to implement proactive decision making.

29. Give positive verbal reinforcement for each timely thought-out decision that the client makes.

30. Refer the client to Alanon or another appropriate self-help group.

31. Assign the client to read *The Verbally Abusive Relationship* (Evans); process key ideas and insights.

32. Refer the client to a safe house.

33. Refer the client to a domestic violence program and monitor and encourage his/her continued involvement in the program.

—. _____
_____

—. _____
_____

—. _____
_____

—. _____
_____

—. _____
_____

—. _____
_____

DIAGNOSTIC SUGGESTIONS

Axis I:	300.4	Dysthymic Disorder
	995.81	Physical Abuse of Adult, Victim
	_____	_____
	_____	_____
Axis II:	301.82	Avoidant Personality Disorder
	301.83	Borderline Personality Disorder
	301.6	Dependent Personality Disorder
	_____	_____
	_____	_____

DEPRESSION

BEHAVIORAL DEFINITIONS

1. Loss of appetite.
2. Depressed affect.
3. Diminished interest in or enjoyment of activities.
4. Psychomotor agitation or retardation.
5. Sleeplessness or hypersomnia.
6. Lack of energy.
7. Poor concentration and indecisiveness.
8. Social withdrawal.
9. Suicidal thoughts and/or gestures.
10. Feelings of hopelessness, worthlessness, or inappropriate guilt.
11. Low self-esteem.
12. Unresolved grief issues.
13. Mood-related hallucinations or delusions.
14. History of chronic or recurrent depression for which the client has taken antidepressant medication, been hospitalized, had outpatient treatment, or had a course of electroconvulsive therapy.

__. _____
   _____
   _____
__. _____
   _____
__. _____
   _____

LONG-TERM GOALS

1. Alleviate depressed mood and return to previous level of effective functioning.

2. Recognize, accept, and cope with feelings of depression.
3. Develop healthy cognitive patterns and beliefs about self and the world that lead to alleviation of depression symptoms.
4. Appropriately grieve the loss in order to normalize mood and to return to previous adaptive level of functioning.

—. _____
   _____
   _____
—. _____
   _____
   _____
—. _____
   _____

SHORT-TERM OBJECTIVES

1. Describe the signs and symptoms of depression that are experienced. (1)

2. Verbally identify, if possible, the source of depressed mood. (2, 3)

3. Express feelings of hurt, disappointment, shame, and anger that are associated with early life experiences. (4, 5)

THERAPEUTIC INTERVENTIONS

1. Explore how depression is experienced in the client's day-to-day living.

2. Ask the client to make a list of what he/she is depressed about; process the list content.

3. Encourage the client to share his/her feelings of depression in order to clarify them and gain insight as to causes.

4. Explore experiences from the client's childhood that contribute to current depressed state.

5. Encourage the client to share feelings of anger regarding pain inflicted on him/her in childhood that contribute to current depressed state.

4. Verbally express understanding of the relationship between depressed mood and repression of feelings—that is, anger, hurt, sadness, and so on. (6)

5. Take prescribed psychotropic medications responsibly at times ordered by physician. (7, 8)

6. Complete psychological testing to assess the depth of depression and the need for antidepressant medication and suicide prevention measures. (9)

7. Verbalize any history of suicide attempts and any current suicidal urges. (10)

8. Identify and replace cognitive self-talk that is engaged in to support depression. (11, 12, 13)

6. Explain a connection between previously unexpressed (repressed) feelings of anger (and helplessness) and current state of depression.

7. Arrange for a physician to give the client a physical examination to rule out organic causes for depression, assess need for antidepressant medication, and order a prescription, if appropriate.

8. Monitor and evaluate the client's psychotropic medication compliance, effectiveness, and side effects.

9. Arrange for the administration of an objective assessment instrument for evaluating the client's depression (e.g., Beck Depression Inventory, Minnesota Multiphasic Personality Inventory-2, or Modified Scale for Suicidal Ideation). Evaluate results and give feedback to the client.

10. Explore the client's history and current state of suicidal urges and behavior (see Suicidal Ideation chapter in this Planner if suicide risk is present).

11. Assist the client in developing an awareness of his/her cognitive messages that reinforce hopelessness and helplessness.

12. Assign the client to keep a daily journal of experiences,

automatic negative thoughts associated with experiences, and the depressive affect that results from that distorted interpretation; process the journal material to diffuse destructive thinking patterns and replace them with alternate realistic, positive thoughts.

13. Reinforce the client's positive, reality-based cognitive messages that enhance self-confidence and increase adaptive action.

9. State no longer having thoughts of self-harm. (14, 15)

14. Assess and monitor the client's suicide potential.

15. Arrange for hospitalization, as necessary, when the client is judged to be harmful to self.

10. Show evidence of daily care for personal grooming and hygiene with minimal reminders from others. (16)

16. Monitor and redirect the client on daily grooming and hygiene.

11. Verbalize hopeful and positive statements regarding self and the future. (13, 17, 18)

13. Reinforce the client's positive, reality-based cognitive messages that enhance self-confidence and increase adaptive action.

17. Assign the client to write at least one positive affirmation statement daily regarding himself/herself and the future.

18. Teach the client more about depression and to accept some sadness as a normal variation in feeling.

12. Utilize behavioral strategies to overcome depression. (19, 20, 21)

19. Assist the client in developing coping strategies (e.g., more physical exercise, less internal focus, increased social involvement, more assertiveness, greater need sharing, more anger expression, etc.) for feelings of depression.

20. Assign the chemically dependent client to read passages related to depression from the books *One Day at a Time* (Hallinan) and *Each Day a New Beginning* (Hazelden Staff).

21. Develop a plan for the client's participation in social and recreational activities; assist him/her in selecting activities that will bring satisfaction.

13. Participate in social contacts and initiate communication of needs and desires. (21, 22)

21. Develop a plan for the client's participation in social and recreational activities; assist him/her in selecting activities that will bring satisfaction.

22. Reinforce the client's participation in social activities and assertive verbalization of feelings, needs, and desires.

14. Verbalize any unresolved grief issues that may be contributing to depression. (23)

23. Explore the role of unresolved grief issues as they contribute to the client's current depression (see the Grief/Loss Unresolved chapter in this Planner).

15. Read books on overcoming depression. (24)

24. Recommend that the client read self-help books on

coping with depression (e.g., *The Feeling Good Handbook* by Burns, *What to Say When You Talk to Yourself* by Helmstetter, or *Talking to Yourself* by Butler); process material read.

16. Use positive conflict resolution skills to resolve interpersonal discord and to make needs and expectations known. (25, 26)

25. Teach the client conflict resolution skills (e.g., empathy, active listening, "I messages," respectful communication, assertiveness without aggression, compromise); then use modeling, role-playing, and behavior rehearsal to work through several current conflicts.

26. In conjoint sessions, help the client resolve interpersonal conflicts.

17. Increase the frequency of assertive behaviors to express needs, desires, and expectations. (22, 27)

22. Reinforce the client's participation in social activities and assertive verbalization of feelings, needs, and desires.

27. Use modeling and/or role-playing to train the client in assertiveness; if indicated, refer him/her to an assertiveness training class/group for further instruction.

18. Decrease the frequency of negative self-descriptive statements and increase the frequency of positive self-descriptive statements. (13, 17, 28, 29)

13. Reinforce the client's positive, reality-based cognitive messages that enhance self-confidence and increase adaptive action.

17. Assign the client to write at least one positive affirmation statement daily regarding himself/herself and the future.

28. Assign the exercise of the client talking positively about himself/herself into a mirror once per day.

29. Reinforce the client's positive statements made about self.

19. Implement a regular exercise regimen as a depression reduction technique. (30, 31)

30. Develop and reinforce a routine of physical exercise for the client to stimulate depression-reducing hormones.

31. Recommend that the client read and implement programs from *Exercising Your Way to Better Mental Health* (Leith).

___. _____

___. _____

___. _____

___. _____

___. _____

___. _____

DIAGNOSTIC SUGGESTIONS

Axis I:	309.0	Adjustment Disorder With Depressed Mood
	296.xx	Bipolar I Disorder
	296.89	Bipolar II Disorder
	300.4	Dysthymic Disorder
	301.13	Cyclothymic Disorder
	296.2x	Major Depressive Disorder, Single Episode
	296.3x	Major Depressive Disorder, Recurrent

	295.70	Schizoaffective Disorder
	310.1	Personality Change Due to (Axis III Disorder)
	V62.82	Bereavement
	_____	_____
Axis II:	301.9	Personality Disorder NOS (Depressive)
	799.9	Diagnosis Deferred
	V71.09	No Diagnosis
	_____	_____
	_____	_____

DISSOCIATION

BEHAVIORAL DEFINITIONS

1. The existence of two or more distinct personality states that recurrently take full control of one's behavior.
2. An episode of the sudden inability to remember important personal identification information that is more than just ordinary forgetfulness.
3. Persistent or recurrent experiences of depersonalization; feeling as if detached from or outside of one's mental processes or body during which reality testing remains intact.
4. Persistent or recurrent experiences of depersonalization; feeling as if one is automated or in a dream.
5. Depersonalization sufficiently severe and persistent as to cause marked distress in daily life.

__. _____

_____

__. _____

_____

__. _____

_____

LONG-TERM GOALS

1. Integrate the various personalities.
2. Reduce the frequency and duration of dissociative episodes.
3. Resolve the emotional trauma that underlies the dissociative disturbance.
4. Reduce the level of daily distress caused by dissociative disturbances.

5. Regain full memory.

—. _____

_____

—. _____

_____

—. _____

_____

SHORT-TERM OBJECTIVES

1. Identify each personality and have each one tell its story. (1, 2)

2. Complete a psychotropic medication evaluation with a physician. (3)

3. Take prescribed psychotropic medications responsibly at times ordered by the physician. (4)

4. Identify the key issues that trigger a dissociative state. (5, 6, 7)

THERAPEUTIC INTERVENTIONS

1. Actively build the level of trust with the client in individual sessions through consistent eye contact, active listening, unconditional positive regard, and warm acceptance to help increase his/her ability to identify and express feelings.

2. Without undue encouragement or leading, probe and assess the existence of the various personalities that take control of the client.

3. Arrange for an evaluation of the client for a psychotropic medication prescription.

4. Monitor and evaluate the client's psychotropic medication prescription for compliance, effectiveness, and side effects.

5. Explore the feelings and circumstances that trigger the client's dissociative state.

6. Explore the client's sources of emotional pain or trauma,

and feelings of fear, inadequacy, rejection, or abuse.

7. Assist the client in accepting a connection between his/her dissociating and avoidance of facing emotional conflicts/issues.

5. Decrease the number and duration of personality changes. (8, 9)

8. Facilitate integration of the client's personality by supporting and encouraging him/her to stay focused on reality rather than escaping through dissociation.

9. Emphasize to the client the importance of a here-and-now focus on reality rather than a preoccupation with the traumas of the past and dissociative phenomena associated with that fixation. Reinforce instances of here-and-now behavior.

6. Practice relaxation and deep breathing as means of reducing anxiety. (10)

10. Train the client in relaxation and deep breathing techniques to be used for anxiety management.

7. Verbalize acceptance of brief episodes of dissociation as not being the basis for panic, but only as passing phenomena. (11)

11. Teach the client to be calm and matter-of-fact in the face of brief dissociative phenomena so as to not accelerate anxiety symptoms, but to stay focused on reality.

8. Discuss the period preceding memory loss and the period after memory returns. (6, 12)

6. Explore the client's sources of emotional pain or trauma, and feelings of fear, inadequacy, rejection, or abuse.

12. Arrange and facilitate a session with the client and significant others to assist him/her in regaining lost personal information.

9. Cooperate with a referral to a neurologist to rule out organic factors in amnestic episodes. (13)

10. Attend family therapy sessions that focus on the recall of personal history information. (12, 14)

11. Utilize photos and other memorabilia to stimulate recall of personal history. (14, 15)

13. Refer the client to a neurologist for evaluation of any organic cause for memory loss experiences.

12. Arrange and facilitate a session with the client and significant others to assist him/her in regaining lost personal information.

14. Calmly reassure the client to be patient in seeking to regain lost memories.

14. Calmly reassure the client to be patient in seeking to regain lost memories.

15. Utilize pictures and other memorabilia to gently trigger the client's memory recall.

__. _____
   _____
__. _____
   _____
__. _____
   _____

__. _____
   _____
__. _____
   _____
__. _____
   _____

DIAGNOSTIC SUGGESTIONS

Axis I: 303.90   Alcohol Dependence
           300.14   Dissociative Identity Disorder
           300.12   Dissociative Amnesia
           300.6   Depersonalization Disorder
           300.15   Dissociative Disorder NOS
           _____   _____
           _____   _____

Axis II: 799.9   Diagnosis Deferred
           V71.09   No Diagnosis
           _____   _____
           _____   _____

EATING DISORDER

BEHAVIORAL DEFINITIONS

1. Chronic, rapid consumption of large quantities of high-carbohydrate food.
2. Self-induced vomiting and/or abuse of laxatives due to fear of weight gain.
3. Extreme weight loss (and amenorrhea in females) with refusal to maintain a minimal healthy weight.
4. Very limited ingestion of food and high frequency of secret self-induced vomiting, inappropriate use of laxatives, and/or excessive strenuous exercise.
5. Persistent preoccupation with body image related to grossly inaccurate assessment of self as overweight.
6. Predominating irrational fear of becoming overweight.
7. Escalating fluid and electrolyte imbalance resulting from eating disorder.
8. Strong denial of seeing self as emaciated even when severely under recommended weight.

—. _____
   _____

—. _____
   _____

—. _____
   _____

LONG-TERM GOALS

1. Restore normal eating patterns, body weight, balanced fluid and electrolytes, and a realistic perception of body size.

2. Terminate the pattern of binge eating and purging behavior with a return to normal eating of enough nutritious foods to maintain a healthy weight.
3. Stabilize the medical conditions, resume patterns of food intake that will sustain life, and gain weight to a normal level.
4. Gain sufficient insight into the cognitive and emotional struggle to allow termination of the eating disorder and responsible maintenance of nutritional food intake.
5. Develop alternate coping strategies (e.g., feeling identification and assertiveness) to deal with underlying emotional issues, making the eating disorder unnecessary.
6. Change the definition of the self, so that it does not focus on body weight, size, and shape as the primary criteria for self-acceptance.
7. Restructure the distorted thoughts, beliefs, and values that contribute to eating disorder development.

—. _____

_____

—. _____

_____

—. _____

_____

SHORT-TERM OBJECTIVES	THERAPEUTIC INTERVENTIONS
1. Honestly describe the pattern of eating as to frequency, amounts, and types of food consumed or hoarded. (1, 2)	1. Document the reality of the client's dysfunctional eating pattern (too little food, too much food and/or binge eating, or hoarding food).
	2. Compare the client's calorie consumption with an average adult rate of 1,500 calories per day to establish the reality of over- or undereating.
2. Describe any regular use of dysfunctional weight control behaviors. (3, 4, 5)	3. Explore for the existence of vomiting behavior by the client to purge himself/herself of calorie intake;

monitor on an ongoing basis.

4. Document the client's abuse of laxatives in an effort to control his/her weight; monitor on an ongoing basis.

5. Explore for a history of too vigorous and too frequent exercise by the client in an effort to control his/her weight; monitor on an ongoing basis.

3. Admit to a persistent preoccupation with body image/size. (6)

6. Explore the client's perception of body image/size and the frequency and intensity of his/her thinking about it; matter-of-factly confront all distortions of body image.

4. Cooperate with a complete physical exam. (7)

7. Refer the client to a physician for a physical exam and stay in close consultation with the physician as to the client's medical condition and nutritional habits.

5. Submit to a dental exam. (8)

8. Refer the client to a dentist for a dental exam.

6. Cooperate with an evaluation for psychotropic medications. (9)

9. Assess the client's need for psychotropic medications; arrange for a physician to evaluate for and then prescribe psychotropic medications, if indicated.

7. Take medications as ordered and report as to effectiveness and side effects. (10)

10. Monitor psychotropic medication prescription compliance, effectiveness, and side effects.

8. Comply with psychological testing. (11)

11. Arrange for the administration of psychological testing to assess the client's current emotional functioning and

aid in differential diagnosis of any coexisting conditions; give feedback to the client (and his/her family) regarding psychological testing results.

9. Cooperate with admission to inpatient treatment if a fragile medical condition necessitates such treatment. (7, 12)

7. Refer the client to a physician for a physical exam and stay in close consultation with the physician as to the client's medical condition and nutritional habits.

12. Refer the client for hospitalization, as necessary, if his/her weight loss becomes severe and physical health is jeopardized.

10. Eat at regular intervals (three meals a day), consuming at least the minimum daily calories necessary to progressively gain weight. (13, 14, 15)

13. Establish a minimum daily caloric intake for the client and assist him/her in meal planning.

14. Monitor the client's weight and give realistic feedback regarding body thinness.

15. Establish healthy weight goals for the client per the Body Mass Index (BMI = pounds of body weight × 700/ height in inches/height in inches; normal range is 20 to 27 and below 18 is medically critical), the Metropolitan Height and Weight Tables, or some other recognized standard.

11. Keep a journal of food consumption. (16)

16. Assign the client to keep a journal of food intake, thoughts, and feelings; process journal information.

12. Attain and maintain balanced fluids and electrolytes as well as resumption of reproductive functions. (7, 17)

7. Refer the client to a physician for a physical exam and stay in close consultation with the physician as to the client's medical condition and nutritional habits.

17. Refer the client back to the physician at regular intervals if fluids and electrolytes need monitoring due to poor nutritional habits.

13. Identify and replace irrational beliefs and distorted self-talk messages associated with eating normal amounts of food. (18, 19)

18. Assist in the identification of negative cognitive messages (e.g., catastrophizing or exaggerating) that mediate the client's avoidance of food intake; train the client to establish realistic cognitive messages regarding food intake and body size.

19. Reinforce the client's use of more realistic, positive messages to himself/herself regarding food intake and body size.

19. Reinforce the client's use of more realistic, positive messages to himself/herself regarding food intake and body size.

14. Verbalize positive, reality-based self-talk regarding weight status and body size. (19, 20)

20. Confront the client's unrealistic and perfectionistic assessment of his/her body image and assign exercises (e.g., positive self-talk in the mirror, shopping for clothes that flatter the appearance) that reinforce a healthy, realistic body appraisal.

15. Verbalize acceptance of sexual impulses and a desire for intimacy. (21)

16. Identify the relationship between the fear of failure, drive for perfectionism, and the roots of low self-esteem. (22, 23, 24)

17. Acknowledge and overcome the role that passive-aggressive control (e.g., the refusal to accept guidance) has in the avoidance of eating. (25, 26)

18. Acknowledge and resolve separation anxiety related to the emancipation process. (27, 28)

21. Explore the client's fear of losing control of sexual impulses and how the fear relates to keeping himself/herself unattractively thin or fat; reinforce acceptance of sexual impulses and a desire for intimacy as normal.

22. Discuss the client's fear of failure and the role of perfectionism in the search for control and the avoidance of failure.

23. Reinforce the client's positive qualities and successes to reduce the fear of failure and build a positive sense of self.

24. Teach and reinforce the client's acceptance of self and others as human and subject to shortcomings and imperfection. If appropriate, use the client's spiritual belief system to strengthen this concept.

25. Process the client's use of passive-aggressive control in rebellion against authority figures.

26. Explore the client's food control as related to fear of losing control of eating or weight.

27. Explore the client's fears related to independence and emancipation from parent figures.

28. Hold family therapy sessions that focus on issues of

separation, dependence, and emancipation; support and encourage the client in identifying fears related to separation and in making a declaration of independence.

19. Develop assertive behaviors that allow for healthy expression of needs and emotions. (29)

29. Train the client in assertiveness or refer him/her to an assertiveness training class, reinforcing assertive behaviors in session and reports of successful assertiveness between sessions.

20. Verbalize the feelings of low self-esteem, depression, loneliness, anger, need for nurturance, or lack of trust that underlie the eating disorder. (30, 31)

30. Facilitate family therapy sessions that focus on owning feelings, clarifying messages, identifying control conflicts, and developing age-appropriate boundaries.

31. Probe the client's emotional struggles that are camouflaged by the eating disorder.

21. State a basis for positive identity that is not based on weight and appearance but on character, traits, relationships, and intrinsic value. (23, 32, 33)

23. Reinforce the client's positive qualities and successes to reduce the fear of failure and build a positive sense of self.

32. Assist the client in identifying a basis for self-worth apart from body image by reviewing his/her talents, successes, positive traits, importance to others, and intrinsic spiritual value.

33. Assign the client the book *Body Traps* (Rodin) and process the key ideas regarding obsessing over body image.

22. Verbalize the connection between suppressed emotional expression, difficulty with interpersonal issues, and unhealthy food usage. (31, 34)

31. Probe the client's emotional struggles that are camouflaged by the eating disorder.

34. Teach the client the connection between suppressed emotions, interpersonal conflict, and dysfunctional eating behavior.

23. Understand and verbalize the connection between too-restrictive dieting and binge episodes. (35, 36)

35. Assist the client in understanding the relationship between binging and lack of regular mealtimes or total deprivation from specific foods.

36. Encourage the client to read book(s) on binge eating (e.g., *Overcoming Binge Eating* by Fairburn) to increase the awareness of the components of eating disorders.

24. Ask significant others to state a detachment from responsibility for the client's eating disorder. (37, 38)

37. Teach parents or partner how to successfully detach from taking responsibility for the client's eating behavior without becoming hostile or indifferent.

38. Recommend that the client's parents, partner, or friends read *Surviving an Eating Disorder* (Siegel, Brisman, and Weinshel) and process the concepts in a family therapy session.

25. Verbalize the acceptance of full responsibility for choices about eating behavior. (39, 40)

39. Refer the client to a dietician for education in healthy eating and nutritional concerns; process the meeting as to concrete plans for meal planning and caloric consumption.

26. Terminate dysfunctional weight control behaviors. (41)

40. Ask the client to commit to setting a goal of a weight gain of two pounds per week; reinforce weight gain and acceptance of personal responsibility for normal food intake.

41. Ask the client to commit to a contract of terminating all dysfunctional weight control behaviors (e.g., use of laxatives, self-induced vomiting, vigorous exercise, etc.).

27. Attend an eating disorder group. (42)

42. Refer the client to a support group for eating disorders.

—. _____
_____

—. _____
_____

—. _____
_____

—. _____
_____

—. _____
_____

—. _____
_____

DIAGNOSTIC SUGGESTIONS

Axis I:	307.1	Anorexia Nervosa
	307.51	Bulimia Nervosa
	307.50	Eating Disorder NOS
	_____	_____
	_____	_____
Axis II:	301.6	Dependent Personality Disorder
	799.9	Diagnosis Deferred
	V71.09	No Diagnosis
	_____	_____
	_____	_____

EDUCATIONAL DEFICITS

BEHAVIORAL DEFINITIONS

1. Failure to complete requirements for high school diploma or GED certificate.
2. Possession of no marketable employment skills and need for vocational training.
3. Functional illiteracy.
4. History of difficulties, not involving behavior, in school or other learning situations.

—. _____

_____

—. _____

_____

—. _____

_____

LONG-TERM GOALS

1. Recognize the need for high school completion or GED certificate and reenroll in the necessary courses.
2. Seek out vocational training to obtain marketable employment skill.
3. Increase literacy skills.
4. Receive high school diploma or GED certificate.
5. Establish the existence of a learning disability and begin the development of skills to overcome it.

—. _____

_____

—. _____
   _____
   _____
—. _____
   _____

SHORT-TERM OBJECTIVES

1. Identify the factors that contributed to termination of education. (1, 2)

2. Verbally verify the need for a high school diploma or GED. (3, 4, 5, 6)

THERAPEUTIC INTERVENTIONS

1. Explore the client's attitude toward education and the family, peer, and/or school experiences that led to termination of education.

2. Gather an educational history from the client that includes family achievement history and difficulties he/she had with regard to specific subjects (e.g., reading, math).

3. Confront the client with his/her need for further education.

4. Assist the client in listing the negative effects that the lack of a GED certificate or high school diploma has had on his/her life.

5. Support and direct the client toward obtaining further academic training.

6. Reinforce and encourage the client in pursuing educational and/or vocational training by pointing out the social, monetary, and self-esteem advantages.

3. Complete an assessment to identify style of learning and to establish or rule out a specific learning disability. (7)

4. Cooperate with a psychological assessment for symptoms of Attention Deficit Disorder (ADD) that may have interfered with educational achievement. (8)

5. Complete an evaluation for psychotropic medications. (9, 10, 11)

6. Implement the recommendations of evaluations. (12)

7. Identify the facts and feelings related to negative, critical education-related experiences endured from parents, teachers, or peers. (13, 14)

7. Administer testing or refer the client to an educational specialist to be tested for learning style, cognitive strengths, and to establish or rule out a learning disability.

8. Refer the client for or perform psychological assessment for Attention Deficit Disorder (see ADD–Adult chapter in this Planner).

9. Refer the client for medication evaluation to treat his/her ADD.

10. Encourage the client to take the prescribed psychotropic medications, reporting as to their effectiveness and side effects.

11. Monitor the client's psychotropic medication prescription compliance, effectiveness, and side effects.

12. Encourage the client to implement the recommendations of the educational, psychological, and medical evaluations.

13. Ask the client to list the negative messages he/she has experienced in learning situations from teachers, parents, and peers, and to process this list with the therapist.

14. Facilitate the client's openness regarding shame or embarrassment surrounding

8. Verbalize decreased anxiety and negativity associated with learning situations. (15, 16)

9. Identify own academic and motivational strengths. (17)

10. Verbalize positive self-talk regarding educational opportunities. (18)

11. Agree to pursue educational assistance to attain reading skills. (19, 20)

12. State commitment to obtain further academic or vocational training. (21)

13. Make the necessary contacts to investigate enrollment in high school, GED, or vocational classes. (22, 23)

lack of reading ability, educational achievement, or vocational skill.

15. Give encouragement and verbal affirmation to the client as he/she works to increase his/her educational level.

16. Assist the client in developing strategies (e.g., deep breathing, muscle relaxation, positive self-talk) for coping with his/her own fears and anxieties in learning situations.

17. Assist the client in identifying his/her realistic academic and motivational strengths.

18. Reframe the client's negative self-talk in light of testing results or overlooked accomplishments.

19. Assess the client's reading deficits.

20. Refer the client to resources for learning to read. Monitor, and encourage the client's follow-through.

21. Elicit a commitment from the client to pursue further academic or vocational training.

22. Provide the client with information regarding community resources available for adult education, GED, high school completion, and vocational skill training.

23. Assign the client to make
preliminary contact with
vocational and/or educa-
tional training agencies and
report back regarding the
experience.

14. Attend classes consistently
to complete academic de-
gree and/or vocational
training course. (24)

24. Monitor and support the
client's attendance at educational or vocational classes.

__. _____

_____

__. _____

_____

__. _____

_____

__. _____

_____

__. _____

_____

__. _____

_____

DIAGNOSTIC SUGGESTIONS

Axis I:	V62.3	Academic Problem
	V62.2	Occupational Problem
	315.2	Disorder of Written Expression
	315.00	Reading Disorder
	_____	_____
Axis II:	V62.89	Borderline Intellectual Functioning
	317	Mild Mental Retardation
	_____	_____
	_____	_____

FAMILY CONFLICT

BEHAVIORAL DEFINITIONS

1. Constant or frequent conflict with parents and/or siblings.
2. A family that is not a stable source of positive influence or support since family members have little or no contact with each other.
3. Ongoing conflict with parents, which is characterized by parents fostering dependence leading to feelings that the parents are overly involved.
4. Maintains a residence with parents and has been unable to live independently for more than a brief period.
5. Long period of noncommunication with parents, and description of self as the "black sheep."
6. Remarriage of two parties, both of whom bring children into the marriage from previous relationships.

__. _____
   _____
__. _____
   _____
__. _____
   _____

LONG-TERM GOALS

1. Resolve fear of rejection, low self-esteem, and/or oppositional defiance by resolving conflicts developed in the family or origin and understanding their connection to current life.
2. Begin the process of emancipating from parents in a healthy way by making arrangements for independent living.

3. Decrease the level of present conflict with parents while beginning to let go of or resolving past conflicts with them.
4. Achieve a reasonable level of family connectedness and harmony where members support, help, and are concerned for each other.
5. Become a reconstituted/blended family unit that is functional and whose members are bonded to each other.

—. _____
   _____
   _____

—. _____
   _____
   _____

—. _____
   _____

SHORT-TERM OBJECTIVES

1. Describe the conflicts and the causes of conflicts between self and parents. (1, 2)

2. Attend and participate in family therapy sessions where the focus is on controlled, reciprocal, respectful communication of thoughts and feelings. (3, 4)

THERAPEUTIC INTERVENTIONS

1. Give verbal permission for the client to have and express own feelings, thoughts, and perspectives in order to foster a sense of autonomy from family.

2. Explore the nature of the client's family conflicts and their perceived causes.

3. Conduct family therapy sessions with the client and his/her parents to facilitate healthy communication, conflict resolution, and emancipation process.

4. Educate family members that resistance to change in styles of relating to one another is usually high and that change takes concerted effort by all members.

3. Identify own as well as others' role in the family conflicts. (5, 6)

5. Confront the client when he/she is not taking responsibility for his/her role in the family conflict and reinforce the client for owning responsibility for his/her contribution to the conflict.

6. Ask the client to read material on resolving family conflict (e.g., *Making Peace with Your Parents* by Bloomfield and Felder); encourage and monitor the selection of concepts to begin using in conflict resolution.

4. Family members demonstrate increased openness by sharing thoughts and feelings about family dynamics, roles, and expectations. (7, 8)

7. Conduct a family session in which a process genogram is formed that is complete with members, patterns of interaction, rules, and secrets.

8. Facilitate each family member in expressing his/her concerns and expectations regarding becoming a more functional family unit.

5. Identify the role that chemical dependence behavior plays in triggering family conflict. (9)

9. Assess for the presence of chemical dependence in the client or family members; emphasize the need for chemical dependence treatment, if indicated, and arrange for such a focus. (See Chemical Dependence and Chemical Dependence—Relapse chapters in this Planner.)

6. Verbally describe an understanding of the role played by family relationship stress in triggering substance abuse or relapse. (10, 11)

10. Help the client to see the triggers for chemical dependence relapse in the family conflicts.

11. Ask the client to read material on the family aspects of chemical dependence (e.g., *It Will Never Happen to Me* by Black, *On the Family* by Bradshaw, etc.); process key family issues from the reading that are triggers for him/her.

7. Increase the number of positive family interactions by planning activities. (12, 13, 14)

12. Refer the family for an experiential weekend at a center for family education to build skills and confidence in working together. (Consider a physical confidence class with low or high ropes courses, etc.).

13. Ask the parents to read material on positive parenting methods (e.g., *Raising Self-Reliant Children* by Glenn and Nelsen, *Between Parent and Child* by Ginott, *Between Parent and Teenager* by Ginott, etc.); process key concepts gathered from their reading.

14. Assist the client in developing a list of positive family activities that promote harmony (e.g., bowling, fishing, playing table games, or doing work projects). Schedule such activities into the family calendar.

8. Parents report how both are involved in the home and parenting process. (15, 16)

15. Elicit from the parents the role each takes in the parental team and his/her perspective on parenting.

16. Read and process in a family therapy session the fable "Raising Cain" or

9. Identify ways in which the parental team can be strengthened. (17, 18, 19, 20)

"Cinderella" (see *Friedman's Fables* by Friedman).

17. Assist the parents in identifying areas that need strengthening in their "parental team," then work with them to strengthen these areas.

18. Refer the parents to a parenting group to help expand their understanding of children and to build discipline skills.

19. Direct the parents to attend a Toughlove group for support and feedback on their situation.

20. Train the parents in the Barkley Method (see *Defiant Children* by Barkley) of understanding and managing defiant and oppositional behavior.

10. Parents report a decrease in the frequency of conflictual interactions with the child and between children. (13, 21, 22)

13. Ask the parents to read material on positive parenting methods (e.g., *Raising Self-Reliant Children* by Glenn and Nelsen, *Between Parent and Child* by Ginott, *Between Parent and Teenager* by Ginott, etc.); process key concepts gathered from their reading.

21. Assign the parents to read material on reducing sibling conflict (e.g., *Siblings Without Rivalry* by Faber and Mazlish); process key concepts and encourage implementation of interventions with their children.

22. Train the parents in a structured approach to discipline for young children (e.g., *1-2-3 Magic* by Phelan or *Parenting with Love and Logic* by Cline and Fay); monitor and readjust their implementation as necessary.

11. Report an increase in resolving conflicts with parent by talking calmly and assertively rather than aggressively and defensively. (23)

23. Use role-playing, role reversal, modeling, and behavioral rehearsal to help the client develop assertive ways to resolve conflict with parents.

12. Parents increase structure within the family. (24, 25)

24. Assist parents in developing rituals (e.g., dinner times, bedtime readings, weekly family activity times, etc.) that will provide structure and promote bonding.

25. Assist the parents in increasing structure within the family by setting times for eating meals together, limiting number of visitors, setting a lights-out time, establishing a phone call cutoff time, curfew time, "family meeting" time, and so on.

13. Each family member represent pictorially and then describe his/her role in the family. (26, 27)

26. Conduct a family session in which all members bring self-produced drawings of themselves in relationship to the family; ask each to describe what they've brought and then have the picture placed in an album.

27. Ask the family to make a collage of pictures cut out from magazines depicting "family" through their eyes

14. Family members report a desire for and vision of a new sense of connectedness. (28, 29, 30)

28. In a family session, assign the family the task of planning and going on an outing or activity; in the following session, process the experience with the family, giving positive reinforcement where appropriate.

and/or ask them to design a coat of arms that will signify the blended unit.

29. Conduct a session with all new family members in which a genogram is constructed gathering the history of both families and that visually shows how the new family connection will be.

30. Assign the parents to read the book *Changing Families* (Fassler, Lash, and Ives) at home with the family and report their impressions in family therapy sessions.

15. Identify factors that reinforce dependence on the family and discover how to overcome them. (31, 32)

31. For each factor that promotes the client's dependence on parents, develop a constructive plan to reduce that dependence.

32. Ask the client to make a list of ways he/she is dependent on parents.

16. Increase the level of independent functioning—that is, finding and keeping a job, saving money, socializing with friends, finding own housing, and so on. (33, 34, 35)

33. Confront the client's emotional dependence and avoidance of economic responsibility that promotes continuing pattern of living with parents.

34. Probe the client's fears surrounding emancipation.

35. Assist the client in developing a plan for healthy and responsible emancipation from parents that is, if possible, complete with their blessing.

—. _____   —. _____
   _____   _____

—. _____   —. _____
   _____   _____

—. _____   —. _____
   _____   _____

DIAGNOSTIC SUGGESTIONS

Axis I: 300.4   Dysthymic Disorder
              300.0   Anxiety Disorder NOS
              312.34   Intermittent Explosive Disorder
              303.90   Alcohol Dependence
              304.20   Cocaine Dependence
              304.80   Polysubstance Dependence

              _____   _____

Axis II: 301.7   Antisocial Personality Disorder
              301.6   Dependent Personality Disorder
              301.83   Borderline Personality Disorder
              301.9   Personality Disorder NOS

              _____   _____
              _____   _____

FEMALE SEXUAL DYSFUNCTION

BEHAVIORAL DEFINITIONS

1. Consistently very low or no pleasurable anticipation of or desire for sexual activity.
2. Strong avoidance of and/or repulsion to any and all sexual contact in spite of a relationship of mutual caring and respect.
3. Recurrent lack of usual physiological response of sexual excitement and arousal (genital lubrication and swelling).
4. Consistent lack of subjective sense of enjoyment and pleasure during sexual activity.
5. Persistent delay in or absence of reaching orgasm after achieving arousal and in spite of sensitive sexual pleasuring by a caring partner.
6. Genital pain before, during, or after sexual intercourse.
7. Consistent or recurring involuntary spasm of the vagina that prohibits penetration for sexual intercourse.

—. _____
   _____

—. _____
   _____

—. _____
   _____

LONG-TERM GOALS

1. Increase desire for and enjoyment of sexual activity.
2. Attain and maintain physiological excitement response during sexual intercourse.

3. Reach orgasm with a reasonable amount of time, intensity, and focus given to sexual stimulation.
4. Eliminate pain and achieve a presence of subjective pleasure before, during, and after sexual intercourse.
5. Eliminate vaginal spasms that prohibit penile penetration during sexual intercourse and achieve a sense of relaxed enjoyment of coital pleasure.

—. _____
   _____

—. _____
   _____

—. _____
   _____

SHORT-TERM OBJECTIVES	THERAPEUTIC INTERVENTIONS
1. Openly reveal conflicts and unfulfilled needs in the relationship that lead to anger and emotional distance. (1, 2)	1. Assess the client's relationship with her sexual partner as to level of harmony and fulfillment (see Intimate Relationship Conflicts chapter in this Planner).
	2. Direct conjoint sessions with the client and her partner that focus on conflict resolution, expression of feelings, and sex education.
2. Provide a detailed sexual history that explores all experiences that have influenced sexual attitudes, feelings, and behavior. (3, 4, 5)	3. Probe the client's family of origin history for causes for her feelings of inhibition, low self-esteem, guilt, fear, or repulsion.
	4. Obtain a detailed sexual history that examines the client's current adult sexual functioning as well as her childhood and adolescent sexual experiences, level and sources of sexual knowledge, typical sexual

practices and their frequency, medical history, and use of mood-altering substances.

5. Explore the role of the client's family of origin in teaching her negative attitudes regarding sexuality.

3. State an understanding of how religious training negatively influenced sexual thoughts, feelings, and behavior. (5, 6)

5. Explore the role of the client's family of origin in teaching her negative attitudes regarding sexuality.

6. Explore the role of the client's religious training in reinforcing her feelings of guilt and shame surrounding her sexual behavior and thoughts.

4. Verbalize a resolution of feelings regarding sexual trauma or abuse experiences. (7, 8)

7. Probe the client's history for experiences of sexual trauma or abuse.

8. Process the client's emotions surrounding an emotional trauma in the sexual arena (see Sexual Abuse chapter in this Planner).

5. Verbalize an understanding of the role of childhood experiences in the development of negative sexual attitudes and responses. (9)

9. Assist the client in developing insight into the role of unhealthy sexual attitudes and experiences of childhood in the development of current adult dysfunction; press for a commitment to try to put negative attitudes and experiences in the past while making a behavioral effort to become free from those influences.

6. Verbalize an understanding of the connection between the lack of a positive sex role model in childhood or adolescence and current adult sexual dysfunction. (5, 10)

7. Identify and replace negative cognitive messages that trigger fears, shame, anger, or grief during sexual activity. (11, 12)

8. Demonstrate healthy acceptance and accurate knowledge of sexuality by freely verbalizing accurate information regarding sexual functioning using appropriate terms for sexually related body parts. (13, 14, 15)

9. Abstain from substance abuse patterns that interfere with sexual response. (16)

5. Explore the role of the client's family of origin in teaching her negative attitudes regarding sexuality.

10. Explore sex role models the client has experienced in childhood or adolescence.

11. Probe automatic thoughts that trigger the client's negative emotions before, during, and after sexual activity.

12. Train the client in healthy alternative thoughts that will mediate pleasure, relaxation, and disinhibition.

13. Disinhibit and educate the client by encouraging her to talk freely and respectfully regarding her sexual body parts, sexual feelings, and sexual behavior.

14. Assign books (e.g., *Sexual Awareness* by McCarthy and McCarthy, *The Gift of Sex* by Penner and Penner, *The New Male Sexuality* by Zilbergeld) that provide the client with accurate sexual information and/or outline sexual exercises that disinhibit and reinforce sexual sensate focus.

15. Reinforce the client for talking freely, knowledgeably, and positively regarding her sexual thoughts, feelings, and behavior.

16. Explore the client's use or abuse of mood-altering substances and their effect on sexual functioning; refer

10. Verbalize an understanding of the role that physical disease or medication has on sexual dysfunction. (17, 18)

11. Cooperate with a physician's complete examination and report results. (19)

12. Discuss feelings of and causes for depression. (20, 21)

13. Verbalize connection between previously failed intimate relationships as to behaviors and emotions that caused failure. (22)

14. Discuss feelings surrounding a secret affair and make a termination decision regarding one of the relationships. (1, 23)

her for focused substance abuse counseling.

17. Assess the possible role that diabetes, hypertension, or thyroid disease may have on the client's sexual functioning.

18. Review medications taken by the client with regard to their possible negative side effects on sexual functioning.

19. Refer the client to a physician for a complete physical to rule out any organic or medication-related basis for the sexual dysfunction.

20. Assess the role of depression in suppressing the client's sexual desire or performance (see Depression chapter in this Planner).

21. Refer the client for antidepressant medication prescription to alleviate depression.

22. Explore the client's fears surrounding intimate relationships and whether there is evidence of repeated failure in this area.

1. Assess the client's relationship with her sexual partner as to level of harmony and fulfillment (see Intimate Relationship Conflicts chapter in this Planner).

23. Explore for any secret sexual affairs that may account for the client's sexual dysfunction with her partner.

15. Openly acknowledge and discuss, if present, homosexual attraction. (24)

16. Practice sensate focus exercises alone and with partner and share feelings associated with activity. (25, 26, 27)

17. Write about sexual feelings and thoughts in a daily journal. (28, 29)

18. Implement new coital positions and settings for sexual activity that enhance pleasure and satisfaction. (14, 30)

24. Explore for a homosexual interest that accounts for the client's heterosexual disinterest.

25. Assign the client body exploration and awareness exercises that reduce inhibition and desensitize her to sexual aversion.

26. Assign the client graduated steps of sexual pleasuring exercises with partner that reduce her performance anxiety and focus on experiencing bodily arousal sensations.

27. Give the client permission for less inhibited, less constricted sexual behavior by assigning her body-pleasuring exercises with partner.

28. Assign the client to keep a journal of her sexual thoughts and feelings to increase her awareness and acceptance of them as normal.

29. Encourage the client's indulgence in her normally occurring sexual fantasies that mediate enhanced sexual desire.

14. Assign books (e.g., *Sexual Awareness* by McCarthy and McCarthy, *The Gift of Sex* by Penner and Penner, or *The New Male Sexuality* by Zilbergeld) that provide the client with accurate sexual information and/or

outline sexual exercises that disinhibit and reinforce sexual sensate focus.

30. Suggest experimentation with coital positions and settings for sexual play that may increase the client's feelings of security, arousal, and satisfaction.

19. Engage in more assertive behaviors that allow for sharing sexual needs, feelings, and desires, behaving more sensuously and expressing pleasure. (27, 31)

27. Give the client permission for less inhibited, less constricted sexual behavior by assigning body-pleasuring exercises with partner.

31. Encourage the client to gradually explore the role of being more sexually assertive, sensuously provocative, and freely uninhibited in sexual play with partner.

20. Resolve conflicts or develop coping strategies that reduce stress interfering with sexual interest or performance. (32)

32. Probe stress in areas such as work, extended family, and social relationships that distract the client from sexual desire or performance (see Anxiety, Family Conflict, and Vocational Stress chapters in this Planner).

21. Discuss low self-esteem issues that impede sexual functioning and verbalize positive self-image. (3, 7, 33)

3. Probe the client's family of origin history for causes for her feelings of inhibition, low self-esteem, guilt, fear, or repulsion.

7. Probe the client's history for experiences of sexual trauma or abuse.

33. Explore the client's fears of inadequacy as a sexual partner that led to her sexual avoidance.

22. Communicate feelings of threat to partner that are based on perception of partner being too sexually aggressive or too critical. (2, 34)

2. Direct conjoint sessions with the client and her partner that focus on conflict resolution, expression of feelings, and sex education.

34. Explore the client's feelings of threat brought on by perception of partner as sexually aggressive.

23. Verbalize a positive body image. (35, 36)

35. Assign the client to list assets of her body; confront unrealistic distortions and critical comments.

36. Explore the client's feelings regarding her body image, focusing on causes for negativism.

24. Verbalize increasing desire for and pleasure with sexual activity. (30, 31, 37)

30. Suggest experimentation with coital positions and settings for sexual play that may increase the client's feelings of security, arousal, and satisfaction.

31. Encourage the client to gradually explore the role of being more sexually assertive, sensuously provocative, and freely uninhibited in sexual play with partner.

37. Reinforce the client's expressions of desire for and pleasure with sexual activity.

25. Report progress on gradual client-controlled vaginal penetration with partner. (25, 38, 39)

25. Assign the client body exploration and awareness exercises that reduce inhibition and desensitize her to sexual aversion.

38. Direct the client's use of masturbation and/or vaginal dilator devices to

reinforce relaxation and success surrounding vaginal penetration.

39. Direct the client's sexual partner in sexual exercises that allow for client-controlled level of genital stimulation and gradually increased vaginal penetration.

__. _____   __. _____
    _____   _____
__. _____   __. _____
    _____   _____
__. _____   __. _____
    _____   _____

DIAGNOSTIC SUGGESTIONS

Axis I: 302.71   Hypoactive Sexual Desire Disorder
              302.79   Sexual Aversion Disorder
              302.72   Female Sexual Arousal Disorder
              302.73   Female Orgasmic Disorder
              302.76   Dyspareunia
              306.51   Vaginismus
              995.53   Sexual Abuse of Child, Victim
              625.8   Female Hypoactive Sexual Desire Disorder
                       Due to (Axis III Disorder)
              625.0   Female Dyspareunia Due to (Axis III Disorder)
              302.70   Sexual Dysfunction NOS
              _____   _____
              _____   _____

FINANCIAL STRESS

BEHAVIORAL DEFINITIONS

1. Indebtedness and overdue bills that exceed ability to meet monthly payments.
2. Loss of income due to unemployment.
3. Reduction in income due to change in employment status.
4. Conflict with spouse over management of money and the definition of necessary expenditures and savings goals.
5. A feeling of low self-esteem and hopelessness that is associated with the lack of sufficient income to cover the cost of living.
6. A long-term lack of discipline in money management that has led to excessive indebtedness.
7. An uncontrollable crisis (e.g., medical bills, job layoff) that has caused past-due bill balances to exceed ability to make payments.
8. Fear of losing housing because of an inability to meet monthly mortgage payments.
9. A pattern of impulsive spending that does not consider the eventual financial consequences.

—. _____
   _____
—. _____
   _____
—. _____
   _____

LONG-TERM GOALS

1. Establish a clear income and expense budget that will meet bill payment demands.

136

2. Contact creditors to develop a revised repayment plan for outstanding bills.
3. Gain a new sense of self-worth in which the substance of one's value is not attached to the capacity to do things or own things that cost money.
4. Understand personal needs, insecurities, and anxieties that make overspending possible.
5. Achieve an inner strength to control personal impulses, cravings, and desires that directly or indirectly increase debt irresponsibly.

—. _____

_____

_____

—. _____

_____

_____

—. _____

_____

SHORT-TERM OBJECTIVES	THERAPEUTIC INTERVENTIONS
1. Describe the details of the current financial situation. (1, 2, 3)	1. Provide the client a supportive, comforting environment by being empathetic, warm, and sensitive to the fact that the topic may elicit guilt, shame, and embarrassment.
	2. Explore the client's current financial situation.
	3. Assist the client in compiling a complete list of financial obligations.
2. Isolate the sources and causes of the excessive indebtedness. (4)	4. Assist in identifying, without projection of blame or holding to excuses, the causes for the financial crisis through a review of the client's history of spending.

3. Verbalize feelings of depression, hopelessness, and/or shame that are related to financial status. (5, 6)

5. Probe the client's feelings of hopelessness or helplessness that may be associated with the financial crisis.

6. Assess the depth or seriousness of the client's despondency over the financial crisis.

4. Describe any suicidal impulses that may accompany financial stress. (6, 7)

6. Assess the depth or seriousness of the client's despondency over the financial crisis.

7. Assess the client's potential risk for suicidal behavior. If necessary, take steps to ensure the client's safety (see chapter on Suicidal Ideation in this Planner).

5. Identify priorities that should control how money is spent. (8, 9)

8. Ask the client to list the priorities that he/she believes should give direction to how his/her money is spent; process those priorities.

9. Review the client's spending history to discover what priorities and values have misdirected spending.

6. Describe the family of origin pattern of money management and how that pattern may be impacting own credit crisis. (10)

10. Explore the client's family of origin patterns of earning, saving, and spending money, focusing on how those patterns are influencing his/her current financial decisions.

7. Meet with community agency personnel to apply for welfare assistance. (11, 12)

11. Review the client's need for filing for bankruptcy, applying for welfare, and/or obtaining credit counseling.

12. Direct the client to the proper church or community resources to seek welfare

assistance and support him/her in beginning the humbling application process.

8. Write a budget that balances income with expenses. (13, 14)

13. If financial planning is needed, refer to a professional planner or ask partners to write a current budget and long-range savings and investment plan.

14. Review the client's budget as to reasonableness and completeness.

9. Attend a meeting with a credit counselor to gain assistance in budgeting and contacting creditors for establishment of a reasonable repayment plan. (15, 16)

15. Refer the client to a non-profit, no-cost credit counseling service for the development of a budgetary plan of debt repayment.

16. Encourage the client's attendance at all credit counseling sessions and his/her discipline of self to control spending within budgetary guidelines.

10. Meet with an attorney to help reach a decision regarding filing for bankruptcy. (11, 17)

11. Review the client's need for filing for bankruptcy, applying for welfare, and/or obtaining credit counseling.

17. Refer the client to an attorney to discuss the feasibility and implications of filing for bankruptcy.

11. Identify personal traits that make undisciplined spending possible. (18, 19)

18. Probe the client for evidence of low self-esteem, need to impress others, loneliness, or depression that may accelerate unnecessary, unwarranted spending.

19. Assess the client for mood swings that are

characteristic of bipolar disorder and could be responsible for careless spending due to the impaired judgment of manic phase.

12. Honestly describe any of own or family members' substance abuse problems that contribute to financial irresponsibility. (20, 21)

20. Probe the client for excessive alcohol or other drug use by asking questions from the CAGE or Michigan Alcohol Screening Test (MAST) screening instruments for substance abuse.

21. Explore the possibility of alcohol or drug use by the client's family members or significant other.

13. Verbalize a plan for seeking employment to raise level of income. (22, 23)

22. Review the client's income from employment and brainstorm ways to increase this (e.g., additional part-time employment, better-paying job, job training).

23. Assist the client in formulating a plan for a job search.

14. Set financial goals and make budgetary decisions with partner, allowing for equal input and balanced control over financial matters. (24, 25)

24. Encourage financial planning by the client that is done in conjunction with his/her partner.

25. Reinforce changes in managing money that reflect compromise, responsible planning, and respectful cooperation with the client's partner.

15. Keep weekly and monthly records of financial income and expenses. (26, 27)

26. Encourage the client to keep a weekly and monthly record of income and outflow; review his/her records weekly, and reinforce

his/her responsible financial decision making.

16. Use cognitive and behavioral strategies to control the impulse to make unnecessary and unaffordable purchases. (28, 29, 30, 31)

27. Offer praise and ongoing encouragement of the client's progress toward debt resolution.

28. Role-play situations in which the client must resist the inner temptation to spend beyond reasonable limits, emphasizing positive self-talk that compliments self for being disciplined.

29. Role-play situations in which the client must resist external pressure to spend beyond what he/she can afford (e.g., friend's invitation to golf or go shopping, child's request for a toy), emphasizing being graciously assertive in refusing the request.

30. Teach the client the cognitive strategy of asking self before each purchase: Is this purchase absolutely necessary? Can we afford this? Do we have the cash to pay for this without incurring any further debt?

31. Urge the client to avoid all impulse buying by delaying every purchase until after 24 hours of thought and by buying only from a prewritten list of items to buy.

17. Report instances of successful control over impulse to spend on unnecessary expenses. (32, 33)

32. Reinforce with praise and encouragement all of the client's reports of resisting the urge to overspend.

33. Hold conjoint or family therapy session in which controlled spending is reinforced and continued cooperation is pledged by everyone.

__. _____   __. _____
    _____   _____
__. _____   __. _____
    _____   _____
__. _____   __. _____
    _____   _____

DIAGNOSTIC SUGGESTIONS

Axis I:	309.0	Adjustment Disorder with Depressed Mood
	296.4x	Bipolar I Disorder, Manic
	296.89	Bipolar II Disorder
	296.xx	Major Depressive Disorder
	_____	_____
	_____	_____
Axis II:	301.83	Borderline Personality Disorder
	301.7	Antisocial Personality Disorder
	799.9	Diagnosis Deferred
	V71.09	No Diagnosis
	_____	_____
	_____	_____

GRIEF/LOSS UNRESOLVED

BEHAVIORAL DEFINITIONS

1. Thoughts dominated by loss coupled with poor concentration, tearful spells, and confusion about the future.
2. Serial losses in life (i.e., deaths, divorces, jobs) that led to depression and discouragement.
3. Strong emotional response exhibited when losses are discussed.
4. Lack of appetite, weight loss, and/or insomnia as well as other depression signs that occurred since the loss.
5. Feelings of guilt that not enough was done for the lost significant other, or an unreasonable belief of having contributed to the death of the significant other.
6. Avoidance of talking on anything more than a superficial level about the loss.
7. Loss of a positive support network due to a geographic move.

__. _____
   _____

__. _____
   _____

__. _____
   _____

LONG-TERM GOALS

1. Begin a healthy grieving process around the loss.
2. Develop an awareness of how the avoidance of grieving has affected life and begin the healing process.
3. Complete the process of letting go of the lost significant other.

4. Resolve the loss and begin renewing old relationships and initiating new contacts with others.

—. _____
_____
_____

—. _____
_____
_____

—. _____
_____

SHORT-TERM OBJECTIVES

THERAPEUTIC INTERVENTIONS

1. Tell in detail the story of the current loss that is triggering symptoms. (1, 2, 3)

1. Actively build the level of trust with the client in individual sessions through consistent eye contact, active listening, unconditional positive regard, and warm acceptance to help increase his/her ability to identify and express thoughts and feelings.

2. Using empathy and compassion, support and encourage the client to tell in detail the story of his/her recent loss.

3. Ask the client to elaborate in an autobiography the circumstances, feelings, and effects of the loss or losses in his/her life.

2. Read books on the topic of grief to better understand the loss experience and to increase a sense of hope. (4, 5)

4. Ask the client to read books on grief and loss (e.g., *Getting to the Other Side of Grief: Overcoming the Loss of a Spouse* by Zonnebelt-Smeenge and De Vries, *How Can It Be All Right When*

Everything Is All Wrong by Smedes, *How to Survive the Loss of a Love* by Colgrove, Bloomfield, and McWilliams, *When Bad Things Happen to Good People* by Kushner); process the content.

5. Ask the parents of a deceased child to read a book on coping with the loss (e.g., *The Bereaved Parent* by Schiff); process the key themes gleaned from the reading.

3. Identify what stages of grief have been experienced in the continuum of the grieving process. (6, 7, 8)

6. Ask the client to talk to several people about losses in their lives and how they felt and coped. Process the findings.

7. Educate the client on the stages of the grieving process and answer any questions he/she may have.

8. Assist the client in identifying the stages of grief that he/she has experienced and which stage he/she is presently working through.

4. Watch videos on the theme of grief and loss to compare own experience with that of the characters in the films. (9)

9. Ask the client to watch the films *Terms of Endearment, Dad, Ordinary People,* or a similar film that focuses on loss and grieving, then discuss how the characters cope with loss and express their grief.

5. Begin verbalizing feelings associated with the loss. (10, 11, 12)

10. Assign the client to keep a daily grief journal to be shared in therapy sessions.

11. Ask the client to bring pictures or mementos

connected with his/her loss to a session and talk about them.

12. Assist the client in identifying and expressing feelings connected with his/her loss.

6. Attend a grief/loss support group. (13)

13. Ask the client to attend a grief/loss support group and report to the therapist how he/she felt about attending.

7. Identify how avoiding dealing with loss has negatively impacted life. (14)

14. Ask the client to list ways that avoidance of grieving has negatively impacted his/her life.

8. Identify how the use of substances has aided the avoidance of feelings associated with the loss. (15, 16)

15. Assess the role that substance abuse has played as an escape for the client from the pain or guilt of loss.

16. Arrange for chemical dependence treatment so that grief issues can be faced while the client is clean and sober. (See Chemical Dependence chapter in this Planner.)

9. Acknowledge dependency on lost loved one and begin to refocus life on independent actions to meet emotional needs. (17, 18)

17. Assist the client in identifying how he/she depended upon the significant other, expressing and resolving the accompanying feelings of abandonment and of being left alone.

18. Explore the feelings of anger or guilt that surround the loss, helping the client understand the sources for such feelings.

10. Verbalize and resolve feelings of anger or guilt focused on self or deceased loved one that block the grieving process. (19, 20)

11. Identify causes for feelings of regret associated with actions toward or relationship with the deceased. (21)

12. Decrease statements and feelings of being responsible for the loss. (22)

13. Express thoughts and feelings about the deceased that went unexpressed while the deceased was alive. (23, 24, 25, 26)

19. Encourage the client to forgive self and/or deceased to resolve his/her feelings of guilt or anger. Recommend books like *Forgive and Forget* (Smedes).

20. Support and assist the client in identifying and expressing angry feelings connected to his/her loss.

21. Assign the client to make a list of all the regrets he/she has concerning the loss; process the list content.

22. Use a Rational Emotive Therapy (RET) approach to confront the client's statements of responsibility for the loss and compare them to factual reality-based statements.

23. Conduct an empty-chair exercise with the client where he/she focuses on expressing to the lost loved one imagined in the chair what he/she never said while that loved one was alive.

24. Assign the client to visit the grave of the lost loved one to "talk to" the deceased and ventilate his/her feelings.

25. Ask the client to write a letter to the lost person describing his/her fond memories, painful and regretful memories, and how he/she currently feels. Process the letter in session.

26. Assign the client to write to the deceased loved one with

a special focus on his/her feelings associated with the last meaningful contact with that person.

14. Identify the positive characteristics of the deceased loved one, the positive aspects of the relationship with the deceased loved one, and how these things may be remembered. (27, 28)

27. Ask the client to list the most positive aspects of and memories about his/her relationship with the lost loved one.

28. Assist the client in developing rituals (e.g., placing memoriam in newspaper on anniversary of death, volunteering time to a favorite cause of the deceased person) that will celebrate the memorable aspects of the loved one and his/her life.

15. Attend and participate in a family therapy session focused on each member sharing his/her experience with grief. (29)

29. Conduct a family and/or group session with the client participating, where each member talks about his/her experience related to the loss.

16. Report decreased time spent each day focusing on the loss. (30, 31)

30. Develop a grieving ritual with an identified feeling state (e.g., dress in dark colors, preferably black, to indicate deep sorrow) which the client may focus on near the anniversary of the loss. Process what he/she received from the ritual.

31. Suggest that the client set aside a specific time-limited period each day to focus on mourning his/her loss. After each day's time is up the client will resume regular activities and put off grieving thoughts until the next scheduled time. For

17. Develop and enact act(s) of penitence. (32)

18. Implement acts of spiritual faith as a source of comfort and hope. (33)

__. _____
    _____

__. _____
    _____

__. _____
    _____

example, mourning times could include putting on dark clothing and/or sad music; clothing would be changed when the allotted time is up.

32. Research with the client the activities, interests, commitments, loves, and passions of the lost loved one, then select a community-service-connected activity as an act of penitence for the feelings of having failed the departed one in some way. (Period of time should not be less than one month, with intensity and duration increasing with the depth of the perceived offense.)

33. Encourage the client to rely upon his/her spiritual faith promises, activities (e.g., prayer, meditation, worship, music), and fellowship as sources of support.

__. _____
    _____

__. _____
    _____

__. _____
    _____

DIAGNOSTIC SUGGESTIONS

Axis I: 296.2x   Major Depressive Disorder, Single Episode
296.3x   Major Depressive Disorder, Recurrent

V62.82	Bereavement
309.0	Adjustment Disorder With Depressed Mood
309.3	Adjustment Disorder With Disturbance of Conduct
300.4	Dysthymic Disorder
_____	_____
_____	_____

IMPULSE CONTROL DISORDER

BEHAVIORAL DEFINITIONS

1. A tendency to act too quickly without careful deliberation, resulting in numerous negative consequences.
2. Loss of control over aggressive impulses resulting in assault, self-destructive behavior, or damage to property.
3. Desire to be satisfied almost immediately—decreased ability to delay pleasure or gratification.
4. A history of acting out in at last two areas that are potentially self-damaging (e.g., spending money, sexual activity, reckless driving, addictive behavior).
5. Overreactivity to mildly aversive or pleasure-oriented stimulation.
6. A sense of tension or affective arousal before engaging in the impulsive behavior (e.g., kleptomania or pyromania).
7. A sense of pleasure, gratification, or release at the time of committing the ego-dystonic, impulsive act.
8. Difficulty waiting for things—that is, restless standing in line, talking out over others in a group, and the like.

—. _____
   _____
   _____
—. _____
   _____
   _____
—. _____
   _____

LONG-TERM GOALS

1. Reduce the frequency of impulsive behavior and increase the frequency of behavior that is carefully thought out.

151

2. Reduce thoughts that trigger impulsive behavior and increase self-talk that controls behavior.
3. Learn to stop, think, listen, and plan before acting.

—. _____

_____

—. _____

_____

—. _____

_____

SHORT-TERM OBJECTIVES

1. Identify the impulsive behaviors that have been engaged in over the last six months. (1)

2. List the reasons or rewards that lead to continuation of an impulsive pattern. (2, 3)

3. List the negative consequences that accrue to self and others as a result of impulsive behavior. (4, 5, 6)

THERAPEUTIC INTERVENTIONS

1. Review the client's behavior pattern to assist him/her in clearly identifying, without minimization, denial, or projection of blame, his/her pattern of impulsivity.

2. Explore whether the client's impulsive behavior is triggered by anxiety and maintained by anxiety relief rewards.

3. Ask the client to make a list of the positive things he/she gets from impulsive actions and process it with the therapist.

4. Assign the client to write a list of the negative consequences that have occurred because of impulsivity.

5. Assist the client in making connections between his/her impulsivity and the negative consequences for himself/herself and others.

4. Identify impulsive behavior's antecedents, mediators, and consequences. (7, 8)

6. Confront the client's denial of responsibility for the impulsive behavior or the negative consequences.

7. Ask the client to keep a log of impulsive acts (time, place, feelings, thoughts, what was going on prior to the act, and what was the result); process log content to discover triggers and reinforcers.

8. Explore the client's past experiences to uncover his/her cognitive, emotional, and situational triggers to impulsive episodes.

5. Verbalize a clear connection between impulsive behavior and negative consequences to self and others. (5, 9)

5. Assist the client in making connections between his/her impulsivity and the negative consequences for himself/herself and others.

9. Reinforce the client's verbalized acceptance of responsibility for and connection between impulsive behavior and negative consequences.

6. Before acting on behavioral decisions, frequently review them with a trusted friend or family member for feedback regarding possible consequences. (10, 11)

10. Conduct a session with the client and his/her partner to develop a contract for receiving feedback prior to impulsive acts.

11. Brainstorm with the client who he/she could rely on for trusted feedback regarding action decisions; use role play and modeling to teach how to ask for and accept this help.

7. Utilize cognitive methods to control trigger thoughts and reduce impulsive reactions to those trigger thoughts. (8, 12, 13)

8. Explore the client's past experiences to uncover his/her cognitive, emotional, and situational triggers to impulsive episodes.

12. Teach the client cognitive methods (thought stopping, thought substitution, reframing, etc.) for gaining and improving control over impulsive urges and actions.

13. Help the client to uncover dysfunctional thoughts that lead to impulsivity; then, replace each thought with a thought that is accurate, positive, self-enhancing, and adaptive.

8. Use relaxation exercises to control anxiety and reduce consequent impulsive behavior. (14)

14. Teach the client techniques such as progressive relaxation, self-hypnosis, or biofeedback; encourage him/her to relax whenever he/she feels uncomfortable.

9. Utilize behavioral strategies to manage anxiety. (15, 16)

15. Teach the use of positive behavioral alternatives to cope with anxiety (e.g., talking to someone about the stress, taking a time-out to delay any reaction, calling a friend or family member, engaging in physical exercise).

16. Review the client's implementation of behavioral coping strategies to reduce urges and tension; reinforce success and redirect for failure.

10. Implement the assertive formula, "I feel . . . When you . . . I would prefer it if. . . ." (17, 18)

11. List instances where "stop, think, listen, and plan" has been implemented, citing the positive consequences. (19, 20)

12. Comply with the recommendations from a physician evaluation regarding the necessity for psychopharmacological intervention. (21, 22)

13. Implement a reward system for replacing impulsive actions with reflection on consequences and choosing wise alternatives. (23, 24)

17. Using modeling, role playing, and behavior rehearsal, teach the client how to use the assertive formula, "I feel . . . When you . . . I would prefer it if . . ." in difficult situations.

18. Review and process the client's implementation of assertiveness and feelings about it as well as the consequences of it.

19. Using modeling, role playing, and behavior rehearsal, teach the client how to use "stop, think, listen, and plan" before acting in several current situations.

20. Review and process the client's use of "stop, think, listen, and plan" in day-to-day living and identify the positive consequences.

21. Refer the client to a physician for an evaluation for a psychotropic medication prescription.

22. Monitor the client for psychotropic medication prescription compliance, side effects, and effectiveness; consult with the prescribing physician at regular intervals.

23. Assist the client in identifying rewards that would be effective in reinforcing himself/herself for suppressing impulsive behavior.

24. Assist the client and significant others in developing

and putting into effect a reward system for deterring
the client's impulsive actions.

14. Attend a self-help recovery
group. (25)

25. Refer the client to a self-
help recovery group (e.g.,
12-step program, ADHD
group, Rational Recovery,
etc.) designed to help terminate self-destructive impulsivity; process his/her
experience in the group.

__. _____   __. _____
    _____   _____
__. _____   __. _____
    _____   _____
__. _____   __. _____
    _____   _____

DIAGNOSTIC SUGGESTIONS

Axis I: 312.34   Intermittent Explosive Disorder
312.32   Kleptomania
312.31   Pathological Gambling
312.39   Trichotillomania
312.30   Impulse Control Disorder NOS
312.33   Pyromania
310.1   Personality Change Due to (Axis III Disorder)

_____   _____

Axis II: 301.7   Antisocial Personality Disorder
301.83   Borderline Personality Disorder
799.9   Diagnosis Deferred
V71.09   No Diagnosis

_____   _____
_____   _____

INTIMATE RELATIONSHIP CONFLICTS

BEHAVIORAL DEFINITIONS

1. Frequent or continual arguing with the partner.
2. Lack of communication with the partner.
3. A pattern of angry projection of responsibility for the conflicts onto the partner.
4. Marital separation.
5. Pending divorce.
6. Involvement in multiple intimate relationships at the same time.
7. Physical and/or verbal abuse in a relationship.
8. A pattern of superficial or no communication, infrequent or no sexual contact, excessive involvement in activities (work or recreation) that allows for avoidance of closeness to the partner.
9. A pattern of repeated broken, conflictual relationships due to personal deficiencies in problem solving, maintaining a trust relationship, or choosing abusive or dysfunctional partners.

___. _____

_____

___. _____

_____

___. _____

_____

LONG-TERM GOALS

1. Accept the termination of the relationship.
2. Develop the necessary skills for effective, open communication, mutually satisfying sexual intimacy, and enjoyable time for companionship within the relationship.

3. Increase awareness of own role in the relationship conflicts.
4. Develop respect for the partner in the relationship.
5. Learn to identify escalating behaviors that lead to abuse.
6. Make a commitment to one intimate relationship at a time.
7. Rebuild positive self-image after acceptance of the rejection associated with the broken relationship.

—. _____
   _____
   _____

—. _____
   _____
   _____

—. _____
   _____

SHORT-TERM OBJECTIVES	THERAPEUTIC INTERVENTIONS
1. Attend and actively participate in conjoint sessions with the partner. (1, 2)	1. Facilitate conjoint sessions that focus on increasing the client's communication and problem-solving skills.
	2. Assist the client in identifying behaviors that focus on relationship building.
2. Identify the positive aspects of the client's present relationship. (3)	3. Assign the couple to spend the time between sessions noticing and recording in journals the positive things about the significant other that are present in their relationship; ask the couple not to show their journal material to each other until the next session, when the material will be processed.
3. Each partner identifies his/her own role in the conflicts. (4, 5, 6)	4. Assign the client to read the book *The Intimate Enemy* (Bach and Wyden); process key ideas.

5. Explore current, ongoing conflicts existent in the client's relationship.

6. Confront each partner for projection of and avoidance of responsibility for conflicts within the relationship.

4. Each partner makes a commitment to attempt to change specific behaviors that have been identified by self or the partner. (7, 8)

7. Assign each partner to list changes he/she needs to make as well as changes the other needs to make to improve the relationship; process the lists in conjoint sessions.

8. Seek a commitment from each partner to begin to work on changing specific behaviors on his/her own list and on the list of the partner for him/her.

5. Increase the frequency and quality of the communication with the partner. (9, 10, 11)

9. Assign the couple to set aside daily 15 minutes that are distraction free during which they can communicate about nonemotional and nonconflictual issues. The couple will practice with the therapist during the session, then follow up at home. As assignment is completed, explore thoughts and feelings with each partner in the following session.

10. Encourage the clients to attend a skills-based marital relationship seminar such as PREP (see *Fighting for Your Marriage* by Markman, Stanley, and Blumberg); encourage them to continue to practice the skills obtained there at

home and in conjoint sessions.

11. Assist each partner in clarifying communication and expression of feelings within sessions.

6. Express thoughts and feelings regarding the relationship in a direct, nonaggressive manner. (12, 13)

12. Teach the couple to reframe complaints into requests and to seek agreement from the partner to meet these requests.

13. Train in assertiveness or refer the client to a group that will educate and facilitate assertiveness skills via lectures and assignments.

7. Both partners identify and verbalize their expectations for the relationship. (14)

14. Confront irrational beliefs and unrealistic expectations regarding relationships and then assist the couple in adopting more realistic beliefs and expectations of each other and of the relationship.

8. Verbally recognize own responsibility to meet some needs of the partner in the relationship. (7, 15)

7. Assign each partner to list changes he/she needs to make as well as changes the other needs to make to improve the relationship; process the lists in conjoint sessions.

15. Teach both partners the key concept that mutually satisfying relationships necessitate each partner being willing at times to sacrifice his/her own needs and desires to chose to meet the needs and desires of the other.

9. Utilize new conflict resolution techniques to resolve issues reasonably. (16)

16. Teach the couple conflict resolution techniques like "Do's & Don'ts List" and "Fair Fighting Steps" (Bach and Wyden) and have them practice these techniques in sessions at home.

10. Identify a pattern of repeatedly forming destructive intimate relationships. (17)

17. Probe the family-of-origin history of each partner to discover patterns of destructive intimate relationship interaction that are being repeated in the present relationship.

11. Both partners agree to a "time out" signal that either partner may give to stop interaction that may escalate into abuse. (18, 19, 20)

18. Ask each partner to make a list of escalating behaviors that occur prior to abusive behavior.

19. Assist the partners in identifying a clear verbal or behavioral signal to be used by either partner to terminate interaction immediately if either fears impending abuse.

20. Solicit a firm agreement from both partners that the "time out" signal will be responded to favorably without debate.

12. Acknowledge the connection between substance abuse and the conflicts present within the relationship. (21)

21. Explore the role of substance abuse in precipitating conflict and/or abuse within the relationship.

13. Chemically dependent partner agrees to pursue treatment and seek clean and sober living. (22)

22. Solicit an agreement for substance abuse treatment for the chemically dependent partner. (See Chemical Dependence chapter in this Planner.)

14. Identify the message, cause, and consequences of the partner's infidelity. (23, 24, 25)

23. Using Emily Brown's "Five Degrees for Affairs" in her book *Patterns of Infidelity and Their Treatment,* assist the couple in identifying the message behind the infidelity.

24. Assign the clients to read *After the Affair* (Abrahms-Spring) and then process key concepts gathered from the reading in conjoint sessions with the therapist.

25. Discuss the consequences to self and others that result from multiple intimate relationships.

15. Discuss the level of closeness/distance desired in a relationship and how this may relate to fears of intimacy. (26, 27, 28)

26. Direct the clients to read *Getting the Love You Want* (Hendrix) and/or attend an Imago workshop to create relationship skills.

27. Explore and clarify feelings associated with loss of the relationship.

28. Explore each partner's fears regarding getting too close and feeling vulnerable to hurt, rejection, or abandonment.

16. Share family and childhood experiences with each other to increase understanding and empathy. (29, 30)

29. Assist the couple in doing an Imago exercise where each shares with the other childhood wounds they experienced to expand understanding and sharing. (Format: Recall the incident; tell what you enjoyed about being with parents; next, tell how you were hurt by parents; and last, tell

what you wanted from them but never got. Repeat for each incident.)

30. Assign each client to complete a genogram; process each genogram in a conjoint session to promote greater empathy and awareness concerning each other.

17. Increase time spent in enjoyable contact with the partner. (31)

31. Assist the client in identifying and planning rewarding social/recreational activities that can be shared with the partner.

18. Initiate verbal and physical affection behaviors toward the partner. (32)

32. Defuse resistance surrounding initiating affectionate or sexual interactions with the partner.

19. Identify or rule out sexual dysfunction. (33, 34)

33. Gather from each partner a thorough sexual history to determine areas of strength and to identify areas of dysfunction. (See Female Sexual Dysfunction and Male Sexual Dysfunction chapters in this Planner.)

34. Refer the client to a physician who specializes in treating sexual dysfunction for an evaluation.

20. Commit to the establishment of healthy, mutually satisfying sexual attitudes and behavior that is not a reflection of destructive earlier experiences. (35, 36)

35. Create a sexual genogram in a conjoint session that identifies sexual behavior, patterns, activities, and beliefs of each partner and the extended family.

36. Assist each partner in committing to attempt to develop healthy, mutually satisfying sexual beliefs, attitudes, and behavior that is

21. Verbalize the various feelings associated with grieving the loss of the relationship. (37, 38)

22. Express plans as to how to cope with loneliness. (39, 40)

independent of previous childhood, personal, or family training or experience.

37. Refer the client to a support group or divorce seminar to assist in resolving the loss and in adjusting to the new life.

38. Assign the client to read *How to Survive the Loss of a Love* (Colgrove, Bloomfield, and McWilliams); process key concepts.

39. Help, support, and encourage the client in his/her adjustment to living alone and being single.

40. Make the client aware of social opportunities within the community and then assist him/her in integrating these resources into a plan to start building new social relationships.

—. _____

_____

—. _____

_____

—. _____

_____

—. _____

_____

—. _____

_____

—. _____

_____

DIAGNOSTIC SUGGESTIONS

Axis I:	312.34	Intermittent Explosive Disorder
	309.0	Adjustment Disorder With Depressed Mood
	309.24	Adjustment Disorder With Anxiety
	300.4	Dysthymic Disorder
	300.0	Anxiety Disorder NOS

	311	Depressive Disorder NOS
	309.81	Posttraumatic Stress Disorder
	_____	_____
	_____	_____
Axis II:	301.20	Schizoid Personality Disorder
	301.81	Narcissistic Personality Disorder
	301.9	Personality Disorder NOS
	_____	_____
	_____	_____

LEGAL CONFLICTS

BEHAVIORAL DEFINITIONS

1. Legal charges pending.
2. On parole or probation subsequent to legal charges.
3. Legal pressure has been central to the decision to enter treatment.
4. A history of criminal activity leading to numerous incarcerations.
5. Most arrests are related to alcohol or drug abuse.
6. Pending divorce accompanied by emotional turmoil.
7. Fear of loss of freedom due to current legal charges.

—. _____
_____

—. _____
_____

—. _____
_____

LONG-TERM GOALS

1. Accept and responsibly respond to the mandates of court.
2. Understand how chemical dependence has contributed to legal problems and accept the need for recovery.
3. Accept responsibility for decisions and actions that have led to arrests and develop higher moral and ethical standards to govern behavior.
4. Internalize the need for treatment so as to change values, thoughts, feelings, and behavior to a more prosocial position.
5. Become a responsible citizen in good standing within the community.

—. _____
    _____

—. _____
    _____

—. _____
    _____

SHORT-TERM OBJECTIVES

1. Describe the behavior that led to current involvement with the court system. (1)

2. Obtain counsel and meet to make plans for resolving legal conflicts. (2)

3. Make regular contact with court officers to fulfill sentencing requirements. (3)

4. Verbalize the role drug and/or alcohol abuse has played in legal problems. (4, 5)

5. Maintain sobriety in accordance with rules of probation/parole. (6, 7)

THERAPEUTIC INTERVENTIONS

1. Explore the client's behavior that led to legal conflicts and assess whether it fits a pattern of antisocial behavior (see Antisocial Behavior chapter in this Planner).

2. Encourage and facilitate the client in meeting with an attorney to discuss plans for resolving legal issues.

3. Monitor and encourage the client to keep appointments with court officers.

4. Explore how chemical dependence may have contributed to the client's legal conflicts.

5. Confront the client's denial of chemical dependence by reviewing the various negative consequences of addiction that have occurred in his/her life.

6. Reinforce the client's need for a plan for recovery and sobriety as a means of improving judgment and control over behavior (see

Chemical Dependence chapter in this Planner).

6. Verbalize and accept responsibility for the series of decisions and actions that eventually led to illegal activity. (8, 9)

7. Monitor and reinforce the client's sobriety, using physiological measures to confirm, if advisable.

8. Assist the client in clarification of values that allow him/her to act illegally.

9. Confront the client's denial and projection of responsibility onto others for his/her own illegal actions.

7. State values that affirm behavior within the boundaries of the law. (8, 10)

8. Assist the client in clarification of values that allow him/her to act illegally.

10. Teach the values associated with respecting legal boundaries and the rights of others as well as the consequences of crossing these boundaries.

8. Verbalize how the emotional state of anger, frustration, helplessness, or depression has contributed to illegal behavior. (11, 12)

11. Probe the client's negative emotional states that could contribute to his/her illegal behavior.

12. Refer the client for ongoing counseling to deal with emotional conflicts and antisocial impulses (see Antisocial Behavior, Anger Management, or Depression chapters in this Planner).

9. Identify the causes for the negative emotional state that was associated with illegal actions. (13, 14)

13. Explore causes for the client's underlying negative emotions that consciously or unconsciously fostered his/her criminal behavior.

14. Interpret the client's antisocial behavior that is linked

to current or past emotional conflicts to foster insights and resolution.

10. Identify and replace cognitive distortions that foster antisocial behavior. (15, 16)

15. Assess and clarify the client's distorted cognitive belief structures that foster illegal behavior.

16. Restructure the client's distorted cognitions to those that foster keeping of legal boundaries and respecting the rights of others.

11. Attend an anger control group. (17)

17. Refer the client to an impulse or anger management group.

12. Identify ways to meet life needs (i.e., social and financial) without resorting to illegal activities. (18, 19)

18. Explore with the client ways he/she can meet social and financial needs without involvement with illegal activity (e.g., employment, further education or skill training, spiritual enrichment group, etc.).

19. Educate the client on the difference between antisocial and prosocial behaviors; assist him/her in writing a list of ways to show respect for the law, help others, and work regularly.

13. Attend class to learn how to successfully seek employment. (20)

20. Refer the client to an ex-offender center for assistance in obtaining employment.

14. Verbalize an understanding of the importance of honesty in earning the trust of others and esteem for self. (21)

21. Help the client understand the importance of honesty in earning the trust of others and self-respect.

15. Develop and implement a plan for restitution for illegal activity. (22, 23)

22. Assist the client in seeing the importance of restitution to self-worth; help him/her develop a plan to provide restitution for the results of his/her behavior.

23. Review the client's implementation of his/her restitution plan; reinforce success and redirect for failure.

—. _____
_____

—. _____
_____

—. _____
_____

—. _____
_____

—. _____
_____

—. _____
_____

DIAGNOSTIC SUGGESTIONS

Axis I:	304.30	Cannabis Dependence
	304.20	Cocaine Dependence
	303.90	Alcohol Dependence
	304.89	Polysubstance Dependence
	312.32	Kleptomania
	V71.01	Adult Antisocial Behavior
	309.3	Adjustment Disorder With Disturbance of Conduct
	_____	_____
	_____	
Axis II:	301.7	Antisocial Personality Disorder
	799.9	Diagnosis Deferred
	V71.09	No Diagnosis
	_____	_____
	_____	

LOW SELF-ESTEEM

BEHAVIORAL DEFINITIONS

1. Inability to accept compliments.
2. Makes self-disparaging remarks; sees self as unattractive, worthless, a loser, a burden, unimportant; takes blame easily.
3. Lack of pride in grooming.
4. Difficulty in saying no to others; assumes not being liked by others.
5. Fear of rejection of others, especially peer group.
6. Lack of any goals for life and setting of inappropriately low goals for self.
7. Inability to identify positive things about self.
8. Uncomfortable in social situations, especially larger groups.

—. _____
   _____
—. _____
   _____
—. _____
   _____

LONG-TERM GOALS

1. Elevate self-esteem.
2. Develop a consistent, positive self-image.
3. Demonstrate improved self-esteem through more pride in appearance, more assertiveness, greater eye contact, and identification of positive traits in self-talk messages.
4. Establish an inward sense of self-worth, confidence, and competence.

—. _____
   _____
—. _____
   _____
—. _____
   _____

SHORT-TERM OBJECTIVES

1. Acknowledge feeling less competent than most others. (1, 2)

2. Increase insight into the historical and current sources of low self-esteem. (3, 4)

3. Decrease the frequency of negative self-descriptive statements and increase frequency of positive self-descriptive statements. (5, 6, 7)

THERAPEUTIC INTERVENTIONS

1. Actively build the level of trust with the client in individual sessions through consistent eye contact, active listening, unconditional positive regard, and warm acceptance to help increase his/her ability to identify and express feelings.

2. Explore the client's assessment of himself/herself.

3. Help the client become aware of his/her fear of rejection and its connection with past rejection or abandonment experiences.

4. Discuss, emphasize, and interpret the client's incidents of abuse (emotional, physical, and sexual) and how they have impacted his/her feelings about himself/herself.

5. Confront and reframe the client's negative assessment of himself/herself.

6. Assist the client in becoming aware of how he/she expresses or acts out negative

feelings about himself/herself.

4. Identify negative self-talk messages used to reinforce low self-esteem. (8, 9)

5. Identify any secondary gain that is received by speaking negatively about self and refusing to take any risks. (10, 11)

6. Decrease the verbalized fear of rejection while increasing statements of self-acceptance. (12, 13)

7. Identify accomplishments that would improve self-image and verbalize a plan to achieve those goals. (14, 15)

7. Assist the client in developing self-talk as a way of boosting his/her confidence and positive self-image.

8. Help the client identify his/her distorted, negative beliefs about self and the world.

9. Ask the client to complete and process an exercise in the book *Ten Days to Self Esteem!* (Burns).

10. Teach the client the meaning and power of secondary gain in maintaining negative behavior patterns.

11. Assist the client in identifying how self-disparagement and avoidance of risk taking could bring secondary gain (e.g., praise from others, others taking over responsibilities, etc.).

12. Ask the client to make one positive statement about self daily and record it on a chart or in a journal.

13. Verbally reinforce the client's use of positive statements of confidence and accomplishments.

14. Help the client analyze his/her goals to make sure they are realistic and attainable.

15. Assign self-esteem-building exercises from a workbook (e.g., *The Six Pillars of*

	Self-Esteem by Branden, *Ten Days to Self Esteem!* by Burns); process the completed assignment.
8. Increase eye contact with others. (16, 17)	16. Assign the client to make eye contact with whomever he/she is speaking to; process the feelings associated with eye contact.
	17. Confront the client when he/she is observed avoiding eye contact with others.
9. Take responsibility for daily grooming and personal hygiene. (18)	18. Monitor and give feedback to the client on his/her grooming and hygiene.
10. Identify positive traits and talents about self. (19, 20, 21)	19. Assign the client the exercise of identifying his/her positive physical characteristics in a mirror to help him/her become more comfortable with himself/herself.
	20. Ask the client to keep a building list of positive traits and have him/her read list at beginning and end of each session.
	21. Reinforce the client's positive self-descriptive statements.
11. Demonstrate an increased ability to identify and express personal feelings. (22, 23)	22. Assign the client to keep a journal of feelings on a daily basis.
	23. Assist the client in identifying and labeling emotions.
12. Articulate a plan to be proactive in trying to get identified needs met. (24, 25, 26)	24. Assist the client in identifying and verbalizing his/her needs, met and unmet.

25. Conduct a conjoint or family therapy session in which the client is supported in expression of unmet needs.

26. Assist the client in developing a specific action plan to get each need met.

13. Positively acknowledge verbal compliments from others. (27)

27. Assign the client to be aware of and acknowledge graciously (without discounting) praise and compliments from others.

14. Increase the frequency of assertive behaviors. (28)

28. Train the client in assertiveness or refer him/her to a group that will educate and facilitate assertiveness skills via lectures and assignments.

15. Form realistic, appropriate, and attainable goals for self in all areas of life. (14, 29)

14. Help the client analyze his/her goals to make sure they are realistic and attainable.

29. Assign the client to make a list of goals for various areas of life and a plan for steps toward goal attainment.

16. Take verbal responsibility for accomplishments without discounting. (30)

30. Ask the client to list accomplishments; process the integration of these into his/her self-image.

17. Use positive self-talk messages to build self-esteem. (31, 32)

31. Assign the client to read *What to Say When You Talk to Yourself* (Helmstetter); process key ideas.

32. Reinforce the client's use of more realistic, positive messages to himself/herself in interpreting life events.

18. Increase the frequency of speaking up with confidence in social situations. (33, 34)

33. Use role playing and behavioral rehearsal to improve the client's social skills in greeting people and carrying a conversation.

34. Recommend that the client read *Shyness* (Zimbardo); process the content.

__. _____
   _____

__. _____
   _____

__. _____
   _____

__. _____
   _____

__. _____
   _____

__. _____
   _____

DIAGNOSTIC SUGGESTIONS

Axis I: 300.23   Social Phobia
           300.4   Dysthymic Disorder
           296.xx   Major Depressive Disorder
           296.xx   Bipolar I Disorder
           296.89   Bipolar II Disorder

           _____   _____

           _____   _____

MALE SEXUAL DYSFUNCTION

BEHAVIORAL DEFINITIONS

1. Consistently very low or no pleasurable anticipation of or desire for sexual activity.
2. Strong avoidance of and/or repulsion to any and all sexual contact in spite of a relationship of mutual caring and respect.
3. Recurrent lack of usual physiological response of sexual excitement and arousal (attaining and/or maintaining an erection).
4. Consistent lack of subjective sense of enjoyment and pleasure during sexual activity.
5. Persistent delay in or absence of reaching ejaculation after achieving arousal and in spite of sensitive sexual pleasuring by a caring partner.
6. Genital pain before, during, or after sexual intercourse.

—. _____
   _____

—. _____
   _____

—. _____
   _____

LONG-TERM GOALS

1. Increase desire for and enjoyment of sexual activity.
2. Attain and maintain physiological excitement response during sexual intercourse.

3. Reach ejaculation with a reasonable amount of time, intensity, and focus to sexual stimulation.
4. Eliminate pain and achieve a presence of subjective pleasure before, during, and after sexual intercourse.

—. _____

_____

—. _____

_____

—. _____

_____

SHORT-TERM OBJECTIVES

1. Openly reveal conflicts and unfulfilled needs in the relationship that lead to anger and emotional distance. (1, 2)

2. Provide a detailed sexual history that explores all experiences that influence sexual attitudes, feelings, and behavior. (3, 4, 5)

THERAPEUTIC INTERVENTIONS

1. Assess the client's relationship with his sexual partner as to level of harmony and fulfillment (see Intimate Relationship Conflicts chapter in this Planner).

2. Direct conjoint sessions with the client and his partner that focus on conflict resolution, expression of feelings, and sex education.

3. Probe the client's family of origin history for causes for his feelings of inhibition, low self-esteem, guilt, fear, or repulsion.

4. Obtain a detailed sexual history that examines the client's current adult sexual functioning as well as his childhood and adolescent sexual experiences, level and sources of sexual knowledge, typical sexual practices and frequency of them, medical history, and

use of mood-altering sub-
stances.

5. Explore the role of the
client's family of origin in
teaching him negative attitudes regarding sexuality.

3. State an understanding of
how religious training negatively influenced sexual
thoughts, feelings, and behavior. (5, 6)

5. Explore the role of the
client's family of origin in
teaching him negative attitudes regarding sexuality.

6. Explore the role of the
client's religious training in
reinforcing his feelings of
guilt and shame surround-
ing his sexual behavior and
thoughts.

4. Verbalize a resolution of
feelings regarding sexual
trauma or abuse experi-
ences. (7, 8)

7. Probe the client's history for
experiences of sexual
trauma or abuse.

8. Process the client's emotions surrounding an emo-
tional trauma in the sexual
arena (see Sexual Abuse
chapter in this Planner).

5. Verbalize an understanding
of the role of childhood experiences in the develop-
ment of negative sexual
attitudes and responses. (9)

9. Assist the client in developing insight into the role of
unhealthy sexual attitudes
and experiences of child-
hood in the development of
current adult dysfunction;
press for a commitment to
try to put negative attitudes
and experiences in the past
while making a behavioral
effort to become free from
those influences.

6. Verbalize an understanding
of the connection between
the lack of a positive sex
role model in childhood and
current adult sexual dys-
function. (5, 10)

5. Explore the role of the
client's family of origin in
teaching his negative attitudes regarding sexuality.

7. Identify and replace negative cognitive messages that trigger fears, shame, anger, or grief during sexual activity. (11, 12)

8. Demonstrate healthy acceptance and accurate knowledge of sexuality by freely verbalizing accurate information regarding sexual functioning using appropriate terms for sexually related body parts. (13, 14, 15)

9. Abstain from substance abuse patterns that interfere with sexual response. (16)

10. Explore sex role models the client has experienced in childhood or adolescence.

11. Probe automatic thoughts that trigger the client's negative emotions before, during, and after sexual activity.

12. Train the client in healthy alternative thoughts that will mediate pleasure, relaxation, and disinhibition.

13. Disinhibit and educate the client by talking freely and respectfully regarding sexual body parts, sexual feelings, and sexual behavior.

14. Assign books (e.g., *Sexual Awareness* by McCarthy and McCarthy, *The Gift of Sex* by Penner and Penner, or *The New Male Sexuality* by Zilbergeld) that provide the client accurate sexual information and/or outline sexual exercises that disinhibit and reinforce sexual sensate focus.

15. Reinforce the client talking freely, knowledgeably, and positively regarding sexual thoughts, feelings, and behavior.

16. Explore the client's use or abuse of mood-altering substances and their effect on sexual functioning; refer him for focused substance abuse counseling.

10. Verbalize an understanding of the role physical disease or medication has in sexual dysfunction. (17, 18)

11. Cooperate with a physician's complete examination and report results. (19)

12. Take medication for impotence as ordered and report as to effectiveness and side effects. (20)

13. Discuss feelings of and causes for depression. (21, 22)

14. Verbalize connection between previously failed intimate relationships as to behaviors and emotions that caused failure. (23)

15. Discuss feelings surrounding secret affair and make termination decision on one of the relationships. (1, 24)

17. Assess the possible role that diabetes, hypertension, or thyroid disease may have on the client's sexual functioning.

18. Review medications taken by the client with regard to their possible negative side effects on sexual functioning.

19. Refer the client to a physician for a complete physical to rule out any organic or medication-related basis for the sexual dysfunction.

20. Refer the client to a physician for an evaluation regarding a prescription of medication to overcome impotence (e.g., Viagra).

21. Assess the role of depression in suppressing the client's sexual desire or performance (see Depression chapter in this Planner).

22. Refer the client for antidepressant medication prescription to alleviate depression.

23. Explore the client's fears surrounding intimate relationships and whether there is evidence of repeated failure in this area.

1. Assess the client's relationship with his sexual partner as to level of harmony and fulfillment (see Intimate Relationship Conflicts chapter in this Planner).

24. Explore for any secret sexual affairs that may account for the client's sexual dysfunction with partner.

16. Openly acknowledge and discuss, if present, homosexual attraction. (25)

25. Explore for a homosexual interest that accounts for the client's heterosexual disinterest (see Sexual Identity Confusion chapter in this Planner).

17. Practice sensate focus exercises alone and with partner and share feelings associated with activity. (26, 27, 28)

26. Assign the client body exploration and awareness exercises that reduce inhibition and desensitize him to sexual aversion.

27. Assign graduated steps of sexual pleasuring exercises with partner that reduce the client's performance anxiety and focus on experiencing bodily arousal sensations.

28. Give the client permission for less inhibited, less constricted sexual behavior by assigning body-pleasuring exercises with partner.

18. Write about sexual feelings and thoughts in a daily journal. (29, 30)

29. Assign the client to keep a journal of sexual thoughts and feelings to increase awareness and acceptance of them as normal.

30. Encourage the client's indulgence in his normally occurring sexual fantasies that mediate enhanced sexual desire.

19. Implement new coital positions and settings for sexual activity that enhance pleasure and satisfaction. (14, 31)

14. Assign books (e.g., *Sexual Awareness* by McCarthy and McCarthy, *The Gift of Sex* by Penner and Penner, or *The New Male Sexuality*

by Zilbergeld) that provide the client accurate sexual information and/or outline sexual exercises that disinhibit and reinforce sexual sensate focus.

31. Suggest experimentation with coital positions and settings for sexual play that may increase the client's feelings of security, arousal, and satisfaction.

20. Engage in more assertive behaviors that allow for sharing sexual needs, feelings, and desires, behaving more sensuously, and expressing pleasure. (28, 32)

28. Give the client permission for less inhibited, less constricted sexual behavior by assigning body-pleasuring exercises with partner.

32. Encourage the client to gradually explore the role of being more sexually assertive, sensuously provocative, and freely uninhibited in sexual play with partner.

21. Resolve conflicts or develop coping strategies that reduce stress interfering with sexual interest or performance. (33)

33. Probe stress in areas such as work, extended family, and social relationships that distract the client from sexual desire of performance (see Anxiety, Family Conflict, and Vocational Stress chapters in this Planner).

22. Discuss low self-esteem issues that impede sexual functioning and verbalize positive self-image. (3, 7, 34)

3. Probe the client's family-of-origin history for causes for his feelings of inhibition, low self-esteem, guilt, fear, or repulsion.

7. Probe the client's history for experiences of sexual trauma or abuse.

34. Explore the client's fears of inadequacy as a sexual

23. Communicate feelings of threat to partner that are based on perception of partner being too sexually aggressive or too critical. (2, 35)

24. Implement the squeeze technique during sexual intercourse and report on success in slowing premature ejaculation. (36)

25. Verbalize increasing desire for and pleasure with sexual activity. (31, 32, 37)

partner that led to his sexual avoidance.

2. Direct conjoint sessions with the client and his partner that focus on conflict resolution, expression of feelings, and sex education.

35. Explore the client's feelings of threat brought on by perception of partner as sexually aggressive.

36. Instruct the client and partner in use of the squeeze technique to retard premature ejaculation; process the procedure and feelings about it, reinforcing success and redirecting for failure.

31. Suggest experimentation with coital positions and settings for sexual play that may increase the client's feelings of security, arousal, and satisfaction.

32. Encourage the client to gradually explore the role of being more sexually assertive, sensuously provocative, and freely uninhibited in sexual play with partner.

37. Reinforce the client's expressions of desire for and pleasure in sexual activity.

__. _____
   _____

__. _____
   _____

__. _____
   _____

__. _____
   _____

__. _____
   _____

__. _____
   _____

DIAGNOSTIC SUGGESTIONS

Axis I:

302.71	Hypoactive Sexual Desire Disorder
302.79	Sexual Aversion Disorder
302.72	Male Erectile Disorder
302.74	Male Orgasmic Disorder
302.76	Dyspareunia
302.75	Premature Ejaculation
608.89	Male Hypoactive Sexual Desire Disorder Due to (Axis III Disorder)
607.84	Male Erectile Disorder Due to (Axis III Disorder)
608.89	Male Dyspareunia Due to (Axis III Disorder)
302.70	Sexual Dysfunction NOS
995.53	Sexual Abuse of Child, Victim
_____	_____
_____	_____

MANIA OR HYPOMANIA

BEHAVIORAL DEFINITIONS

1. Loquaciousness or pressured speech.
2. Flight of ideas or reports of thoughts racing.
3. Grandiosity and/or persecutory beliefs.
4. Decreased need for sleep, often with little or no appetite.
5. Increased motor activity or agitation.
6. Poor attention span and easily distracted.
7. Loss of normal inhibition leading to impulsive, pleasure-oriented behavior without regard for painful consequences.
8. Bizarre dress and grooming.
9. Expansive mood that can easily turn to impatience and irritable anger if behavior is blocked or confronted.
10. Lack of follow-through in projects, even though energy is very high, since behavior lacks discipline and goal-directedness.

—. _____
_____
_____

—. _____
_____
_____

—. _____
_____

LONG-TERM GOALS

1. Reduce psychic energy and return to normal activity levels, good judgment, stable mood, and goal-directed behavior.
2. Reduce agitation, impulsivity, and pressured speech while achieving sensitivity to the consequences of behavior and having more realistic expectations.

3. Talk about underlying feelings of low self-esteem or guilt and fears of rejection, dependency, and abandonment.
4. Achieve controlled behavior, moderated mood, and more deliberative speech and thought process through psychotherapy and medication.

___. _____
    _____
___. _____
    _____
___. _____
    _____

SHORT-TERM OBJECTIVES

1. Describe mood state, energy level, amount of control over thoughts, and sleeping pattern. (1, 2)

2. Cooperate with psychiatric evaluation as to the need for medication and/or hospitalization to stabilize mood and energy. (3, 4)

3. Take psychotropic medications as directed. (5, 6)

THERAPEUTIC INTERVENTIONS

1. Assess the client for classic signs of mania: pressured speech, impulsive behavior, euphoric mood, flight of ideas, reduced need for sleep, inflated self-esteem, and high energy.

2. Assess the client's stage of elation: hypomanic, manic, or psychotic.

3. Arrange for or continue hospitalization if the client is judged to be potentially harmful to self or others, or unable to care for his/her own basic needs.

4. Arrange for a psychiatric evaluation of the client for pharmacotherapy (e.g., lithium carbonate or Depakote).

5. Monitor the client's reaction to the psychotropic

medication prescription
(e.g., compliance, side effects, and effectiveness).

6. Continually evaluate the
client's compliance with the
psychotropic medication
prescription as manic
clients often want to terminate medication because
they "don't feel normal."

4. Differentiate between real
and imagined losses, rejec-
tions, and abandonments.
(7, 8, 9)

7. Pledge to be there consistently to help, listen to, and
support the client.

8. Explore the client's fears of
abandonment by sources of
love and nurturance.

9. Help the client differentiate
between real and imagined,
actual and exaggerated
losses.

5. Verbalize grief, fear, and
anger regarding real or
imagined losses in life.
(10, 11)

10. Probe real or perceived
losses in the client's life.

11. Review ways for the client
to replace the losses and
put them in perspective.

6. Acknowledge the low self-
esteem and fear of rejection
that underlie the braggadocio. (12, 13)

12. Probe the causes for the
client's low self-esteem and
abandonment fears in the
family-of-origin history.

13. Confront the client's
grandiosity and demanding-
ness gradually but firmly.

7. Identify the psychosocial
stressors that may trigger
manic behavior. (14)

14. Explore the stressors that
precipitate the client's
manic behavior (e.g., school
failure, social rejection, or
family trauma).

8. Terminate self-destructive
behaviors such as promiscu-

15. Repeatedly focus on the
consequences of the client's

ity, substance abuse, and the expression of overt hostility or aggression. (15, 16, 17, 18)

9. Speak more slowly and be more subject focused. (19, 20)

10. Dress and groom in a less attention-seeking manner. (21)

11. Decrease grandiose statements and express self more realistically. (22, 23)

behavior to reduce his/her thoughtless impulsivity.

16. Facilitate the client's impulse control by using role playing, behavioral rehearsal, and role reversal to increase his/her sensitivity to consequences of his/her behavior.

17. Calmly listen to the client's expressions of hostility while setting limits on his/her aggressive or impulsive behavior.

18. Set limits on the client's manipulation or acting out by making clear rules and establishing clear consequences for breaking rules.

19. Provide structure and focus for the client's thoughts and actions by regulating the direction of conversation and establishing plans for behavior.

20. Verbally reinforce the client's slower speech and more deliberate thought process.

21. Encourage and reinforce the client's appropriate dress and grooming.

22. Interpret the fear and insecurity underlying the client's braggadocio, hostility, and denial of dependency.

23. Encourage the client to share feelings at a deeper level to facilitate openness

and intimacy in relation-
ships, counteracting denial
and superficiality.

12. Identify positive traits and
behaviors that build gen-
uine self-esteem. (24)

24. Assist the client in identifying strengths and assets to
build self-esteem and confidence.

13. Be less agitated and distracted—that is, able to sit
quietly and calmly for 30
minutes. (4, 25)

4. Arrange for a psychiatric
evaluation of the client
for pharmacotherapy (e.g.,
lithium carbonate or
Depakote).

25. Reinforce increased control
over hyperactivity and help
the client set goals and limits on agitation.

14. Sleep about five hours or
more per night. (4, 26)

4. Arrange for a psychiatric
evaluation of the client
for pharmacotherapy (e.g.,
lithium carbonate or
Depakote).

26. Monitor the client's sleep
pattern and encourage a
steady return to five or
more hours sleep per night.

15. Report more control over
impulses and thoughts, and
a slower thinking process.
(4, 27, 28)

4. Arrange for a psychiatric
evaluation of the client
for pharmacotherapy (e.g.,
lithium carbonate or
Depakote).

27. Monitor the patient's energy level and reinforce increased control over
behavior, pressured speech,
and expression of ideas.

28. Reinforce the client's reports of behavior that is
more focused on goal attain-
ments and less distractible.

16. Verbalize an understanding that behavior and judgment were under poor control during manic phase. (16, 29)

16. Facilitate the client's impulse control by using role playing, behavioral rehearsal, and role reversal to increase his/her sensitivity to consequences of his/her behavior.

29. Explore the client's understanding of his/her illness and reinforce a realistic appraisal of his/her impulsivity and loss of judgment.

17. Verbalize acceptance of the need for ongoing supportive treatment and medication because without it a destructive, manic swing could redevelop. (6, 30)

6. Continually evaluate the client's compliance with the psychotropic medication prescription as manic clients often want to terminate medication because they "don't feel normal."

30. Teach the client his/her need for ongoing care of a condition that is usually chronic in nature and often misleads a client into thinking there is no need for medication or therapy.

18. Family of client verbalizes an understanding of the serious nature of the client's illness, its behavioral manifestations, and the need for continuing treatment. (31, 32)

31. Meet with the family to allow ventilation of their feelings of guilt, shame, fear, concern, confusion, or anger regarding the client's behavior.

32. Meet with the family to educate them regarding the client's illness and emphasize the need for ongoing treatment.

__. _____

_____

__. _____

_____

___. _____   ___. _____
      _____   _____
___. _____   ___. _____
      _____   _____

DIAGNOSTIC SUGGESTIONS

Axis I:	296.xx	Bipolar I Disorder
	298.89	Bipolar II Disorder
	301.13	Cyclothymic Disorder
	295.70	Schizoaffective Disorder
	296.80	Bipolar Disorder NOS
	310.1	Personality Change Due to (Axis III Disorder)
	_____	_____
	_____	_____

MEDICAL ISSUES

BEHAVIORAL DEFINITIONS

1. A diagnosis of a chronic illness that is not life threatening but necessitates changes in living.
2. A diagnosis of an acute, serious illness that is life threatening.
3. A diagnosis of a chronic illness that eventually will lead to an early death.
4. Sad affect, social withdrawal, anxiety, loss of interest in activities, and low energy.
5. Suicidal ideation.
6. Denial of the seriousness of the medical condition.
7. Refusal to cooperate with recommended medical treatments.
8. A positive test for human immunodeficiency virus (HIV).
9. Acquired immune deficiency syndrome (AIDS).
10. Medical complications secondary to chemical dependence.
11. Psychological or behavioral factors that influence the course of the medical condition.
12. History of neglecting physical health.

—. _____
   _____
—. _____
   _____
—. _____
   _____

LONG-TERM GOALS

1. Medically stabilize physical condition.

2. Work through the grieving process and face with peace the reality of own death.
3. Accept emotional support from those who care, without pushing them away in anger.
4. Live life to the fullest extent possible, even though remaining time may be limited.
5. Cooperate with the medical treatment regimen without passive-aggressive or active resistance.
6. Become as knowledgeable as possible about the diagnosed condition and about living as normally as possible.
7. Reduce fear, anxiety, and worry associated with the medical condition.
8. Accept the illness, and adapt life to the necessary limitations.
9. Accept the role of psychological or behavioral factors in development of medical condition and focus on resolution of these factors.

—. _____
   _____

—. _____
   _____

—. _____
   _____

SHORT-TERM OBJECTIVES	THERAPEUTIC INTERVENTIONS
1. Describe history, symptoms, and treatment of the medical condition. (1, 2)	1. Gather a history of the facts regarding the client's medical condition, including symptoms, treatment, and prognosis.
	2. With the client's informed consent, contact treating physician and family members for additional medical information regarding the client's diagnosis, treatment, and prognosis.
2. Identify feelings associated with the medical condition. (3)	3. Assist the client in identifying, sorting through, and verbalizing the various

3. Family members share with each other feelings that are triggered by the client's medical condition. (4)

4. Identify the losses or limitations that have been experienced due to the medical condition. (5)

5. Verbalize an increased understanding of the steps to grieving the losses brought on by the medical condition. (6, 7)

6. Verbalize feelings associated with the losses related to the medical condition. (3, 8)

7. Decrease time spent focusing on the negative aspects of the medical condition. (9, 10)

feelings generated by his/her medical condition.

4. Meet with family members to facilitate their clarifying and sharing possible feelings of guilt, anger, helplessness, and/or sibling attention jealousy associated with the client's medical condition.

5. Ask the client to list the changes, losses, or limitations that have resulted from the medical condition.

6. Educate the client on the stages of the grieving process and answer any questions that he/she may have.

7. Suggest that the client read a book on grief and loss (e.g., *Good Grief* by Westberg, *How Can It Be Right When Everything Is All Wrong?* by Smedes, *When Bad Things Happen to Good People* by Kushner).

3. Assist the client in identifying, sorting through, and verbalizing the various feelings generated by his/her medical condition.

8. Assign the client to keep a daily grief journal to be shared in therapy sessions.

9. Suggest that the client set aside a specific time-limited period each day to focus on mourning his/her medical condition. After each day's time period has elapsed, the client will resume regular

activities and put off grieving thoughts until the next
scheduled time. For exam-
ple, mourning times could
include putting on dark
clothing and/or sad music;
the clothing would be
changed when the allotted
time has ended.

10. Challenge the client to focus
his/her thoughts on the positive aspects of life rather
than on the losses associated
with his/her medical condition; reinforce instances of
such a positive focus.

8. Implement faith-based activities as a source of comfort and hope. (11)

11. Encourage the client to rely
upon his/her spiritual faith
promises, activities (e.g.,
prayer, meditation, worship,
music), and fellowship as
sources of support.

9. Verbalize acceptance of the
reality of the medical condition and the need for treatment. (12, 13, 14, 15)

12. Gently confront the client's
denial of the seriousness of
his/her condition and need
for compliance with medical
treatment procedures; reinforce the client's acceptance
of his/her medical condition
and compliance with treatment.

13. Explore and process the
client's fears associated with
medical treatment, deterio-
ration of physical health,
and subsequent death.

14. Normalize the client's feelings of grief, sadness, or
anxiety associated with
medical condition; encourage verbal expression of

these emotions to significant others and medical personnel.

15. Assess the client for and treat his/her depression and anxiety. (See Depression and Anxiety chapters in this Planner).

10. Attend a support group of others diagnosed with a similar illness. (16)

16. Refer the client to a support group of others living with a similar medical condition.

11. Partner and family members attend a support group. (17)

17. Refer family members to a community-based support group associated with the client's medical condition.

12. Comply with the medication regimen and necessary medical procedures, reporting any side effects or problems to physicians or therapists. (2, 18, 19, 20)

2. With the client's informed consent, contact treating physician and family members for additional medical information regarding the client's diagnosis, treatment, and prognosis.

18. Monitor and reinforce the client's compliance with medical treatment regimen.

19. Explore and address the client's misconceptions, fears, and situational factors that interfere with medical treatment compliance.

20. Confront any manipulative, passive-aggressive, and denial mechanisms that block the client's compliance with the medical treatment regimen.

13. Engage in social, productive, and recreational activities that are possible in spite of medical condition. (21, 22)

21. Sort out with the client activities that he/she can still enjoy either alone or with others.

22. Solicit a commitment from the client to increase his/her activity level by engaging in enjoyable and challenging activities; reinforce such engagement.

14. Implement behavioral stress-reduction skills to terminate exacerbation of medical condition due to tension. (23, 24, 25)

23. To reduce tension and stress, teach the client deep muscle relaxation and deep-breathing methods along with positive imagery.

24. Utilize electromyograph (EMG) biofeedback to monitor, increase, and reinforce the client's depth of relaxation.

25. Develop and encourage a routine of physical exercise for the client.

15. Identify and replace negative self-talk and catastrophizing that is associated with the medical condition. (26, 27)

26. Assist the client in identifying the cognitive distortions and negative automatic thoughts that contribute to his/her negative attitude and hopeless feelings associated with the medical condition.

27. Generate with the client a list of positive, realistic self-talk that can replace the cognitive distortions and catastrophizing regarding his/her medical condition and its treatment.

16. Implement positive imagery as a means of triggering peace of mind and reducing tension. (28, 29)

28. Teach the client the use of positive, relaxing, healing imagery to reduce stress and promote peace of mind.

29. Encourage the client to rely on faith-based promises of God's love, presence, caring,

17. Verbalize increased factual understanding of medical condition. (30, 31)

18. Identify the sources of emotional support that have been beneficial and additional sources that could be tapped. (32, 33)

19. Client's partner and family members verbalize their fears regarding the client's severely disabled life or possible death. (34)

20. Maintain a life of sobriety that supports recovery from medical condition. (35, 36)

and support to bring peace of mind.

30. Provide the client with accurate information regarding the symptoms, causes, treatment, and prognosis for his/her medical condition.

31. Refer the client and his/her family to reading material and reliable Internet resources for accurate information regarding the medical condition.

32. Probe and evaluate the client's and family members' resources of emotional support.

33. Encourage the client and his/her family members to reach out for support from church leaders, extended family, hospital social services, community support groups, and God.

34. Draw out from the client's partner and family members their unspoken fears about his/her possible death; empathize with their feelings of panic, helpless frustration, and anxiety. Reassure them of God's presence as the giver and supporter of life.

35. Explore and assess the role of chemical abuse on the client's medical condition.

36. Recommend that the client pursue treatment for his/her chemical dependence. (See Chemical Dependence chapter in this Planner.)

21. Acknowledge any high-risk behaviors associated with sexually transmitted disease (STD). (37)

22. Accept the presence of an STD or HIV and follow through with medical treatment. (38, 39)

23. Identify sources of emotional distress that could have a negative impact on physical health. (40, 41)

37. Assess the client's behavior for the presence of high-risk behaviors (e.g., IV drug use, unprotected sex, gay lifestyle, promiscuity) related to STD and HIV.

38. Refer the client to public health or a physician for STD and/or HIV testing, education, and treatment.

39. Encourage and monitor the client's follow-through on pursuing medical treatment for STD and HIV at a specialized treatment program, if necessary.

40. Teach the client how lifestyle and emotional distress can have negative impacts on medical condition; review his/her lifestyle and emotional status to identify negative factors for physical health.

41. Assign the client to make a list of lifestyle changes he/she could make to help maintain physical health; process list.

__. _____
   _____

__. _____
   _____

__. _____
   _____

__. _____
   _____

__. _____
   _____

__. _____
   _____

DIAGNOSTIC SUGGESTIONS

Axis I: 316   Psychological Symptoms Affecting (Axis II Disorder)

309.0   Adjustment Disorder With Depressed Mood

309.24   Adjustment Disorder With Anxiety

309.28   Adjustment Disorder With Mixed Anxiety and Depressed Mood

309.3   Adjustment Disorder With Disturbance of Conduct

309.4   Adjustment Disorder With Mixed Disturbance of Emotions and Conduct

296.xx   Major Depressive Disorder

311   Depressive Disorder NOS

300.02   Generalized Anxiety Disorder

300.00   Anxiety Disorder NOS

_____   _____

_____   _____

Axis II: 799.9   Diagnosis Deferred

V71.09   No Diagnosis on Axis II

_____   _____

_____   _____

OBSESSIVE-COMPULSIVE DISORDER
(OCD)

BEHAVIORAL DEFINITIONS

1. Recurrent and persistent ideas, thoughts, or impulses that are viewed as intrusive, senseless, and time-consuming, or that interfere with the client's daily routine, job performance, or social relationships.
2. Failed attempts to ignore or control these thoughts or impulses or neutralize them with other thoughts and actions.
3. Recognition that obsessive thoughts are a product of his/her own mind.
4. Repetitive and intentional behaviors that are done in response to obsessive thoughts or according to eccentric rules.
5. Repetitive and excessive behavior that is done to neutralize or prevent discomfort or some dreaded situation; however, that behavior is not connected in any realistic way with what it is designed to neutralize or prevent.
6. Recognition of repetitive behaviors as excessive and unreasonable.

__. _____

_____

__. _____

_____

__. _____

_____

LONG-TERM GOALS

1. Reduce time involved with or interference from obsessions and compulsions.
2. Function daily at a consistent level with minimal interference from obsessions and compulsions.
3. Resolve key life conflicts and the emotional stress that fuels obsessive-compulsive behavior patterns.
4. Let go of key thoughts, beliefs, and past life events in order to maximize time free from obsessions and compulsions.

__. _____

_____

_____

__. _____

_____

_____

__. _____

_____

SHORT-TERM OBJECTIVES

1. Describe the nature, history, and severity of obsessive thoughts and/or compulsive behavior. (1)

2. Comply with psychological testing evaluation to assess the nature and severity of the obsessive-compulsive problem. (2)

3. Take medication as prescribed and report any improvement or side effects to therapist. (3, 4)

THERAPEUTIC INTERVENTIONS

1. Assess the nature, severity, and history of the obsessive-compulsive problems using clinical interview.

2. Arrange for psychological testing to further evaluate the nature and severity of the client's obsessive-compulsive problem.

3. Arrange for a physician evaluation for a psychotropic medication prescription to aid in the control of the client's OCD.

4. Monitor and evaluate the client's psychotropic medication prescription compliance, effectiveness, and side effects.

4. Implement thought-stopping technique to interrupt obsessions. (5)

5. Assign thought-stopping technique that cognitively interferes with obsessions by thinking of a stop sign and then a pleasant scene.

5. Implement relaxation methods to reduce tension. (6, 7)

6. Train in relaxation methods (e.g., deep breathing, muscle tension, positive imagery, etc.) to counteract high anxiety.

7. Administer biofeedback to deepen the client's relaxation skills.

6. Report a decreased level of emotional intensity around conflicts. (4, 8)

4. Monitor and evaluate the client's psychotropic medication prescription compliance, effectiveness, and side effects.

8. Monitor the client's implementation of thought-stopping and relaxation techniques in counteracting his/her activity. Give encouragement and redirection as appropriate.

7. Identify key life conflicts that raise anxiety. (9, 10, 11)

9. Explore the client's life circumstances to help identify key unresolved conflicts.

10. Read with the client the fable "The Friendly Forest" or "Round in Circles" from *Friedman's Fables* (Friedman), and then process using discussion questions.

11. Assign the client to read or read to him/her the story "The Little Clock That Couldn't Tell Time" or "The Little Centipede Who Didn't Know How to Walk" from *Stories for the Third Ear*

8. Verbalize and clarify feelings connected to key life conflicts. (12)

9. Identify and replace distorted thinking and belief errors and reduce the impact each has on daily functioning. (13, 14, 15, 16)

10. Decrease ruminations about death and other perplexing life issues. (17, 18)

(Wallas); process the stories as they are applied to the client's current life.

12. Encourage, support, and assist the client in identifying and expressing feelings related to key unresolved life issues.

13. Ask the client to read "The Perfectionist's Script for Self-Defeat" in *Ten Days to Self-Esteem!* (Burns). Discuss key concepts gathered from the information.

14. Assign the client to complete exercises that focus on cost benefit analysis (Perfectionist Exercise 1) and distorted thinking (Perfectionist Exercise 2) from *Ten Days to Self-Esteem!* (Burns). Process exercises.

15. Assist the client in identifying distorted automatic thoughts and beliefs.

16. Assist the client in developing reality-based self-talk as a strategy to help abate his/her obsessive thoughts.

17. Use a Rational Emotive Therapy approach and teach the client to analyze, attack, and destroy his/her self-defeating beliefs. Monitor and offer appropriate encouragement.

18. Develop and assign a cognitive/behavioral intervention task that will help disrupt the obsessive patterns.

11. Implement the Ericksonian task designed to interfere with OCD. (19)

19. Develop and assign an Ericksonian task (e.g., if obsessed with a loss, give the client the task to visit, send a card, or bring flowers to someone who has lost someone) to the client that is centered around the obsession or compulsion and assess the results with the client.

12. Engage in a strategic ordeal to overcome OCD impulses. (20)

20. Create and sell a strategic ordeal that offers a guaranteed cure to the client for the obsession or compulsion. Note that Haley emphasizes that the "cure" offers an intervention to achieve a goal and is not a promise to cure the client at the beginning of the therapy. (See *Ordeal Therapy* by Haley.)

13. Develop and implement a daily ritual that interrupts the current pattern of compulsions. (21)

21. Help the client create and implement a ritual (e.g., find a job that the client finds necessary but very unpleasant, and have him/her do this job each time he/she finds thoughts becoming obsessive). Follow up with the client on the outcome of its implementation and make and necessary adjustments.

__. _____

__. _____

__. _____

__. _____

__. _____

__. _____

DIAGNOSTIC SUGGESTIONS

Axis I: 300.3   Obsessive-Compulsive Disorder
              300.0   Anxiety Disorder NOS
              296.xx   Major Depressive Disorder
              303.90   Alcohol Dependence
              304.10   Sedative, Hypnotic, or Anxiolytic Dependence

              _____   _____

              _____   _____
Axis II: 301.82   Avoidant Personality Disorder
              301.4   Obsessive-Compulsive Personality Disorder

              _____   _____

              _____   _____

PARANOID IDEATION

BEHAVIORAL DEFINITIONS

1. Extreme or consistent distrust of others generally or someone specifically, without sufficient basis.
2. Expectation of being exploited or harmed by others.
3. Misinterpretation of benign events as having threatening personal significance.
4. Hypersensitivity to hints of personal critical judgment by others.
5. Inclination to keep distance from others out of fear of being hurt or taken advantage of.
6. Tendency to be easily offended and quick to anger; defensiveness is common.
7. A pattern of being suspicious of the loyalty or fidelity of spouse or significant other without reason.
8. Level of mistrust is obsessional to the point of disrupting daily functioning.

—. _____

_____

—. _____

_____

—. _____

_____

LONG-TERM GOALS

1. Show more trust in others by speaking positively of them and reporting comfort in socializing.
2. Interact with others without defensiveness or anger.

3. Verbalize trust of significant other and eliminate accusations of disloyalty.
4. Report reduced vigilance and suspicion around others as well as more relaxed, trusting, and open interaction.
5. Concentrate on important matters without interference from suspicious obsessions.
6. Function appropriately at work, in social activities, and in the community with only minimal interference from distrustful obsessions.

__. _____
_____
__. _____
_____
__. _____
_____

SHORT-TERM OBJECTIVES

1. Demonstrate a level of trust with therapist by disclosing feelings and beliefs. (1, 2)

2. Identify those people or agencies that are distrusted and why. (3, 4)

THERAPEUTIC INTERVENTIONS

1. Actively build level of trust with the client through consistent eye contact, active listening, unconditional positive regard, and warm acceptance to help increase his/her ability to identify and express feelings.

2. Demonstrate a calm, tolerant demeanor in sessions to decrease the client's fear of others.

3. Explore the nature and extent of the client's paranoia, probing for delusional components.

4. Explore the client's basis for fears; assess his/her degree of irrationality and ability to acknowledge that he/she is thinking irrationally.

3. Identify feelings of vulnerability. (5, 6, 7)

5. Probe the client's fears of personal inadequacy and vulnerability.

6. Interpret the client's fears of his/her own anger as the basis for his/her mistrust of others.

7. Explore historical sources of the client's feelings of vulnerability in family-of-origin experiences.

4. Identify and replace core belief that others are untrustworthy and malicious. (4, 8)

4. Explore the client's basis for fears; assess his/her degree of irrationality and ability to acknowledge that he/she is thinking irrationally.

8. Review the client's social interactions and explore his/her distorted cognitive beliefs operative during interactions; replace those core beliefs that are distorted and that trigger paranoid feelings.

5. Comply with a psychiatric evaluation and take psychotropic medication prescribed. (9, 10, 11)

9. Assess the necessity of the use of antipsychotic medication to counteract the client's altered thought processes. (See Psychoticism chapter in this Planner).

10. Arrange for the client to be evaluated by a physician for a psychotropic medication prescription.

11. Monitor the client's psychotropic medication prescription for compliance, effectiveness, and side effects; report to the prescribing physician and confront the client if he/she is not

6. Complete a psychological evaluation to assess the depth of paranoia. (12)

7. Comply with a neuropsychological evaluation to rule out the possibility of organic etiology. (13)

8. Acknowledge that the belief about others being threatening is based more on subjective interpretation than on objective data. (4, 8, 14, 15)

9. Verbalize trust in significant other and feel relaxed when not in his/her presence. (16, 17)

taking medication as prescribed.

12. Arrange for a psychological evaluation to assess the client for possible psychotic process; give feedback as to results.

13. Refer the client for or perform neuropsychological evaluation; if organic factors are found refer him/her to a neurologist for consultation.

4. Explore the client's basis for fears; assess his/her degree of irrationality and ability to acknowledge that he/she is thinking irrationally.

8. Review the client's social interactions and explore his/her distorted cognitive beliefs operative during interactions; replace those core beliefs that are distorted and that trigger paranoid feelings.

14. Assist the client in seeing the pattern of distrusting others as being related to his/her own fears of inadequacy.

15. Ask the client to complete a cost-benefit analysis (see *The Feeling Good Handbook* by Burns) around his/her specific fears; process the exercise.

16. Conduct conjoint sessions to assess and reinforce the client's verbalizations of trust toward significant other.

17. Provide alternative explanations for significant other's behavior that counters the client's pattern of assumption of other's malicious intent.

10. Increase social interaction without fear or suspicion being reported. (18, 19)

18. Encourage the client to check out his/her beliefs regarding others by assertively verifying conclusions with others.

19. Use role playing, behavioral rehearsal, and role reversal to increase the client's empathy for others and his/her understanding of the impact that his/her distrustful, defensive behavior has on others.

__. _____
   _____
__. _____
   _____
__. _____
   _____

__. _____
   _____
__. _____
   _____
__. _____
   _____

DIAGNOSTIC SUGGESTIONS

Axis I:	300.23	Social Phobia
	310.1	Personality Change Due to (Axis III Disorder)
	295.30	Schizophrenia, Paranoid Type
	297.1	Delusional Disorder
	_____	_____
	_____	_____
Axis II:	301.0	Paranoid Personality Disorder
	310.22	Schizotypal Personality Disorder
	_____	_____
	_____	_____

PARENTING

BEHAVIORAL DEFINITIONS

1. Expression of feelings of inadequacy in setting effective limits with their child.
2. Frequently struggle to control their emotional reactions to their child's misbehavior.
3. Increasing conflict between spouses over how to parent/discipline their child.
4. A pattern of lax supervision and inadequate limit setting.
5. A pattern of overindulgence of the child's wishes and demands.
6. A pattern of harsh, rigid, and demeaning behavior toward their child.
7. A pattern of physically and emotionally abusive parenting.
8. Lack of knowledge regarding reasonable expectations for a child's behavior at a given developmental level.
9. Have exhausted their ideas and resources in attempting to deal with their child's behavior.

—. _____
   _____
—. _____
   _____
—. _____
   _____

LONG-TERM GOALS

1. Achieve a level of competent, effective parenting.
2. Reach a realistic view and approach to parenting, given the child's developmental level.

3. Terminate ineffective and/or abusive parenting and implement positive, effective techniques.
4. Strengthen the parental team by resolving marital conflicts.
5. Establish and maintain a healthy functioning parental team.
6. Resolve own childhood or adolescent issues that prevent effective parenting.
7. Adopt appropriate expectations for their adolescent and themselves as parents.
8. Achieve a level of greater family connectedness.

—. _____

_____

—. _____

_____

—. _____

_____

SHORT-TERM OBJECTIVES

1. Provide information on the marital relationship, child behavior expectations, and style of parenting. (1)

2. Identify specific marital conflicts and work toward their resolution. (2, 3)

THERAPEUTIC INTERVENTIONS

1. Engage the parents through the use of empathy and normalization of their struggles with parenting and obtain information on their marital relationship, child behavior expectations, and parenting style.

2. Analyze the data received from the parents about their relationship and parenting and establish or rule out the presence of marital conflicts.

3. Conduct or refer the parents to marital/relationship therapy to resolve the conflicts that are preventing them from being effective parents.

3. Complete recommended evaluation instruments and receive the results. (4, 5, 6)

4. Administer or arrange for the parents to complete assessment instruments to evaluate their parenting strengths and weaknesses [e.g., the Parenting Stress Index (PSI) or the Parent-Child Relationship Inventory (PCRI)].

5. Share results of assessment instruments with the parents and identify issues to begin working on to strengthen the parenting team.

6. Use testing results to identify parental strengths and begin to build the confidence and effectiveness level of the parental team.

4. Express feelings of frustration, helplessness, and inadequacy that each experiences in the parenting role. (7, 8, 9)

7. Create a compassionate, empathetic environment where the parents become comfortable enough to let their guard down and express the frustrations of parenting.

8. Educate the parents on the full scope of parenting by using humor and normalization.

9. Help the parents reduce their unrealistic expectations of themselves.

5. Identify unresolved childhood issues that affect parenting and work toward their resolution. (10, 11)

10. Explore each parent's story of his/her childhood to identify any unresolved issues that are present and to identify how these issues are now affecting the ability to effectively parent.

11. Assist the parents in working through issues from childhood that are unresolved.

6. Decrease reactivity to the child's behaviors. (12, 13, 14)

12. Evaluate the level of the parental team's reactivity to the child's behavior and then help them to learn to respond in a more modulated, thoughtful, planned manner.

13. Help the parents become aware of the "hot buttons" they have that the child can push to get a quick negative response and how this overreactive response reduces their effectiveness as parents.

14. Role-play reactive situations with the parents to help them learn to thoughtfully respond instead of automatically reacting to their child's demands or negative behaviors.

7. Identify the child's personality/temperament type that causes challenges and develop specific strategies to more effectively deal with that personality/temperament type. (15, 16, 17)

15. Have the parents read *The Challenging Child* (Greenspan) and then identify which type of difficult behavior pattern their child exhibits; encourage implementation of several of the parenting methods suggested for that type of child.

16. Expand the parents' repertoire of intervention options by having them read material on parenting difficult children (e.g., *The Difficult Child* by Turecki and Tonner, *The Explosive Child* by

Greene, or *How to Handle a Hard to Handle Kid* by Edwards).

17. Support, empower, monitor, and encourage the parents in implementing new strategies for parenting their child, giving feedback and redirection as needed.

8. Verbalize a sense of increased skill, effectiveness, and confidence in parenting. (17, 18, 19, 20)

17. Support, empower, monitor, and encourage the parents in implementing new strategies for parenting their child, giving feedback and redirection as needed.

18. Train the parents or refer them to structured training in effective parenting methods (e.g., *1-2-3 Magic* by Phelan or *Parenting With Love and Logic* by Cline and Fay).

19. Educate the parents on the numerous key differences between boys and girls such as rate of development, perspectives, impulse control, and anger, and how to handle these differences in the parenting process.

20. Have the children complete the "Parent Report Card" (Berg-Gross) and then give feedback to the parents; support areas of parenting strength and identify weaknesses that need to be bolstered.

9. Partners express verbal support of each other in the parenting process. (21, 22)

21. Assist the parental team in identifying areas of parenting weaknesses; help the

parents improve their skills and boost their confidence and follow-through.

22. Help the parents identify and implement specific ways they can support each other as parents and in realizing the ways children work to keep the parents from cooperating in order to get their way.

10. Decrease outside pressures, demands, and distractions that drain energy and time from the family. (23, 24)

23. Give the parents permission to not involve their child and themselves in too numerous activities, organizations, or sports.

24. Ask the parents to provide a weekly schedule of their entire family's activities and then evaluate the schedule with them, looking for which activities are valuable and which can possibly be eliminated to create a more focused and relaxed time to parent.

11. Develop skills to talk openly and effectively with the children. (25, 26, 27)

25. Use modeling and role play to teach the parents to listen more than talk to their child and to use open-ended questions that encourage openness, sharing, and ongoing dialogue.

26. Encourage the parents to balance the role of limit setting with affirmations of praise, compliments, and appreciation to the child whenever it is possible and appropriate.

27. Ask the parents to read material on parent-child communication (e.g., *How to Talk So Kids Will Listen and Listen So Kids Will Talk* by Faber and Mazlish or *Parent Effectiveness Training* by Gordon); help them implement the new communication style in daily dialogue with their children and to see the positive responses each child had to it.

12. Parents verbalize a termination of their perfectionist expectations of the child. (28, 29)

28. Point out to the parents any unreasonable and perfectionist expectations of their child they hold and help them to modify these expectations.

29. Help the parents identify the negative consequences/outcomes that perfectionist expectations have on a child and on the relationship between the parents and the child.

13. Verbalize an increased awareness and understanding of the unique issues and trials of parenting adolescents. (30, 31, 32, 33)

30. Provide the parents with a balanced view of the impact that adolescent peers have on their child.

31. Teach the parents the concept that adolescence is a time of "normal psychosis" (see *Turning Points* by Pittman) in which the parents need to "ride the adolescent rapids" (see *Preparing for Adolescence: How to Survive the Coming Years of Change* by Dobson) until both survive.

32. Educate the parents on the "second family" (see *The Second Family* by Taffel) concept and how to react to this influence while staying connected to their teen.

33. Assist the parents in coping with the issues and reducing their fears regarding negative peer groups, negative peer influences, and losing their influence to these groups.

14. Decrease negative parenting discipline techniques while replacing them with positive, respectful techniques. (34, 35, 36)

34. Help the parental team identify any negative parenting methods they employ (e.g., overly harsh consequences, demeaning name calling, physical abuse, etc.) and to recognize how this negatively impacts the children; assist them in implementing new, positive methods.

35. Ask the parents to read *Positive Parenting From A to Z* (Renshaw-Joslin) to gain new methods of positive parenting to implement.

36. Encourage, reinforce, and redirect the parents in their efforts to implement and maintain positive methods of parenting.

15. Develop and implement realistic and age-appropriate expectations for the children. (37, 38)

37. Have the parents read books to help them develop appropriate limits and expectations for their child (e.g., *Between Parent and Teenager* by Ginott, *Get Out of My Life but First Could You Drive Me and Cheryl to*

the Mall? by Wolf, *Grounded For Life* by Tracy, or one of the books from the Gesell Development Series by Ames and Ilg.

38. Assist the parents in developing appropriate and realistic behavioral expectations based on their child's age and level of maturity; encourage them to implement these expectations in a nurturing, instructive manner.

16. Increase the gradual letting go of their adolescent in constructive, affirmative ways. (39, 40)

39. Help, encourage, and support the parents in expressing their concerns and fears about "letting go" of their adolescent (include in this their stories of how they separated from their parents).

40. Guide the parents in identifying and implementing constructive, affirmative ways they can allow and support the healthy separation of their adolescent.

17. Parents and child report an increased feeling of connectedness between them. (41, 42)

41. Assist the parents in removing and resolving any barriers that prevent or limit connectedness between family members and in identifying activities that will promote connectedness (e.g., games, one-to-one time).

42. Plant the thought with the parents that just "hanging out at home" or being around/available is what quality time is about.

—. _____   —. _____
   _____   _____
—. _____   —. _____
   _____   _____
—. _____   —. _____
   _____   _____

DIAGNOSTIC SUGGESTIONS

Axis I: 309.3   Adjustment Disorder With Disturbance of
                         Conduct
              309.4   Adjustment Disorder With Mixed Disturbances
                         of Emotions and Conduct
              V61.21   Neglect of Child
              V61.2   Parent-Child Relational Problem
              V61.1   Partner Relational Problem
              V61.21   Physical Abuse of Child
              V61.21   Sexual Abuse of Child
              313.81   Oppositional Defiant Disorder
              312.9   Disruptive Behavior Disorder NOS
              312.8   Conduct Disorder, Adolescent Onset Type
              314.01   Attention-Deficit/Hyperactivity Disorder,
                         Combined Type

              _____   _____
              _____   _____

Axis II: 301.7   Antisocial Personality Disorder
              301.6   Dependent Personality Disorder
              301.81   Narcissistic Personality Disorder
              301.83   Borderline Personality Disorder
              799.9   Diagnosis Deferred
              V71.09   No Diagnosis on Axis II

              _____   _____
              _____   _____

PHASE OF LIFE PROBLEMS

BEHAVIORAL DEFINITIONS

1. Difficulty adjusting to the accountability and interdependence of a new marriage.
2. Anxiety and depression related to the demands of being a new parent.
3. Grief related to children emancipating from the family ("empty nest stress").
4. Restlessness and feelings of lost identity and meaning due to retirement.
5. Feelings of isolation, sadness, and boredom related to quitting employment to be a full-time homemaker and parent.
6. Frustration and anxiety related to providing oversight and caretaking to an aging, ailing, and dependent parent.

__. _____
   _____
   _____
__. _____
   _____
   _____
__. _____
   _____

LONG-TERM GOALS

1. Resolve conflicted feelings and adapt to the new life circumstances.
2. Reorient life view to recognize the advantages of the current situation.
3. Find satisfaction in serving, nurturing, and supporting significant others who are dependent and needy.

4. Balance life activities between consideration of others and development of own interests.

—. _____
_____

—. _____
_____

—. _____
_____

SHORT-TERM OBJECTIVES	THERAPEUTIC INTERVENTIONS
1. Describe the circumstances of life that are contributing to stress, anxiety, or lack of fulfillment. (1, 2, 3)	1. Explore the client's current life circumstances that are causing frustration, anxiety, depression, or lack of fulfillment.
	2. Assign the client to write a list of those circumstances that are causing concern and how or why each is contributing to his/her dissatisfaction.
	3. Assist the client in listing those desirable things that are missing from his/her life that could increase his/her sense of fulfillment.
2. Identify values that guide life's decisions and determine fulfillment. (4, 5)	4. Assist the client in clarifying and prioritizing his/her values.
	5. Assign the client to read books on values clarification (e.g., *Values Clarification* by Simon, Howe, and Kirschenbaum, *In Search of Values: 31 Strategies for Finding Out What Really Matters*

Most to You by Simon); process the content and list values that he/she holds as important.

3. Implement new activities that increase a sense of satisfaction. (6, 7)

6. Develop a plan with the client to include activities that will increase his/her satisfaction, fulfill his/her values, and improve the quality of his/her life.

7. Review the client's attempts to modify his/her life to include self-satisfying activities; reinforce success and redirect for failure.

4. Identify and implement changes that will reduce feelings of being overwhelmed by caretaking responsibilities. (8, 9)

8. Brainstorm with the client possible sources of support or respite (e.g., parent support group, engaging spouse in more child care, respite care for elderly parent, sharing parent-care responsibilities with a sibling, utilizing home health-care resources, taking a parenting class) from the responsibilities that are overwhelming him/her.

9. Encourage the client to implement the changes that will reduce the burden of responsibility felt; monitor progress, reinforcing success and redirecting for failure.

5. Implement increased assertiveness to take control of conflicts. (10, 11, 12)

10. Use role playing, modeling, and behavior rehearsal to teach the client assertiveness skills that can be applied to reducing conflict or dissatisfaction.

11. Refer the client to an assertiveness training class.

12. Encourage the client to read
books on assertiveness and
boundary setting (e.g., *Asserting Yourself* by Bower
and Bower, *When I Say No,
I Feel Guilty* by Smith, *Your
Perfect Right* by Alberti and
Emmons, or *Boundaries:
Where You End and I Begin*
by Katherine); process the
content and its application
to the client's daily life.

6. Apply problem-solving skills
to current circumstances.
(13, 14)

13. Teach the client problem-
resolution skills (e.g., defining the problem clearly,
brainstorming multiple so-
lutions, listing the pros and
cons of each solution, seeking input from others, selecting and implementing a
plan of action, evaluating
outcome, and readjusting
plan as necessary).

14. Use modeling and role playing with the client to apply
the problem-solving ap-
proach to his/her current
circumstances; encourage
implementation of action
plan, reinforcing success
and redirecting for failure.

7. Increase communication
with significant others regarding current life stress
factors. (15, 16)

15. Teach the client communication skills (e.g., "I messages," active listening, eye
contact) to apply to his/her
current life stress factors.

16. Invite the client's partner
and/or other family mem-
bers for conjoint sessions to

address the client's concerns; encourage open communication and group problem solving.

8. Identify five advantages of current life situation. (17)

17. Assist the client in identifying at least five advantages to his/her current life circumstance that may have been overlooked or discounted (e.g., opportunity to make own decisions, opportunity for intimacy and sharing with a partner, a time for developing personal interests or meeting the needs of a significant other).

9. Implement changes in time and effort allocation to restore balance to life. (18)

18. Assist the client in identifying areas of life that need modification in order to restore balance in his/her life (e.g., adequate exercise, proper nutrition and sleep, socialization and recreation activities, spiritual development, conjoint activities with partner as well as individual activities and interests, service to others as well as self-indulgence); develop a plan of implementation.

10. Increase activities that reinforce a positive self-identity. (19, 20)

19. Assist the client in clarifying his/her identity and meaning in life by listing his/her strengths, positive traits and talents, potential ways to contribute to society, and areas of interest and ability that have not yet been developed.

20. Develop an action plan with the client to increase activities that give meaning and

expand his/her sense of identity at a time of transition in life phases (e.g., single to married, employed to homemaker, childless to parent, employed to retired); monitor implementation.

11. Increase social contacts to reduce sense of isolation. (21, 22)

21. Explore opportunities for the client to overcome his/her sense of isolation (e.g., joining a community recreational or educational group, becoming active in church or synagogue activities, taking formal education classes, enrolling in an exercise group, joining a hobby support group); encourage implementation of these activities.

22. Use role playing and modeling to teach the client social skills needed to reach out to build new relationships (e.g., starting conversations, introducing self, asking questions of others about themselves, smiling and being friendly, inviting new acquaintances to his/her home, initiating a social engagement or activity with a new acquaintance).

12. Share emotional struggles related to current adjustment stress. (23, 24)

23. Explore the client's feelings, coping mechanisms, and support system as he/she tries to adjust to the current life stress factors; assess for depth of depression, anxiety, or grief and recommend treatment focused on these problems if warranted (see Depression, Anxiety,

and Grief chapters in this Planner).

24. Assess the client for suicide potential if feelings of depression, helplessness, and isolation are present; initiate suicide prevention precautions, if necessary (see Suicidal Ideation chapter in this Planner).

13. Significant others offer support to reduce the client's stress. (25)

25. Hold family therapy sessions in which significant others are given the opportunity to support the client and offer suggestions for reducing his/her stress; challenge the client to share his/her needs assertively and challenge significant others to take responsibility for support (e.g., partner to increasing parenting involvement, partner to support the client's need for affirmation and stimulation outside the home, family members to take more responsibility for elderly parent's care).

__. _____
   _____
__. _____
   _____
__. _____
   _____

__. _____
   _____
__. _____
   _____
__. _____
   _____

DIAGNOSTIC SUGGESTIONS

Axis I:	V62.89	Phase of Life Problem
	313.82	Identity Problem
	V61.1	Partner Relational Problem
	V61.20	Parent-Child Relational Problem
	309.0	Adjustment Disorder With Depressed Mood
	309.28	Adjustment Disorder With Mixed Anxiety and Depressed Mood
	309.24	Adjustment Disorder With Anxiety
	_____	_____
	_____	_____
Axis II:	799.9	Diagnosis Deferred
	V71.09	No Diagnosis
	_____	_____
	_____	_____

PHOBIA-PANIC/AGORAPHOBIA

BEHAVIORAL DEFINITIONS

1. A persistent and unreasonable fear of a specific object or situation that promotes avoidance behaviors because an encounter with the phobic stimulus provokes an immediate anxiety response.
2. Unexpected, sudden, debilitating panic symptoms (shallow breathing, sweating, heart racing or pounding, dizziness, depersonalization or derealization, trembling, chest tightness, fear of dying or losing control, nausea) that have occurred repeatedly resulting in persisting concern about having additional attacks or behavioral changes to avoid attacks.
3. Fear of being in an environment that may trigger intense anxiety symptoms (panic) and, therefore, avoidance of traveling in an enclosed environment.
4. Avoidance or endurance of the phobic stimulus or feared environment with intense anxiety resulting in interference of normal routines or marked distress.
5. Persistence of fear in spite of recognition that the fear is unreasonable.
6. No evidence of agoraphobia.
7. No evidence of panic disorder.

___. _____
_____

___. _____
_____

___. _____
_____

LONG-TERM GOALS

1. Reduced fear, leading to the ability to independently and freely leave home and comfortably be in public environment.
2. Travel away from home in some form of enclosed transportation.
3. Reduced fear of the specific stimulus object or situation that previously provoked immediate anxiety.
4. Eliminate interference in normal routines and remove distress from feared object or situation.
5. Remove panic symptoms and the fear they will recur without an ability to cope with and control them.

—. _____

_____

—. _____

_____

—. _____

_____

SHORT-TERM OBJECTIVES	THERAPEUTIC INTERVENTIONS
1. Verbalize phobic fear and focus on describing the specific stimuli for it. (1, 2, 3)	1. Discuss and assess the phobic fear, its depth, and the stimuli for it.
	2. Administer a fear survey to further assess the depth and breadth of phobic responses.
	3. Probe, discuss, and interpret possible symbolic meaning of the phobia stimulus object or situation.
2. Identify and replace the cognitive beliefs and messages that mediate the anxiety response. (4)	4. Explore the client's distorted schemas and related negative automatic thoughts that mediate his/her anxiety response; replace the distorted messages with realistic, positive cognitions.

3. Cooperate with systematic desensitization to the anxiety-provoking stimulus object or situation. (5, 6, 7, 8, 9)

4. Undergo in vivo desensitization to the stimulus object or situation. (10)

5. Encounter the phobic stimulus object or situation feeling in control, calm, and comfortable. (9, 10, 11)

6. Verbalize the separate realities of the irrationally feared object or situation and the emotionally painful experience from the past that has been evoked by the phobic stimulus. (12, 13, 14)

5. Direct and assist the client in construction of a hierarchy of anxiety-producing situations associated with the phobic response.

6. Train the client in progressive relaxation methods and deep breathing.

7. Utilize biofeedback techniques to facilitate the client's relaxation skills.

8. Train the client in the use of positive guided imagery for anxiety relief.

9. Direct systematic desensitization procedures to reduce the client's phobic response.

10. Assign and/or accompany the client in in vivo desensitization contact with phobic stimulus object or situation.

9. Direct systematic desensitization procedures to reduce the client's phobic response.

10. Assign and/or accompany the client in in vivo desensitization contact with phobic stimulus object or situation.

11. Review and verbally reinforce the client's progress toward overcoming anxiety.

12. Clarify and differentiate between the client's current irrational fear and past emotional pain.

13. Encourage the client's sharing of feelings associated with past traumas through active listening, positive regard, and questioning.

7. Cooperate with an evaluation by a physician for organic causes of symptoms and for psychotropic medication. (15, 16)

8. Describe the history and nature of the panic symptoms. (17, 18)

9. Identify any secondary gain that accrues due to modification of life related to panic. (19)

10. Verbalize an understanding that panic symptoms do not precipitate a serious mental illness, loss of control over self, or heart attack. (20)

11. Utilize deep muscle relaxation and deep breathing skills to terminate panic symptoms and return to a feeling of peace. (21, 22)

14. Reinforce the client's insights into past emotional pain and present anxiety.

15. Arrange for an evaluation for a prescription of psychotropic medications to alleviate the client's symptoms.

16. Monitor the client for prescription compliance, side effects, and overall effectiveness of the medication; consult with the prescribing physician at regular intervals.

17. Explore the client's symptoms, severity, and history of panic attacks.

18. Explore the nature of any stimulus, thoughts, or situations that precipitate the client's panic.

19. Probe for the presence of secondary gain that reinforces the client's panic symptoms through escape or avoidance mechanisms.

20. Consistently reassure the client of no connection between panic symptoms and heart attack, loss of control over behavior, or serious mental illness ("going crazy").

21. Train the client in the use of coping strategies (e.g., diversion, deep breathing, positive self-talk, muscle relaxation, etc.) to alleviate symptoms.

12. Practice positive self-talk that reassures self of the ability to endure anxiety symptoms without serious consequences. (20, 23, 24)

13. Commit self to not allowing panic symptoms to take control of life and lead to a consistent avoidance of and escape from normal responsibilities and activities. (25)

22. Encourage and monitor the client's use of deep muscle relaxation and deep breathing skills to manage panic symptoms; reinforce success and redirect for failure.

20. Consistently reassure the client of no connection between panic symptoms and heart attack, loss of control over behavior, or serious mental illness ("going crazy").

23. Use modeling and behavioral rehearsal to train patient in positive self-talk that reassures self of ability to work through and endure anxiety symptoms without serious consequences.

24. Urge the patient to keep focus on external stimuli and behavioral responsibilities rather than being preoccupied with internal focus on physiological changes.

25. Support the patient in follow-through with work, family, and social activities rather than escaping or avoiding them to focus on panic.

__. _____

__. _____

__. _____

__. _____

__. _____

__. _____

DIAGNOSTIC SUGGESTIONS

Axis I: 300.01   Panic Disorder Without Agoraphobia
300.21   Panic Disorder With Agoraphobia
300.22   Agoraphobia Without History of Panic
Disorder
300.29   Specific Phobia

_____   _____

_____   _____

POSTTRAUMATIC STRESS DISORDER (PTSD)

BEHAVIORAL DEFINITIONS

1. Exposure to actual or threatened death or serious injury that resulted in an intense emotional response of fear, helplessness, or horror.
2. Intrusive, distressing thoughts or images that recall the traumatic event.
3. Disturbing dreams associated with the traumatic event.
4. A sense that the event is reoccurring, as in illusions or flashbacks.
5. Intense distress when exposed to reminders of the traumatic event.
6. Physiological reactivity when exposed to internal or external cues that symbolize the traumatic event.
7. Avoidance of thoughts, feelings, or conversations about the traumatic event.
8. Avoidance of activity, places, or people associated with the traumatic event.
9. Inability to recall some important aspect of the traumatic event.
10. Lack of interest and participation in significant activities.
11. A sense of detachment from others.
12. Inability to experience the full range of emotions, including love.
13. A pessimistic, fatalistic attitude regarding the future.
14. Sleep disturbance.
15. Irritability.
16. Lack of concentration.
17. Hypervigilance.
18. Exaggerated startle response.
19. Sad or guilty affect and other signs of depression.
20. Alcohol and/or drug abuse.
21. Suicidal thoughts.

22. A pattern of interpersonal conflict, especially in intimate relationships.
23. Verbally and/or physically violent threats of behavior.
24. Inability to maintain employment due to supervisor/coworker conflict of anxiety symptoms.
25. Symptoms have been present for more than one month.

__. _____

_____

__. _____

_____

__. _____

_____

LONG-TERM GOALS

1. Reduce the negative impact that the traumatic event has had on many aspects of life and return to the pretrauma level of functioning.
2. Develop and implement effective coping skills to carry out normal responsibilities and participate constructively in relationships.
3. Recall the traumatic event without becoming overwhelmed with negative emotions.
4. Terminate the destructive behaviors that serve to maintain escape and denial while implementing behaviors that promote healing, acceptance of the past events, and responsible living.

__. _____

_____

__. _____

_____

__. _____

_____

SHORT-TERM OBJECTIVES	THERAPEUTIC INTERVENTIONS
1. Cooperate with psychological testing to assess for symptoms of PTSD. (1)	1. Administer or refer the client for administration of

psychological testing to assess for the presence of strength of PTSD symptoms (e.g., MMPI-2, Impact of Events Scale, PTSD Symptom Scale, or Mississippi Scale for Combat Related PTSD).

2. Identify the symptoms of PTSD that have caused distress and impaired functioning. (2, 3, 4)

2. Ask the client to identify how the traumatic event has negatively impacted his/her personal relationships, functioning at work or school, and social/recreational life.

3. Use the Clinician Administered PTSD Scales (CAPS-1) to assess the client's PTSD status.

4. Ask the client to list and then rank order the strength of his/her symptoms of PTSD.

3. Describe the traumatic event in as much detail as possible. (5, 6)

5. Gently and sensitively explore the client's recollection of the facts of the traumatic incident.

6. Explore the client's emotional reaction at the time of the trauma.

4. Provide honest and complete information for a chemical dependence biopsychosocial history. (7, 8)

7. Assess for the presence of chemical dependence as the client's means of escape from negative emotions (e.g., fear, guilt, rage, etc.) associated with the trauma.

8. Complete a family and personal biopsychosocial history focusing on the client's substance abuse.

5. Verbalize a recognition that mood-altering chemicals were used as the primary coping mechanism to escape from stress or pain, and that their use resulted in negative consequences. (9, 10, 11)

6. Acknowledge the need to implement anger control techniques. (12, 13)

7. Verbalize an awareness of how PTSD develops and its impact on self and others. (14)

8. Practice and implement relaxation training as a coping mechanism for tension, panic, stress, anger, and anxiety. (15, 16)

9. Probe the sense of shame, guilt, and low self-worth that has resulted from the client's substance abuse and its consequences.

10. Use the biopsychosocial history to help the client understand the familial, emotional, and social factors that contributed to the development of chemical dependence.

11. Refer the client for treatment for chemical dependence. (See Chemical Dependence chapter in this Planner.)

12. Assess the client for instances of poor anger management that have led to threats or actual violence that caused damage to property and/or injury to people.

13. Teach the client anger management techniques. (See Anger Management chapter in this Planner.)

14. Refer for didactic sessions or teach the client the facts about trauma and its impact on survivors and their subsequent adjustment.

15. Teach deep muscle relaxation methods along with deep breathing and positive imagery to induce relaxation.

16. Utilize electromyographic (EMG) biofeedback to increase the client's depth of relaxation.

9. Implement a regular exercise regimen as a stress release technique. (17, 18)

17. Develop and encourage a routine of physical exercise for the client.

18. Recommend that the client read and implement programs from *Exercising Your Way to Better Mental Health* (Leith).

10. Report increased comfort and ability to talk and/or think about the traumatic incident without emotional turmoil. (19, 20)

19. Utilize gradual exposure to the traumatic event through systematic desensitization and guided imagery to reduce the client's emotional reactivity to the traumatic event.

20. Explore in detail the client's feelings surrounding the traumatic incident, allowing for a gradual reduction in the intensity of the emotional response with repeated storytelling.

11. Identify and replace negative self-talk and catastrophizing that is associated with past trauma and current stimulus triggers for anxiety. (21, 22)

21. Explore the client's negative self-talk that is associated with the past trauma and his/her predictions of unsuccessful coping or catastrophizing.

22. Assist the client in listing his/her negative, self-defeating thinking and in replacing each thought with self-enhancing self-talk.

12. Approach actual stimuli (in vivo) that trigger memories and feelings associated with past trauma, staying calm by using relaxation techniques and positive self-talk. (15, 22, 23)

15. Teach deep muscle relaxation methods along with deep breathing and positive imagery to induce relaxation.

22. Assist the client in listing his/her negative, self-defeating thinking and in

replacing each thought with self-enhancing self-talk.

23. Encourage the client to approach previously avoided stimuli that trigger thoughts and feelings associated with the past trauma; urge his/her use of relaxation, deep breathing, and positive self-talk during the approach to the stimulus.

13. Sleep without being disturbed by dreams of the trauma. (15, 17, 24)

15. Teach deep muscle relaxation methods along with deep breathing and positive imagery to induce relaxation.

17. Develop and encourage a routine of physical exercise for the client.

24. Monitor the client's sleep pattern and encourage use of relaxation and positive imagery as aids to sleep. (See Sleep Disturbance chapter in this Planner.)

14. Cooperate with eye movement desensitization and reprocessing (EMDR) technique to reduce emotional reaction to the traumatic event. (25)

25. Utilize EMDR technique to reduce the client's emotional reactivity to the traumatic event.

15. Participate in group therapy sessions focused on PTSD. (26)

26. Refer the client to or conduct group therapy sessions where the focus is on sharing traumatic events and their effects with other PTSD survivors.

16. Take medication as prescribed and report as to the effectiveness and side effects. (27, 28)

27. Assess the client's need for medication (e.g., selective serotonin reuptake

inhibitors) and arrange for prescription if appropriate.

28. Monitor and evaluate the client's psychotropic medication prescription compliance and the effectiveness of the medication on his/her level of functioning.

17. Participate in conjoint and/or family therapy sessions. (29)

29. Conduct family and conjoint sessions to facilitate healing of hurt caused by the client's symptoms of PTSD.

18. Describe any dissociative symptoms associated with a reaction to the trauma. (30)

30. Assess the client for dissociative symptoms (e.g., flashbacks, memory loss, identity disorder, etc.) and treat or refer for treatment. (See Dissociation chapter in this Planner.)

19. Verbalize an understanding of the negative impact PTSD has had on vocational functioning and cooperate with treatment for vocational conflicts. (31)

31. Explore the client's vocational history and treat his/her vocational issues as appropriate. (See Vocational Stress chapter in this Planner.)

20. Verbalize the symptoms of depression, including any suicidal ideation. (32)

32. Assess the client's depth of depression and suicide potential and treat appropriately, taking the necessary safety precautions as indicated. (See Depression and Suicidal Ideation chapters in this Planner.)

21. Verbalize hopeful and positive statements regarding the future. (33, 34)

33. Assist the client in developing an awareness of cognitive messages that reinforce hopelessness and helplessness.

34. Reinforce the client's positive, reality-based cognitive

messages that enhance self-confidence and increase adaptive action.

—. _____   —. _____
   _____   _____
—. _____   —. _____
   _____   _____
—. _____   —. _____
   _____   _____

DIAGNOSTIC SUGGESTIONS

Axis I:
309.81	Posttraumatic Stress Disorder
300.14	Dissociative Identify Disorder
300.6	Depersonalization Disorder
300.15	Dissociative Disorder NOS
995.54	Physical Abuse of Child, Victim
995.81	Physical Abuse of Adult, Victim
995.53	Sexual Abuse of Child, Victim
995.83	Sexual Abuse of Adult, Victim
308.3	Acute Stress Disorder
304.80	Polysubstance Dependence
305.0	Alcohol Abuse
303.90	Alcohol Dependence
304.30	Cannabis Dependence
304.20	Cocaine Dependence
304.0	Opioid Dependence
296.xx	Major Depression
_____	_____
_____	_____

Axis II:
301.83	Borderline Personality Disorder
301.9	Personality Disorder NOS
_____	_____
_____	_____

PSYCHOTICISM

BEHAVIORAL DEFINITIONS

1. Bizarre content of thought (delusions of grandeur, persecution, reference, influence, control, somatic sensations, or infidelity).
2. Illogical form of thought/speech (loose association of ideas in speech, incoherence; illogical thinking; vague, abstract, or repetitive speech; neologisms, perseverations, clanging).
3. Perception disturbance (auditory, visual, or olfactory hallucinations).
4. Disturbed affect (blunted, none, flattened, or inappropriate).
5. Lost sense of self (loss of ego boundaries, lack of identity, blatant confusion).
6. Volition diminished (inadequate interest, drive, or ability to follow a course of action to its logical conclusion; pronounced ambivalence or cessation of goal-directed activity).
7. Relationship withdrawal (withdrawal from involvement with external world and preoccupation with egocentric ideas and fantasies, alienation feelings).
8. Psychomotor abnormalities (marked decrease in reactivity to environment; various catatonic patterns such as stupor, rigidity, excitement, posturing, or negativism; unusual mannerisms or grimacing).
9. Extreme agitation, including a high degree of irritability, anger, unpredictability, or impulsive physical acting out.
10. Bizarre dress or grooming.

—. _____
   _____
—. _____
   _____
—. _____
   _____

LONG-TERM GOALS

1. Control or eliminate active psychotic symptoms so that supervised functioning is positive and medication is taken consistently.
2. Eliminate acute, reactive, psychotic symptoms and return to normal functioning in affect, thinking, and relating.
3. Increase goal-directed behaviors.
4. Focus thoughts on reality.
5. Normalize speech patterns, which can be evidenced by coherent statements, attentions to social cues, and remaining on task.

—. _____
   _____
   _____
—. _____
   _____
   _____
—. _____
   _____

SHORT-TERM OBJECTIVES	THERAPEUTIC INTERVENTIONS
1. Describe the type and history of the psychotic symptoms. (1, 2, 3)	1. Demonstrate acceptance to the client through calm, nurturing manner; good eye contact; and active listening.
	2. Assess the pervasiveness of the client's thought disorder through clinical interview and/or psychological testing.
	3. Determine whether the client's psychosis is of a brief reactive nature or long-term with prodromal and reactive elements.
2. Client or significant other provides family history of serious mental illness. (4)	4. Explore the client's family history for serious mental illness.
3. Accept and understand that distressing symptoms are due to mental illness. (5, 6)	5. Provide supportive therapy to alleviate the client's fears

and reduce feelings of alienation.

4. Take antipsychotic medications consistently with or without supervision. (7, 8)

6. Explain to the client the nature of the psychotic process, its biochemical components, and the confusing effect on rational thought.

7. Refer the client for an immediate evaluation by a psychiatrist regarding his/her psychotic symptoms and a possible prescription for antipsychotic medication.

8. Monitor the client for psychotropic medication prescription compliance, effectiveness, and side effects; redirect if the client is noncompliant.

5. Accept the need for a supervised living environment. (9, 10)

9. Arrange for the client to remain in a stable, supervised situation (e.g., crisis adult foster care placement or a friend's/family member's home).

10. Make arrangements for involuntary commitment to an inpatient psychiatric facility if the client is assessed to be unable to care for his/her basic needs or is potentially harmful to himself/herself or others.

6. Describe recent perceived severe stressors that may have precipitated the acute psychotic break. (11, 12, 13)

11. Probe causes for the client's reactive psychosis.

12. Explore the client's feelings surrounding the stressors that triggered his/her psychotic episodes.

13. Assist the client in reducing threat in the environment

(e.g., finding a safer place to live, arranging for regular visits from caseworker, arranging for family members to call more frequently).

7. Report diminishing or absence of hallucinations and/or delusions. (7, 8, 14, 15, 16)

7. Refer the client for an immediate evaluation by a psychiatrist regarding his/her psychotic symptoms and a possible prescription for antipsychotic medication.

8. Monitor the client for psychotropic medication prescription compliance, effectiveness, and side effects; redirect if the client is noncompliant.

14. Assist the client in restructuring his/her irrational beliefs by reviewing reality-based evidence and his/her misinterpretation.

15. Encourage the client to focus on the reality of the external world versus his/her distorted fantasy.

16. Differentiate for the client the source of stimuli between self-generated messages and the reality of the external world.

8. Begin to show limited social functioning by responding appropriately to friendly encounters. (14, 17)

14. Assist the client in restructuring his/her irrational beliefs by reviewing reality-based evidence and his/her misinterpretation.

17. Reinforce the client's socially and emotionally appropriate responses to others.

9. Think more clearly as demonstrated by logical, coherent speech. (7, 18, 19)

7. Refer the client for an immediate evaluation by a psychiatrist regarding his/her psychotic symptoms and a possible prescription for antipsychotic medication.

18. Gently confront the client's illogical thoughts and speech to refocus disordered thinking.

19. Reinforce the client's clarity and rationality of thought and speech.

10. Verbalize an understanding of the underlying needs, conflicts, and emotions that support the irrational beliefs. (14, 20)

14. Assist the client in restructuring his/her irrational beliefs by reviewing reality-based evidence and his/her misinterpretation.

20. Probe the client's underlying needs and feelings (e.g., inadequacy, rejection, anxiety, guilt) that trigger irrational thought.

11. Family members increase their positive support of the client to reduce changes of acute exacerbation of psychotic episodes. (21, 22)

21. Arrange family therapy sessions to educate regarding the client's illness, treatment, and prognosis.

22. Assist the family in avoiding double-bind messages that increase anxiety and psychotic symptoms in the client.

12. Family members share their feelings of guilt, frustration, and fear associated with the client's mental illness. (23, 24)

23. Encourage the family members to share their feelings of frustration, guilt, fear, or depression surrounding the client's mental illness and behavior patterns.

24. Refer the family members to a community-based support

13. Gradually return to premorbid level of functioning and accept responsibility of caring for own basic needs, including medication regimen. (8, 25)

group designed for the families of psychotic patients.

8. Monitor the client for psychotropic medication prescription compliance, effectiveness, and side effects; redirect if the client is noncompliant.

25. Monitor the client's daily level of functioning (i.e., reality orientation, personal hygiene, social interactions, and affect appropriateness) and give feedback that either redirects or reinforces the client's progress.

—. _____

_____

—. _____

_____

—. _____

_____

—. _____

_____

—. _____

_____

—. _____

_____

DIAGNOSTIC SUGGESTIONS

Axis I:	297.1	Delusional Disorder
	298.8	Brief Psychotic Disorder
	295.xx	Schizophrenia
	295.30	Schizophrenia, Paranoid Type
	295.70	Schizoaffective Disorder
	295.40	Schizophreniform Disorder
	296.xx	Bipolar I Disorder
	298.89	Bipolar II Disorder
	298.xx	Major Depressive Disorder
	310.1	Personality Change Due to (Axis III Disorder)
	_____	_____
	_____	_____

SEXUAL ABUSE

BEHAVIORAL DEFINITIONS

1. Vague memories of inappropriate childhood sexual contact that can be corroborated by significant others.
2. Self-report of being sexually abused with clear, detailed memories.
3. Inability to recall years of childhood.
4. Extreme difficulty becoming intimate with others.
5. Inability to enjoy sexual contact with a desired partner.
6. Unexplainable feelings of anger, rage, or fear when coming into contact with a close family relative.
7. Pervasive pattern of promiscuity or the sexualization of relationships.

__. _____

_____

__. _____

_____

__. _____

_____

LONG-TERM GOALS

1. Resolve the issue of being sexually abused with an increased capacity for intimacy in relationships.
2. Begin the healing process from sexual abuse with resultant enjoyment of appropriate sexual contact.
3. Work successfully through the issues related to being sexually abused with consequent understanding and control of feelings.
4. Recognize and accept the sexual abuse without inappropriate sexualization of relationships.

251

5. Establish whether sexual abuse occurred.
6. Begin the process of moving away from being a victim of sexual abuse and toward becoming a survivor of sexual abuse.

__. _____
   _____
   _____

__. _____
   _____
   _____

__. _____
   _____
   _____

SHORT-TERM OBJECTIVES

1. Tell the story of the nature, frequency, and duration of the abuse. (1, 2, 3)

2. Identify a support system of key individuals who will be encouraging and helpful in aiding the process of resolving the issue. (4, 5)

THERAPEUTIC INTERVENTIONS

1. Actively build the level of trust with the client in individual sessions through consistent eye contact, unconditional positive regard, and warm acceptance to help increase his/her ability to identify and express feelings.

2. Gently explore the client's sexual abuse experience without pressing early for unnecessary details.

3. Ask the client to draw a diagram of the house in which he/she was raised, complete with where everyone slept.

4. Help the client identify those individuals who would be compassionate and encourage him/her to enlist their support.

5. Encourage the client to attend a support group for survivors of sexual abuse.

3. Verbalize an increased knowledge of sexual abuse and its effect. (6, 7)

6. Assign the client to read material on sexual abuse (e.g., *The Courage to Heal* by Bass and Davis, *Betrayal of Innocence* by Forward and Buck, *Outgrowing the Pain* by Gil, etc.); process key concepts.

7. Assign and process a written exercise from *The Courage to Heal Workbook* (Davis).

4. Identify and express the feelings connected to the abuse. (8, 9)

8. Explore, encourage, and support the client in verbally expressing and clarifying feelings associated with the abuse.

9. Encourage the client to be open in talking of the abuse without shame or embarrassment as if he/she was responsible for the abuse.

5. Decrease the secrecy in the family by informing key nonabusive members regarding the abuse. (10, 11, 12)

10. Guide the client in an empty chair conversation exercise with a key figure connected to the abuse (e.g., perpetrator, sibling, or parent) telling them of the sexual abuse and its effects.

11. Hold conjoint session where the client tells his/her spouse of the abuse.

12. Facilitate family session with the client, assisting and supporting him/her in revealing the abuse to parent(s).

6. Describe how sex abuse experience is part of a family pattern of broken boundaries through physical contact or verbal suggestiveness. (13)

13. Develop with the client a genogram and assist in illuminating key family patterns of broken boundaries related to sex and intimacy.

7. Verbalize the ways the sexual abuse has had an impact on life. (14, 15)

8. Clarify memories of the abuse. (16, 17)

9. Decrease statements of shame, being responsible for the abuse, or being a victim, while increasing statements that reflect personal empowerment. (18, 19, 20, 21)

14. Ask the client to make a list of the ways sexual abuse has impacted his/her life; process the list content.

15. Develop with the client a symptom line connected to the abuse.

16. Refer or conduct hypnosis with the client to further uncover or clarify the nature and extent of the abuse.

17. Facilitate the client's recall of the details of the abuse by asking him/her to keep a journal and talk and think about the incident(s). Caution him/her against embellishment based on book, video, or drama material, and be very careful not to lead the client into only confirming therapist-held suspicions.

18. Assign the client to read material on overcoming shame (e.g., *Healing the Shame That Binds You* by Bradshaw, *Shame* by Kaufman, *Facing Shame* by Fossum and Mason, etc.); process key concepts.

19. Encourage, support, and assist the client in identifying, expressing, and processing any feelings of guilt related to feelings of physical pleasure, emotional fulfillment, or responsibility connected with the events.

20. Confront and process with the client any statements

that reflect taking responsibility for the abuse or indicating he/she is a victim. Then assist the client in feeling empowered by working through the issues and letting go of the abuse.

21. Assign the client to complete a cost-benefit exercise (see *Ten Days to Self-Esteem!* by Burns), or a similar exercise, on being a victim versus a survivor or on holding on versus forgiving; process completed exercises.

10. Identify the positive benefits for self of being able to forgive all those involved with the abuse. (22, 23, 24)

22. Read and process the story from *Stories for the Third Ear* (Wallas) titled "The Seedling." (A story for a client who has been abused as a child.)

23. Assist the client in removing any barriers that prevent him/her from being able to identify the benefits of forgiving those responsible for the abuse.

24. Recommend that the client read *Forgive and Forget* (Smedes).

11. Express feelings to and about the perpetrator, including the impact the abuse has had both at the time of occurrence and currently. (25, 26, 27)

25. Assign the client to write an angry letter to the perpetrator; process the letter within the session.

26. Prepare the client for a face-to-face meeting with the perpetrator of the abuse by processing the feelings that arise around the event and role-playing the meeting.

27. Hold a conjoint session where the client confronts the perpetrator of the abuse; afterward, process his/her feelings and thoughts related to the experience.

12. Increase level of forgiveness of self, perpetrator, and others connected with the abuse. (28)

28. Assign the client to write a forgiveness letter and/or complete a forgiveness exercise (see *Forgiving* by Simon and Simon) and to process each with therapist.

13. Increase level of trust of others as shown by more socialization and greater intimacy tolerance. (29, 30)

29. Teach the client the share-check method of building trust in relationships (i.e., share only a little of self and then check to be sure that the shared data is treated respectfully, kindly, and confidentially; as proof of trustworthiness is verified, share more freely).

30. Use role playing and modeling to teach the client how to establish reasonable personal boundaries that are neither too porous nor too restrictive.

14. Report increased ability to accept and initiate appropriate physical contact with others. (31, 32)

31. Encourage the client to give and receive appropriate touches; help him/her define what is appropriate.

32. Ask the client to practice one or two times a week initiating appropriate touching or a touching activity (i.e., giving a back rub to spouse, receiving a professional massage, hugging a friend, etc.).

15. Verbally identify self as a survivor of sexual abuse. (33, 34)

33. Reinforce with the client the benefits of seeing himself/herself as a survivor rather than the victim and work to remove any barriers that remain in the way of him/her doing so.

34. Give positive verbal reinforcement when the client identifies himself/herself as a survivor.

__. _____
    _____

__. _____
    _____

__. _____
    _____

__. _____
    _____

__. _____
    _____

__. _____
    _____

DIAGNOSTIC SUGGESTIONS

Axis I:	303.90	Alcohol Dependence
	304.80	Polysubstance Dependence
	300.4	Dysthymic Disorder
	296.xx	Major Depressive Disorder
	300.02	Generalized Anxiety Disorder
	300.14	Dissociative Identity Disorder
	300.15	Dissociative Disorder NOS
	995.53	Sexual Abuse of Child, Victim
	995.83	Sexual Abuse of Adult, Victim
	_____	_____
Axis II:	301.82	Avoidant Personality Disorder
	301.6	Dependent Personality Disorder
	_____	_____
	_____	_____

SEXUAL IDENTITY CONFUSION*

BEHAVIORAL DEFINITIONS

1. Uncertainty about basic sexual orientation.
2. Difficulty in enjoying sexual activities with opposite-sex partner because of low arousal.
3. Sexual fantasies and desires about same-sex partners, which causes distress.
4. Sexual activity with person of same sex that has caused confusion, guilt, and anxiety.
5. Depressed mood, diminished interest in activities.
6. Marital conflicts caused by uncertainty about sexual orientation.
7. Feelings of guilt, shame, and/or worthlessness.
8. Concealing sexual identity from significant others (e.g., friends, family, spouse).

__. _____
   _____
__. _____
   _____
__. _____
   _____

---

*Most of the content of this chapter (with only slight revisions) originates from J. M. Evosevich and M. Avriette, *The Gay and Lesbian Psychotherapy Treatment Planner* (New York: John Wiley & Sons, 2000. Copyright © 2000 by J. M. Evosevich and M. Avriette. Reprinted with permission.

LONG-TERM GOALS

1. Identify sexual identity and engage in a wide range of relationships that are supportive of that identity.
2. Reduce overall frequency and intensity of the anxiety associated with sexual identity so that daily functioning is not impaired.
3. Disclose sexual orientation to significant others.
4. Return to previous level of emotional, psychological, and social functioning.
5. Eliminate all feelings of depression (e.g., depressed mood, guilt, worthlessness).

—. _____

_____

—. _____

_____

—. _____

_____

SHORT-TERM OBJECTIVES	THERAPEUTIC INTERVENTIONS
1. Describe fear, anxiety, and distress about confusion over sexual identity. (1)	1. Actively build trust with the client and encourage his/her expression of fear, anxiety, and distress over sexual identity confusion.
2. Identify sexual experiences that have been a source of excitement, satisfaction, and emotional gratification. (2, 3, 4, 5)	2. Assess the client's current sexual functioning by asking him/her about previous sexual history, fantasies, and thoughts.
	3. Assist the client in identifying sexual experiences that have been a source of excitement, satisfaction, and emotional gratification.
	4. To assist the client in increasing his/her awareness of sexual attractions and

conflicts, assign him/her to write a journal describing sexual thoughts, fantasies, and conflicts that occur throughout the week.

5. Have the client rate his/her sexual attraction to both men and women on a scale of 1 to 10 (with 10 being extremely attracted and 1 being not at all attracted).

3. Verbalize an understanding of how cultural, racial, and/or ethnic identity factors contribute to confusion about sexual identity. (6)

6. Explore with the client how cultural, racial and/or ethnic factors contribute to confusion about homosexual behavior and/or identity.

4. Write a "future" biography detailing life as a heterosexual and as a homosexual to assist in identifying primary orientation. (7)

7. Assign the client the homework of writing a "future" biography describing his/her life 20 years in the future, once as a heterosexual, another as a homosexual; read and process in session (e.g., ask him/her which life was more satisfying, which life had more regret).

5. Verbalize an understanding of the range of sexual identities possible. (8, 9)

8. Educate the client about the range of sexual identities possible (i.e., heterosexual, homosexual, bisexual).

9. Have the client read *The Invention of Heterosexuality* by Katz; process the client's thoughts and feelings about its content.

6. Identify the negative emotions experienced by hiding sexuality. (10, 11)

10. Explore the client's negative emotions (e.g., shame, guilt, anxiety, loneliness) related to hiding/denying his/her sexuality.

7. Verbalize an understanding of safer-sex practices. (12)

8. Verbalize an increased understanding of homosexuality. (8, 13, 14)

9. List the advantages and disadvantages of disclosing sexual orientation to significant people in life. (15)

10. Watch films/videos that depict lesbian women/gay men in positive ways. (16)

11. Explore the client's religious convictions and how these may conflict with identifying himself/herself as homosexual and cause feelings of shame or guilt (see Spiritual Confusion chapter in this Planner).

12. Teach the client the details of safer-sex guidelines and encourage him/her to include them in all future sexual activity.

8. Educate the client about the range of sexual identities possible (i.e., heterosexual, homosexual, bisexual).

13. Assign the client homework to identify 10 myths about homosexuals and assist him/her in replacing them with more realistic, positive beliefs.

14. Assign the client to read books that provide accurate, positive messages about homosexuality (e.g., *Is It a Choice?* by Marcus, *Outing Yourself* by Signorile, or *Coming Out: An Act of Love* by Eichberg).

15. Assign the client to list advantages and disadvantages of disclosing sexual orientation to significant others; process the list content.

16. Ask the client to watch movies/videos that depict lesbians/gay men as healthy and happy (e.g., *Desert Hearts, In and Out, Jeffrey,*

and *When Night is Falling*); process his/her reactions to the films.

11. Attend a support group for those who want to disclose themselves as homosexual. (17)

12. Identify gay/lesbian people to socialize with or to obtain support from. (18, 19, 20)

17. Refer the client to a coming-out support group (e.g., at Gay and Lesbian Community Service Center or AIDS Project).

18. Assign the client to read lesbian/gay magazines and newspapers (e.g., *The Advocate*).

19. Encourage the client to gather information and support from the Internet (e.g., coming-out bulletin boards on AOL, lesbian/gay organizations' web sites).

20. Encourage the client to identify gay men or lesbians to interact with by reviewing people he/she has met in support groups, at work, and so on, and encourage him/her to initiate social activities.

13. Develop a plan detailing when, where, how, and to whom sexual orientation is to be disclosed. (21, 22)

21. Have the client role-play disclosure of sexual orientation to significant others (e.g., family, friends, coworkers). (See Family Conflict chapter in this Planner.)

22. Assign the client homework to write a detailed plan to disclose his/her sexual orientation, including to whom it will be disclosed, where, when, and possible questions and reactions recipient(s) might have.

14. Identify one friend who is likely to have a positive reaction to homosexuality disclosure. (23, 24)

23. Encourage the client to identify one friend who is likely to be accepting of his/her homosexuality.

24. Suggest the client have casual talks with a friend about lesbian/gay rights, or some item in the news related to lesbians and gay men to "test the water" before disclosing sexual orientation to that friend.

15. Reveal sexual orientation to significant others according to written plan. (25, 26)

25. Encourage the client to disclose sexual orientation to friends/family according to the written plan.

26. Probe the client about reactions of significant others to disclosure of homosexuality (e.g., acceptance, rejection, shock); provide encouragement and positive feedback.

__. _____
_____
__. _____
_____
__. _____
_____

__. _____
_____
__. _____
_____
__. _____
_____

DIAGNOSTIC SUGGESTIONS

Axis I: 309.0   Adjustment Disorder With Depressed Mood
309.28   Adjustment Disorder With Mixed Anxiety and Depressed Mood
300.00   Anxiety Disorder NOS
309.24   Adjustment Disorder With Anxiety
300.4   Dysthymic Disorder
302.85   Gender Identity Disorder in Adults
300.02   Generalized Anxiety Disorder

313.82	Identity Problem
296.2x	Major Depressive Disorder, Single Episode
296.3x	Major Depressive Disorder, Recurrent
V62.89	Phase of Life Problem
V61.20	Parent-Child Relational Problem
302.9	Sexual Disorder NOS
_____	_____
_____	_____

Axis II:	301.82	Avoidant Personality Disorder
	301.83	Borderline Personality Disorder
	301.81	Narcissistic Personality Disorder
	_____	_____
	_____	_____

SLEEP DISTURBANCE

BEHAVIORAL DEFINITIONS

1. Difficulty getting to sleep or remaining asleep.
2. Sleeping adequately but not feeling refreshed or rested after waking.
3. Predominately daytime sleepiness or falling asleep too easily during daytime.
4. Insomnia or hypersomnia complaints due to a reversal of the normal sleep-wake schedule.
5. Distress resulting from repeated awakening with detailed recall of extremely frightening dreams involving threats to self.
6. Abrupt awakening with a panicky scream followed by intense anxiety and autonomic arousal, no detailed dream recall, and confusion or disorientation.
7. Repeated incidents of sleepwalking accompanied by amnesia for the episode.

LONG-TERM GOALS

1. Restore restful sleep pattern.
2. Feel refreshed and energetic during wakeful hours.
3. Terminate anxiety-producing dreams that cause awakening.

4. End abrupt awakening in terror and return to peaceful, restful sleep pattern.
5. Restore restful sleep with reduction of sleepwalking incidents.

___. _____
_____

___. _____
_____

___. _____
_____

SHORT-TERM OBJECTIVES

THERAPEUTIC INTERVENTIONS

1. Describe the history and details of sleep pattern. (1, 2)

1. Assess the exact nature of sleep pattern, including bedtime routine, activity level while awake, nutritional habits, napping practice, actual sleep time, rhythm of time for being awake versus sleeping, and so on.

2. Assign the client to keep a journal of daily stressors and nightly sleep patterns; process the material for details of the sleep-wake cycle.

2. Share history of substance abuse or medication use. (3)

3. Assess the contribution of the client's medication or substance abuse to his/her sleep disorder; refer him/her for chemical dependence treatment, if indicated (see Chemical Dependence chapter in this Planner).

3. Verbalize depressive or anxious feelings and share possible causes. (4)

4. Assess the role of depression or anxiety as the cause of the client's sleep disturbance.

4. Keep physician appointment to assess organic contributions to sleep disorder and the need for psychotropic medications. (5)

5. Take psychotropic medication daily for three weeks to assess the effect on sleep. (6)

6. Discuss experiences of emotional traumas that continue to disturb sleep. (7, 8)

7. Discuss fears regarding relinquishing control. (9)

8. Disclose fears of death that may contribute to sleep disturbance. (10)

9. Identify current stressors that may be interfering with sleep. (2, 7, 11)

5. Refer the client to a physician to rule out physical and pharmacological causes for sleep disturbance and evaluate him/her for a prescription for psychotropic medications.

6. Monitor the client for psychotropic medication prescription compliance, effectiveness, and side effects.

7. Explore recent traumatic events that interfere with the client's sleep.

8. Probe the client for the presence and nature of disturbing dreams and their relationship to his/her life stress; assign him/her to keep a dream journal to be processed in future appointments.

9. Probe the client's fears related to letting go of control.

10. Probe a fear of death that may contribute to the client's sleep disturbance.

2. Assign the client to keep a journal of daily stressors and nightly sleep patterns; process the material for details of the sleep-wake cycle.

7. Explore recent traumatic events that interfere with the client's sleep.

11. Explore the client's current life circumstances for causes of anxiety that may be interfering with his/her sleep.

268 THE COMPLETE ADULT PSYCHOTHERAPY TREATMENT PLANNER

10. Verbalize a plan to deal with stressors proactively. (12)

11. Share childhood traumatic experiences associated with sleep experience. (8, 13)

12. Reveal sexual abuse incidents that continue to be disturbing. (8, 14)

13. Follow sleep induction schedule of events. (15, 16)

14. Practice deep muscle relaxation exercises. (17, 18)

12. Assist the client in formulating a plan to modify his/her life situation to reduce stress and anxiety.

8. Probe the client for the presence and nature of disturbing dreams and their relationship to his/her life stress; assign him/her to keep a dream journal to be processed in future appointments.

13. Explore traumas of the client's childhood that surround the sleep experience.

8. Probe the client for the presence and nature of disturbing dreams and their relationship to his/her life stress; assign him/her to keep a dream journal to be processed in future appointments.

14. Explore for possible sexual abuse to the client that has not been revealed.

15. Assign the client to adhere to a strict sleep induction routine: daily exercise, low stimulation prior to sleep, relaxation training, bland diet, warm bath, reading a book, set time to retire, and so forth.

16. Review the client's implementation of a sleep induction routine; reinforce success and redirect for failure.

17. Train the client in deep muscle relaxation and deep

breathing exercises with and without audiotape instruction; encourage use of this technique at bedtime.

18. Administer electromyographic (EMG) biofeedback to reinforce the client's successful relaxation response.

15. Cooperate with sleep clinic referral and evaluation. (19)

19. Refer the client to a sleep clinic for assessment of sleep apnea or other physiological factors.

__. _____
     _____
__. _____
     _____
__. _____
     _____

__. _____
     _____
__. _____
     _____
__. _____
     _____

DIAGNOSTIC SUGGESTIONS

Axis I:	307.42	Primary Insomnia
	307.44	Primary Hypersomnia
	307.45	Circadian Rhythm Sleep Disorder
	307.47	Nightmare Disorder
	307.46	Sleep Terror Disorder
	307.46	Sleepwalking Disorder
	309.81	Posttraumatic Stress Disorder
	296.xx	Major Depressive Disorder
	300.4	Dysthymic Disorder
	_____	_____
	_____	_____

SOCIAL DISCOMFORT

BEHAVIORAL DEFINITIONS

1. Overall pattern of social anxiety, shyness, or timidity that presents itself in most social situations.
2. Hypersensitivity to the criticism or disapproval of others.
3. No close friends or confidants outside of first-degree relatives.
4. Avoidance of situations that require a degree of interpersonal contact.
5. Reluctant involvement in social situations out of fear of saying or doing something foolish or of becoming emotional in front of others.
6. Abuse of alcohol or chemicals to help ease the anxiety of becoming involved in social situations.
7. Isolation or involvement in solitary activities during most waking hours.
8. Increased heart rate, sweating, dry mouth, muscle tension, and shakiness in most social situations.

__. _____
   _____

__. _____
   _____
   _____

__. _____
   _____

LONG-TERM GOALS

1. Interact socially without excessive fear or anxiety.
2. Develop the essential social skills that will enhance the quality of relationship life.

3. Develop the ability to form relationships that will enhance recovery support system.
4. Reach a personal balance between solitary time and interpersonal interaction with others.
5. Terminate use of alcohol or chemicals to relieve social anxiety and learn constructive coping behaviors.

—. _____
_____
_____

—. _____
_____
_____

—. _____
_____

SHORT-TERM OBJECTIVES

THERAPEUTIC INTERVENTIONS

1. Identify and clarify nature of fears connected to associating with others. (1, 2)

1. Explore childhood and adolescent experiences of rejection and neglect that would foster fear of associating with others.

2. Assist the client in identifying fears tied to relating with others.

2. Identify sources of low self-esteem. (3, 4)

3. Probe childhood experiences of criticism, abandonment, or abuse that would foster low self-esteem and shame.

4. Assign the client to read the books *Healing the Shame That Binds You* (Bradshaw) and *Facing Shame* (Fossum and Mason), and process key ideas.

3. Identify and replace negative self-talk that fosters social anxiety. (5, 6, 7, 8)

5. Assist the client in identifying distorted automatic thoughts associated with anxiety over social interaction.

6. Ask the client to read the "Social Anxiety" section in *The Feeling Good Handbook* (Burns) and process key ideas with the therapist.

7. Assign the client to complete and process exercises on social anxiety and thought distortion in *Ten Days to Self-Esteem!* (Burns).

8. Assist the client in developing positive self-talk that will aid in overcoming fear of relating with others or participating in social activities.

4. Identify and implement again successful social skills from the past. (9, 10, 11)

9. Ask the client to list and process positive experiences from previous social encounters.

10. Utilize a brief solution-oriented approach to identify a time where the client socialized with enjoyment and little anxiety, then create a situation that involves the same elements and have the client use this social coping skill consistently in the following weeks.

11. Monitor the client's solution-oriented approach to his/her social anxiety; reinforce success and redirect for failure.

5. Initiate one social contact per day with a familiar person for increasing lengths of time. (12)

12. Assign the client to initiate one conversation daily, increasing time from one minute to five minutes per

6. Verbally report positive outcomes of participation in social and support groups. (13, 14, 15, 16)

7. Initiate a social contact with a stranger. (17, 18)

8. Identify ways he/she is like other people and therefore acceptable to others. (19, 20, 21)

interaction, and report results to therapist.

13. Ask the client to attend and participate in available social and recreational activities within treatment program or the community.

14. Refer the client to a self-help group (i.e., AA, NA, Emotions Anonymous, or Recovery, Inc.) and to self-disclose two times in each session; process the experience.

15. Refer the client to attend a communication improvement seminar or a Dale Carnegie course.

16. Monitor, encourage, redirect, and give positive feedback to the client as he/she increases his/her interaction with others.

17. Encourage and support the client in his/her effort to initiate and build social relationships.

18. Facilitate a role play with the client around initiating a conversation with another person for the first time. Process the experience.

19. Read either "Jean and Jane" or "The Wallflower" from *Friedman's Fables* (Friedman) to the client, then use the accompanying questions to process the fable with him/her.

20. Assign the client to read books on self-understanding (e.g., *Born to Win* by James and Jongeward, *Pulling Your Own Strings* by Dyer, or *I'm OK You're OK* by Harris and Harris) to help him/her see himself/herself more clearly and in a more hopeful light.

21. Assist the client in recognizing how he/she is like or similar to others.

9. Verbally describe the defense mechanisms used to avoid close relationships. (22)

22. Utilize a transactional analysis (TA) approach to undercover and identify the client's beliefs and fears. Then use the TA approach to alter beliefs and actions.

10. Implement assertiveness skills. (23)

23. Train the client in assertiveness skills or refer him/her to an assertiveness training class.

11. Verbally report and demonstrate a renewed sense of trust in others. (24, 25, 26)

24. Assist the client in identifying defense mechanisms that keep others at a distance and in identifying ways to keep defensiveness at a minimum.

25. Guide and encourage the client's use of new assertiveness skills providing reinforcement and redirect as needed.

26. Point out to the client incidents where he/she demonstrates an inappropriate sense of mistrust in others. Process situations to help the client identify and remove the barrier.

12. Develop a written plan that divides non-workdays between social and solitary activities. (27)

27. Assign the client to develop a plan for nonworking hours that contains both social and solitary activities; review plan and give feedback.

__. _____
_____

__. _____
_____

__. _____
_____

__. _____
_____

__. _____
_____

__. _____
_____

DIAGNOSTIC SUGGESTIONS

Axis I:

300.23	Social Phobia
300.4	Dysthymic Disorder
296.xx	Major Depressive Disorder
300.21	Panic Disorder With Agoraphobia
309.81	Posttraumatic Stress Disorder
_____	_____
_____	_____

Axis II:

301.82	Avoidant Personality Disorder
301.20	Schizoid Personality Disorder
301.0	Paranoid Personality Disorder
301.21	Schizotypal Personality Disorder
_____	_____
_____	_____

SOMATIZATION

BEHAVIORAL DEFINITIONS

1. Preoccupation with some imagined defect in appearance or excessive concern regarding a minor physical abnormality.
2. A physical malady caused by a psychosocial stressor triggering a psychological conflict.
3. Preoccupation with the fear of having serious physical disease, without any medical basis for concern.
4. A multitude of physical complaints that have no organic foundation but have led to life changes (e.g., seeing doctors often, taking prescriptions, withdrawing from responsibilities).
5. Preoccupation with chronic pain beyond what is expected for a physical malady or in spite of no known organic cause.
6. One or more physical complaints (usually vague) that have no known organic basis, or complaining and impairment in life functioning in excess of what is expected.
7. Preoccupation with pain in one or more anatomical sites with both psychological factors and a medical condition as a basis for the pain.

__. _____
_____

__. _____
_____

__. _____
_____

LONG-TERM GOALS

1. Reduce frequency of physical complaints and improve the level of independent functioning.

2. Reduce verbalizations focusing on pain while increasing productive activities.
3. Accept body appearance as normal even with insignificant flaws.
4. Accept self as relatively healthy with no known medical illness.
5. Improve physical functioning due to development of adequate coping mechanisms for stress management.

—. _____
   _____
   _____

—. _____
   _____
   _____

—. _____
   _____

SHORT-TERM OBJECTIVES

1. Verbalize negative feelings regarding body and discuss self-prediction of catastrophized consequences of perceived body abnormality. (1)

2. Discuss causes for emotional stress in life that underlie the focus on physical complaints. (2, 3, 4)

3. Identify family patterns that exist around exaggerated focus on physical maladies. (5)

THERAPEUTIC INTERVENTIONS

1. Build a level of trust and understanding with client by listening to his/her initial complaints without rejection or confrontation.

2. Refocus the client's discussion from physical complaints to emotional conflicts and expression of feelings.

3. Explore the client's sources of emotional pain—feelings of fear, inadequacy, rejection, or abuse.

4. Assist the client in acceptance of connection between physical focus and avoidance of facing emotional conflicts.

5. Explore the client's family history for modeling and reinforcement of physical complaints.

4. Verbalize the secondary gain that results from physical complaints. (6)

6. Assist the client in developing insight into the secondary gain received from physical illness, complaints, and the like.

5. Identify causes for anger. (7)

7. Explore for causes for the client's anger.

6. Express angry feelings assertively and directly. (8, 9, 10)

8. Using role-playing and behavioral rehearsal, teach the client assertive, respectful expression of angry feelings.

9. Train the client in assertiveness or refer him/her to an assertiveness training class.

10. Reinforce the client's assertiveness as a means of him/her attaining healthy need satisfaction in contrast to whining helplessness.

7. Identify the connection between negative body image and general low self-esteem. (11, 12)

11. Probe the client for causes for low self-esteem and fears of inadequacy in his/her childhood experiences.

12. Teach the client the connection between low self-esteem and preoccupation with body image.

8. Increase social and productive activities rather than being preoccupied with self and physical complaints. (13, 14)

13. Assign the client to develop a list of pleasurable activities that can serve as rewards and diversions from bodily focus.

14. Assign diversion activities that take the client's focus off himself/herself and redirect it toward hobbies,

9. Implement the use of relaxation skills and exercise to reduce tension in response to stress. (15, 16)

10. Decrease physical complaints, doctor visits, and reliance on medication while increasing verbal assessment of self as able to function normally and productively. (17, 18, 19)

11. Poll family and friends regarding their concern about the client's physical complaints. (20)

social activities, assisting others, completing projects, or returning to work.

15. Train the client in relaxation techniques using biofeedback, deep breathing, and positive imagery techniques.

16. Assign the client to a daily exercise routine.

17. Challenge the client to endure pain and carry on with responsibilities so as to build self-esteem and a sense of contribution.

18. Structure specific times each day for the client to think about, talk about, and write down his/her physical problems. Outside of those times the client will not focus on his/her physical condition. Monitor and process intervention's effectiveness.

19. Create an ordeal for the client to do each time the symptom (physical complaint) occurs. (An ordeal is a specific task that is necessary in the client's daily life but one that he/she finds unpleasant.) Convince the client of the effectiveness of this prescription and monitor for compliance and results.

20. Assign to the client the ritual of polling spouse, friends, neighbors, pastors, and so on about how

concerned they feel he/she should be, and what they would recommend he/she do each time a physical complaint/concern occurs. Process results.

12. List coping behaviors that will be implemented when physical symptoms appear. (21)

21. Ask the client to try to predict the next attack or physical issue and then plan how he/she will cope with it when it comes.

13. Report on instances of taking active control over environmental events versus passively reacting like a victim. (22)

22. Empower the client to take control of his/her environment rather than continuing in his/her attitude of helplessness, frustration, anger, and "poor me."

14. Engage in normal responsibilities vocationally and socially without complaining or withdrawing into avoidance while using physical problems as an excuse. (23, 24, 25)

23. Reframe the client's worries into a metaphor of "making sure he/she stays healthy." Then issue a prescription and a plan for implementing increased exercise, sex, or joy.

24. Give positive feedback when the client is symptom-free and accepting of his/her body as normal and healthy.

25. Discuss with client the destructive social impact that consistent complaintive verbalizations or negative body focus have on friends and family.

15. Accept referral to a pain clinic to learn pain management techniques. (26)

26. Refer the client to a pain clinic.

__. _____
_____

__. _____
_____

___. _____   ___. _____
      _____   _____
___. _____   ___. _____
      _____   _____

DIAGNOSTIC SUGGESTIONS

Axis I: 300.7   Body Dysmorphic Disorder
              300.11   Conversion Disorder
              300.7   Hypochondriasis
              300.81   Somatization Disorder
              307.80   Pain Disorder Associated With Psychological
                         Factors
              307.89   Pain Disorder Associated With Both
                         Psychological Factors and an Axis III Disorder
              300.81   Undifferentiated Somatoform Disorder
              300.4   Dysthymic Disorder

              _____   _____
              _____   _____

SPIRITUAL CONFUSION

BEHAVIORAL DEFINITIONS

1. Verbalization of a desire for a closer relationship to a higher power.
2. Feelings and attitudes about a higher power that are characterized by fear, anger, and distrust.
3. Verbalization of a feeling of emptiness in his/her life, as if something were missing.
4. A negative, bleak outlook on life and regarding others.
5. A felt need for a higher power, but because upbringing contained no religious education or training, does not know where or how to begin.
6. An inability to connect with a higher power, due to anger, hurt, and rejection from religious upbringing.
7. A struggle with understanding and accepting Alcoholics Anonymous (AA) Steps 2 and 3 (i.e., difficulty in believing in a higher power).

—. _____
   _____

—. _____
   _____
   _____

—. _____
   _____

LONG-TERM GOALS

1. Clarify spiritual concepts and instill a freedom to approach a higher power as a resource for support.
2. Increase belief in and development of a relationship with a higher power.

3. Begin a faith in a higher power and incorporate it into support system.

4. Resolve issues that have prevented faith or belief from developing and growing.

—. _____

_____

—. _____

_____

—. _____

_____

SHORT-TERM OBJECTIVES

1. Summarize the highlights of own spiritual quest or journey to this date. (1)

2. Describe beliefs and feelings around the idea of a higher power. (2, 3, 4)

3. Describe early life training in spiritual concepts and identify its impact on current religious beliefs. (5)

THERAPEUTIC INTERVENTIONS

1. Ask the client to write the story of his/her spiritual quest/journey; process the journey material.

2. Assign the client to list all of his/her beliefs related to a higher power; process the beliefs.

3. Assist the client in processing and clarifying his/her feelings regarding a higher power.

4. Explore the causes for the emotional components (e.g., fear, rejection, peace, acceptance, abandonment) of the client's reaction to a higher power.

5. Review the client's early life experiences surrounding belief in a higher power.

4. Verbalize an increased knowledge and understanding of concept of a higher power. (6, 7)

5. Identify specific blocks to believing in a higher power. (8, 9)

6. Identify the difference between religion and faith. (10)

7. Replace the concept of a higher power as harsh and judgmental with a belief in a higher power as forgiving and loving. (9, 11)

6. Ask the client to talk with a chaplain, pastor, rabbi, or priest regarding the client's spiritual struggles, issues, or questions, and record the feedback.

7. Assign the client to read *God: A Biography* (Miles) or *The History of God* (Armstrong) to build knowledge and a concept of a higher power.

8. Assist the client in identifying specific issues or blocks that prevent the development of his/her spirituality.

9. Encourage the client to read books dealing with conversion experiences (e.g., *Surprised by Joy* by Lewis, *Confessions of St. Augustine* by Augustine, *The Seven Storey Mountain* by Merton, *Soul on Fire* by Cleaver).

10. Educate the client on the difference between religion and spirituality.

9. Encourage the client to read books dealing with conversion experiences (e.g., *Surprised by Joy* by Lewis, *Confessions of St. Augustine* by Augustine, *The Seven Storey Mountain* by Merton, *Soul on Fire* by Cleaver).

11. Emphasize that the higher power is characterized by love and gracious forgiveness for anyone with remorse and who seeks forgiveness.

8. Implement daily attempts to be in contact with higher power. (12, 13, 14)

9. Verbalize separation of beliefs and feelings regarding one's earthly father from those regarding a higher power. (15, 16)

10. Acknowledge the need to separate negative past experiences with religious people from the current spiritual evaluation. (17, 18)

11. Verbalize acceptance of forgiveness from a higher power. (19, 20)

12. Recommend that the client implement daily meditations and/or prayer; process the experience.

13. Assign the client to write a daily note to his/her higher power.

14. Encourage and assist the client in developing and implementing a daily devotional time or other ritual that will foster his/her spiritual growth.

15. Assist the client in comparing his/her beliefs and feelings about his/her earthly father with those about a higher power.

16. Urge separating the feelings and beliefs regarding the earthly father from those regarding a higher power to allow for spiritual growth and maturity.

17. Assist the client in evaluating religious tenets separated from painful emotional experiences with religious people in his/her past.

18. Explore the religious distortions and judgmentalism that the client has been subjected to by others.

19. Ask the client to read the books *Serenity* (Helmfelt and Fowler)—all readings related to AA Steps 2 and 3; *The Road Less Traveled* (Peck); and *Search for Serenity* (Presnall); process the concept of forgiveness.

12. Ask a respected person who has apparent spiritual depth to serve as a mentor. (21)

13. Attend groups dedicated to enriching spirituality. (22, 23)

20. Explore the client's feelings of shame and guilt that led to him/her feeling unworthy before a higher power and others.

21. Help the client find a mentor to guide his/her spiritual development.

22. Make the client aware of opportunities for spiritual enrichment (e.g., Bible studies, study groups, fellowship groups); process the experiences he/she decides to pursue.

23. Suggest that the client attend a spiritual retreat (e.g., DeColores or Course in Miracles) and report to therapist what the experience was like for him/her and what he/she gained from the experience.

14. Read books that focus on furthering a connection with a higher power. (24)

24. Ask the client to read books to cultivate his/her spirituality (e.g., *Cloistered Walk* by Norris, *Hymns to an Unknown God* by Keen, and *The Care of the Soul* by Moore).

__. _____
   _____

__. _____
   _____

__. _____
   _____

__. _____
   _____

__. _____
   _____

__. _____
   _____

DIAGNOSTIC SUGGESTIONS

Axis I: 300.4   Dysthymic Disorder
               311   Depressive Disorder NOS
               300.0   Anxiety Disorder NOS
               296.xx   Major Depressive Disorder
               _____   _____
               _____   _____

SUICIDAL IDEATION

BEHAVIORAL DEFINITIONS

1. Recurrent thoughts of or preoccupation with death.
2. Recurrent or ongoing suicidal ideation without any plans.
3. Ongoing suicidal ideation with a specific plan.
4. Recent suicide attempt.
5. History of suicide attempts that required professional or family/ friend intervention on some level (e.g., inpatient, safe house, outpatient, or supervision).
6. Positive family history of depression and/or a preoccupation with suicidal thoughts.
7. A bleak, hopeless attitude regarding life coupled with recent life events that support this (e.g., divorce, death of a friend or family member, or loss of job).
8. Social withdrawal, lethargy, and apathy coupled with expressions of wanting to die.
9. Sudden change from being depressed to upbeat and at peace, while actions indicate the client is "putting his/her house in order" and there has been no genuine resolution of conflict issues.
10. Engages in self-destructive or dangerous behavior (e.g., chronic drug or alcohol abuse; promiscuity, unprotected sex; reckless driving, etc.) that appears to invite death.

—. _____

    _____

—. _____

    _____

—. _____

    _____

LONG-TERM GOALS

1. Alleviate the suicidal impulses/ideation and return to the highest level of previous daily functioning.
2. Stabilize the suicidal crisis.
3. Placement in an appropriate level of care to safely address the suicidal crisis.
4. Reestablish a sense of hope for self and the future.
5. Cease the perilous lifestyle and resolve the emotional conflicts that underlie the suicidal pattern.

—. _____
_____
—. _____
_____
—. _____
_____

SHORT-TERM OBJECTIVES

1. State the strength of the suicidal feelings, the frequency of the thoughts, and the detail of the plans. (1, 2, 3, 4)

THERAPEUTIC INTERVENTIONS

1. Assess the client's suicidal ideation, taking into account the extent of his/her ideation, the presence of a primary and backup plan, past attempts, and family history.

2. Assess and monitor the client's suicidal potential on an ongoing basis.

3. Notify the client's family and significant others of his/her suicidal ideation; ask them to form a 24-hour suicide watch until the crisis subsides.

4. Arrange for the client to take the Minnesota Multiphasic Personality Inventory

(MMPI), Beck Depression Inventory (BDI), or Modified Scale for Suicide Ideation (MSSI); evaluate the results for the client's degree of depression and suicide risk.

2. Verbalize a promise to contact the therapist or some other emergency helpline if a serious urge toward self-harm arises. (5, 6, 7, 8)

5. Elicit a promise from the client that he/she will initiate contact with the therapist or a helpline if the suicidal urge becomes strong and before any self-injurious behavior.

6. Provide the client with an emergency helpline telephone number that is available 24 hours a day.

7. Make a contract with the client, identifying what he/she will and won't do when experiencing suicidal thoughts or impulses.

8. Offer to be available to the client through telephone contact if a life-threatening urge develops.

3. Client and/or significant others increase the safety of the home by removing firearms or other lethal weapons from easy access. (3, 9)

3. Notify the client's family and significant others of his/her suicidal ideation; ask them to form a 24-hour suicide watch until the crisis subsides.

9. Encourage significant others to remove firearms or other lethal weapons from the client's easy access.

4. Report suicidal impulses to a designated significant other or helping professional. (3, 5, 10)

3. Notify the client's family and significant others of his/her suicidal ideation; ask them to form a 24-hour suicide watch until the crisis subsides.

5. Elicit a promise from the client that he/she will initiate contact with the therapist or a helpline if the suicidal urge becomes strong and before any self-injurious behavior.

10. Encourage the client to be open and honest regarding suicidal urges, reassuring him/her regularly of caring concern by therapist and significant others.

5. Cooperate with hospitalization if the suicidal urge becomes uncontrollable. (4, 11)

4. Arrange for the client to take the Minnesota Multiphasic Personality Inventory (MMPI), Beck Depression Inventory (BDI), or Modified Scale for Suicide Ideation (MSSI); evaluate the results for the client's degree of depression and suicide risk.

11. Arrange for hospitalization when the client is judged to be uncontrollably harmful to self.

6. Identify life factors that preceded the suicidal ideation. (12, 13, 14)

12. Explore the client's sources of emotional pain and hopelessness.

13. Encourage the client to express feelings related to his/her suicidal ideation in order to clarify them and increase insight as to the causes for them.

14. Assist the client in becoming aware of life factors that were significant precursors to the beginning of his/her suicidal ideation.

7. Increase communication with significant others, resulting in a feeling of understanding, empathy, and being attended to. (15, 16, 17)

15. Probe the client's feelings of despair related to his/her family relationships.

16. Hold family therapy sessions to promote communication of the client's feelings of sadness, hurt, and anger.

17. Meet with significant others to assess their understanding of the causes for the client's distress.

8. Significant others verbalize an understanding of the client's feelings of alienation and hopelessness. (16, 17)

16. Hold family therapy sessions to promote communication of the client's feelings of sadness, hurt, and anger.

17. Meet with significant others to assess their understanding of the causes for the client's distress.

9. Cooperate with a referral to a physician for an evaluation for antidepressant medication. (18)

18. Assess the client's need for antidepressant medication and arrange for a prescription, if necessary.

10. Take medications as prescribed and report all side effects. (19)

19. Monitor the client for effectiveness and compliance with prescribed psychotropic medication; confer with prescribing physician on a regular basis.

11. Identify how previous attempts to solve interpersonal problems have failed, leading to feelings of abject loneliness and rejection. (14, 20, 21)

14. Assist the client in becoming aware of life factors that were significant precursors to the beginning of his/her suicidal ideation.

20. Encourage the client to share feelings of grief related to broken close relationships.

21. Review with the client previous problem-solving

attempts and discuss new alternatives that are available.

12. Reestablish a consistent eating and sleeping pattern. (22)

22. Encourage normal eating and sleeping patterns by the client and monitor his/her compliance.

13. Verbally report no longer feeling the impulse to take own life and demonstrate an increased sense of hope for self. (2, 23, 24)

2. Assess and monitor the client's suicidal potential on an ongoing basis.

23. Assist the client in developing coping strategies for suicidal ideation (e.g., more physical exercise, less internal focus, increased social involvement, and more expression of feelings).

24. Assist the client in finding positive, hopeful things in his/her life at the present time.

14. Identify the positive aspects, relationships, and achievements in his/her life. (24, 25)

24. Assist the client in finding positive, hopeful things in his/her life at the present time.

25. Review with the client the success he/she has had and the sources of love and concern that exist in his/her life; ask him/her to write a list of positive aspects of his/her life.

15. Identify and replace negative thinking patterns that mediate feelings of hopelessness and helplessness. (26, 27, 28, 29)

26. Assist the client in developing an awareness of the cognitive messages that reinforce hopelessness and helplessness.

27. Identify and confront catastrophizing tendencies in the client's cognitive processing,

allowing for a more realistic perspective of hope in the face of pain.

28. Train the client in revising core schemas using cognitive restructuring techniques.

29. Require the client to keep a daily record of self-defeating thoughts (thoughts of hopelessness, helplessness, worthlessness, catastrophizing, negatively predicting the future, etc.); challenge each thought for accuracy, then replace each dysfunctional thought with one that is positive and self-enhancing.

16. Develop and implement a penitence ritual in which one expresses grief for victims and absolves self of guilt for surviving an incident fatal to others. (30)

30. Develop a penitence ritual for the client with suicidal ideation connected with being a survivor and implement it with him/her.

17. Verbalize a feeling of support that results from spiritual faith. (31, 32)

31. Explore the client's spiritual belief system as to it being a source of acceptance and peace.

32. Arrange for the client's spiritual leader to meet with and support the client.

—. _____

_____

—. _____

_____

—. _____

_____

—. _____

_____

—. _____

_____

—. _____

_____

DIAGNOSTIC SUGGESTIONS

Axis I: 296.xx   Bipolar I Disorder
300.4   Dysthymic Disorder
296.2x   Major Depressive Disorder, Single Episode
296.3x   Major Depressive Disorder, Recurrent
296.89   Bipolar II Disorder

_____   _____

_____   _____

Axis II: 301.83   Borderline Personality Disorder

_____   _____

_____   _____

TYPE A BEHAVIOR

BEHAVIORAL DEFINITIONS

1. A pattern of pressuring self and others to accomplish more because there is never enough time.
2. A spirit of intense competition in all activities.
3. Intense compulsion to win at all costs regardless of the activity or cocompetitor.
4. Inclination to dominate all social or business situations, being too direct and overbearing.
5. Propensity to become irritated by the action of others who do not conform to own sense of propriety or correctness.
6. A state of perpetual impatience with any waiting, delays, or interruptions.
7. Difficulty in sitting and quietly relaxing or reflecting.
8. Psychomotor facial signs of intensity and pressure (e.g., muscle tension, scowling, glaring, or tics).
9. Psychomotor voice signs (e.g., irritatingly forceful speech or laughter, rapid and intense speech, and frequent use of obscenities).

__. _____
_____

__. _____
_____

__. _____
_____

LONG-TERM GOALS

1. Formulate and implement a new life attitudinal pattern that allows for a more relaxed pattern of living.

2. Reach a balance between work/competitive and social/noncompetitive time in daily life.
3. Achieve an overall decrease in pressured, driven behaviors.
4. Develop social and recreational activities as a routine part of life.
5. Alleviate sense of time urgency, free-floating anxiety, and self-destructive behaviors.

—. _____
_____
—. _____
_____
—. _____
_____

SHORT-TERM OBJECTIVES

1. Describe the pattern of pressured, driven living. (1, 2)

2. Comply with psychological assessment. (3, 4)

3. Identify the beliefs that support driven, overachieving behavior. (5, 6, 7)

THERAPEUTIC INTERVENTIONS

1. Ask the client to give examples of pressured lifestyle.

2. Assist the client to see self as others do.

3. Administer or refer the client for personality testing.

4. Review and process results of testing with the client.

5. Probe family of origin history for role models of or parental pressure for high achievement and compulsive drive.

6. Ask the client to make a list of his/her beliefs about self-worth and the worth of others. Process it with the therapist.

7. Assist the client in making key connections between his/her overachieving/

driven behavior and the desire to please key parental figures.

4. Verbalize a desire to reprioritize values toward less self-focus, more inner and other orientation. (8, 9)

8. Explore and clarify the client's value system and assist in developing new priorities on the importance of relationships, recreation, spiritual growth, reflection time, giving to others, and so on.

9. Ask the client to read biographies or autobiographies of spiritual people (e.g., St. Augustine, Thomas Merton, Albert Schweitzer, C. S. Lewis); process the key beliefs they lived by.

5. Decrease the number of hours worked daily and the frequency of taking work home. (10, 11)

10. Assign the client to read the books on creating positive habits (e.g., *Positive Addiction* by Glasser) and *Overdoing It* by Robinson); select key ideas to discuss.

11. Review the client's pattern of hours spent working (at home and office) and recommend a significant reduction.

6. Identify and replace distorted automatic thoughts that motivate pressured living. (12)

12. Assist the client in identifying distorted automatic thoughts that lead to feeling pressured to achieve; assist him/her in replacing these distortions with positive, realistic cognitions.

7. Develop the pattern of doing one task at a time with less emphasis on pressure to complete it quickly. (13)

13. Encourage and reinforce the client focusing on one activity at a time without a sense of urgency.

8. Increase daily time involved in relaxing activities. (14, 15, 16, 17, 18)

9. Verbalize a recognition of hostility toward and impatience with others. (19, 20, 21, 22)

10. Verbalize the distinction between respectful

14. Train the client in deep muscle relaxation and breathing exercises to slow the pace of his/her life.

15. Assign the client to do one noncompetitive activity each day for a week; process this experience.

16. Ask the client to try one area of interest outside of his/her vocation that he/she will do two times weekly for one month.

17. Assign the client to watch comedy movies and identify the positive aspects of them.

18. Reinforce all the client changes that reflect a greater sense of life balance.

19. Explore the client's pattern of intolerant, impatient interaction with others.

20. Assist the client in identifying his/her critical beliefs about other people and connecting them to behavior patterns in daily life.

21. Reflect the client's hostility and assist in identifying its source.

22. Give the client an Ericksonian assignment—that is, at a certain time drive ____ miles exactly, stop, pull over, and think about ____ for ____ minutes, then return; process assignment.

23. Train the client in assertiveness to learn to avoid

assertiveness and insensi-
tive directness or verbal aggression that is controlling.
(23, 24)

11. Demonstrate decreased impatience with others by
talking of appreciating and
understanding the good
qualities in others.
(25, 26, 27, 28)

12. Increase interest in the
lives of others as evidenced
by listening to others talk of
their life experiences, and
by engaging in one act of
kindness per day.
(29, 30, 31)

aggression and trampling
on rights of others.

24. Confront and reframe the
client's actions or verbalizations when he/she is self-
centered or reflects a lack of
feeling for others. Use role-
playing and role reversal
exercises to increase empathy for others' feelings.

25. Assign the client to talk to
an associate or child, focusing on listening to the other
person and learning several
good things about that person.

26. Train the client in self-talk
that will alter beliefs that
foster the compulsive critical behaviors and foster tolerance.

27. Assign the client and family
to attend an experiential
weekend that promotes self-
awareness (e.g., high-low
ropes course or cooperative
tasks); process the experience afterwards.

28. Assign the client to go with
a group on a wilderness
camping and canoeing trip,
on a work camp project, or
with the Red Cross as a dis-
aster worker.

29. Encourage the client to volunteer for a nonprofit social
agency, school, or the like
for one year, doing direct
work with people (i.e., serving food at a soup kitchen
or tutoring an inner-city

child); process the positive consequences.

30. Encourage and monitor the client in doing one random, spontaneous act of kindness on a daily basis and explore the positive results.

31. Encourage the client to express warmth, appreciation, affection, and gratitude to others.

13. Develop a daily routine that reflects a balance between the quest for achievement and appreciation of aesthetic things. (32, 33, 34)

32. Assign the client to read the book *The Road Less Traveled* (Peck) and to process key ideas with therapist.

33. Assign the client to read "List of Aphorisms" in *Treating Type A Behavior and Your Heart* (Friedman and Ulmer) three times daily for one or two weeks; then to pick several to incorporate into his/her life.

34. Ask the client to list activities he/she could engage in for purely aesthetic enjoyment (e.g., visit an art museum, attend a symphony concert, hike in the woods, take painting lessons, etc.) and incorporate these into his/her life.

___. _____
_____

___. _____
_____

___. _____
_____

___. _____
_____

___. _____
_____

___. _____
_____

DIAGNOSTIC SUGGESTIONS

Axis I:	300.3	Obsessive-Compulsive Disorder
	300.02	Generalized Anxiety Disorder
	296.89	Bipolar II Disorder, Hypomanic
	_____	_____
	_____	_____
Axis II:	301.4	Obsessive-Compulsive Personality Disorder
	_____	_____
	_____	_____

VOCATIONAL STRESS

BEHAVIORAL DEFINITIONS

1. Feelings of anxiety and depression secondary to interpersonal conflict (perceived feelings of inadequacy, fear, and failure) secondary to severe business losses.
2. Fear of failure secondary to success or promotion that increases perceived expectations for greater success.
3. Rebellion against and/or conflicts with authority figures in the employment situation.
4. Feelings of anxiety and depression secondary to being fired or laid off, resulting in unemployment.
5. Anxiety related to perceived or actual job jeopardy.
6. Feelings of depression and anxiety related to complaints of job dissatisfaction or the stress of employment responsibilities.

—. _____

_____

—. _____

_____

—. _____

_____

LONG-TERM GOALS

1. Improve satisfaction and comfort surrounding coworker relationships.
2. Increase sense of confidence and competence in dealing with work responsibilities.
3. Be cooperative with and accepting of supervision of direction in the work setting.

4. Increase sense of self-esteem and elevation of mood in spite of unemployment.
5. Increase job security as a result of more positive evaluation of performance by a supervisor.
6. Pursue employment consistency with a reasonably hopeful and positive attitude.
7. Increase job satisfaction and performance due to implementation of assertiveness and stress management strategies.

__. _____
   _____
   _____
__. _____
   _____
   _____
__. _____
   _____

SHORT-TERM OBJECTIVES

1. Identify own role in the conflict with coworkers or supervisor. (1, 2)

2. Identify any personal problems that may be causing conflict in the employment setting. (3, 4)

3. Review family of origin history to determine roots for interpersonal conflict that are being reenacted in the work atmosphere. (5)

THERAPEUTIC INTERVENTIONS

1. Clarify the nature of the client's conflicts in the work setting.

2. Help the client identify his/her own role in the conflict, attempting to represent the other party's point of view.

3. Explore possible role of substance abuse in the client's vocational conflicts.

4. Explore the client's transfer of personal problems to the employment situation.

5. Probe the client's family of origin history for causes of current interpersonal conflict patterns.

4. Identify patterns of similar conflict with people outside the work environment. (6)

5. Replace projection or responsibility for conflict, feelings, or behavior with acceptance of responsibility for own behavior, feelings, and role in conflict. (7, 8)

6. Identify and implement behavioral changes that could be made in workplace interactions to help resolve conflicts with coworkers or supervisors. (9, 10)

7. Implement assertiveness skills that allow for effective communication of needs and feelings without aggression or defensiveness. (11)

8. Verbalize more healthy, realistic cognitive messages that promote harmony with others, self-acceptance, and self-confidence. (12, 13)

6. Explore the client's patterns of interpersonal conflict that occur beyond the work setting but are repeated in the work setting.

7. Confront the client's projection of responsibility for his/her behavior and feelings onto others.

8. Reinforce the client's acceptance of responsibility for personal feelings and behavior.

9. Assign the client to write a plan for constructive action (e.g., polite compliance with directedness, initiate a smiling greeting, compliment other's work, avoid critical judgments) that contains various alternatives to coworker or supervisor conflict.

10. Use role-playing, behavioral rehearsal, and role rehearsal to increase the client's probability of positive encounters and to reduce anxiety with others in employment situation or job search.

11. Train the client in assertiveness skills or refer to assertiveness training class.

12. Train the client in the development of more realistic, healthy cognitive messages that relieve anxiety and depression.

13. Require the client to keep a daily record of self-defeating thoughts (e.g., thoughts of hopelessness, worthlessness, rejection, catastrophizing, negatively predicting the future); challenge each thought for accuracy, then replace each dysfunctional thought with one that is positive and self-enhancing.

9. Identify and replace distorted cognitive messages associated with feelings of job stress. (14, 15, 16)

14. Probe and clarify the client's emotions surrounding his/her vocational stress.

15. Assess the client's distorted cognitive messages and schema that foster his/her vocational stress; replace these messages with positive cognitions.

16. Confront the client's pattern of catastrophizing situations leading to immobilizing anxiety; replace these messages with realistic thoughts.

10. Identify the effect that vocational stress has on feelings toward self and relationships with significant others. (17, 18)

17. Explore the effect of the client's vocational stress on his/her intra- and interpersonal dynamics with friends and family.

18. Facilitate a family therapy session in which feelings of family members can be aired and clarified regarding the client's vocational situation.

11. Develop and verbalize a plan for constructive action

19. Assist the client in developing a plan to react

to reduce vocational stress. (19)

positively to his/her vocational situation; process the proactive plan and assist in its implementation.

12. Verbalize an understanding of circumstances that led up to being terminated from employment. (20)

20. Explore the causes for client's termination of employment that may have been beyond his/her control.

13. Cease self-disparaging comments that are based on perceived failure at workplace. (21, 22, 23, 24)

21. Probe childhood history for roots of feelings of inadequacy, fear of failure, or fear of success.

22. Reinforce realistic self-appraisal of the client's successes and failures at workplace.

23. Assign the client to separately list his/her positive traits, talents, and successful accomplishments, and then the people who care for, respect, and value him/her. Process these lists as a basis for genuine gratitude and self-worth.

24. Teach the client that the ultimate worth of an individual is not measured in material or vocational success but in service to a higher power and others.

14. Outline plan for job search. (25, 26, 27)

25. Help the client develop a written job plan that contains specific attainable objectives for job search.

26. Assign the client to choose jobs for follow up in the want ads and to ask friends and family about job opportunities.

27. Assign the client to attend a job search class or resumé-writing seminar.

15. Report on job search experiences and feelings surrounding these experiences. (28)

28. Monitor, encourage, and process the client's search for employment.

__. _____
   _____

__. _____
   _____

__. _____
   _____

__. _____
   _____

__. _____
   _____

__. _____
   _____

DIAGNOSTIC SUGGESTIONS

Axis I:	309.0	Adjustment Disorder With Depressed Mood
	300.4	Dysthymic Disorder
	296.xx	Major Depressive Disorder
	V62.2	Occupational Problem
	309.24	Adjustment Disorder With Anxiety
	303.90	Alcohol Dependence
	304.20	Cocaine Dependence
	304.80	Polysubstance Dependence
	_____	_____
	_____	_____
Axis II:	301.0	Paranoid Personality Disorder
	301.81	Narcissistic Personality Disorder
	301.7	Antisocial Personality Disorder
	301.9	Personality Disorder NOS
	_____	_____
	_____	_____

Appendix A

SAMPLE CHAPTER WITH QUANTIFIED LANGUAGE

BORDERLINE PERSONALITY

BEHAVIORAL DEFINITIONS*

1. A minor stress leads to extreme emotional reactivity (expressions of anger, anxiety, or depression) that usually does not last more than a few hours to a few days.
2. A pattern of intense, chaotic interpersonal relationships that occurs with ____ (enter percentage) of the client's personal and/or professional relationships.
3. Marked identity disturbance.
4. Impulsive behaviors that are potentially self-damaging and occur ____ (enter percentage) of the time or ____ (list frequency) times per day/week.
5. Suicidal gestures, threats, or self-mutilating behavior that occur ____ (enter percentage) of the time or ____ (list frequency) times per day/week.
6. Feelings of emptiness and boredom that occur ____ (enter percentage) of the time or ____ (list frequency) times per day/week.

Note: For each behavioral definition, look for or include valid reports of differential levels of occurrence (both higher and lower) between certain times of the day; with certain days of the week; with certain friends, siblings, and peers; under certain circumstances; and so on.

7. Eruptions of intense, inappropriate anger that occur ____ (enter percentage) of the time or ____ (list frequency) times per day/week.
8. Easily feels unfairly treated and that others can't be trusted (enter percentage) of the time.
9. Analyzes most issues in simple terms (e.g., right/wrong, black/white, trustworthy/deceitful) without regard for extenuating circumstances or complex situations ____ (enter percentage) of the time.
10. Becomes very anxious with any hint of perceived abandonment in a relationship, ____ (enter percentage) of the time or ____ (list frequency) times per day/week.

__. _____

_____

__. _____

_____

__. _____

_____

LONG-TERM GOALS

1. Develop and demonstrate coping skills to deal with mood swings.
2. Develop the ability to control impulsive behavior.
3. Replace dichotomous thinking with the ability to tolerate ambiguity and complexity in people and issues.
4. Develop and demonstrate anger management skills.
5. Learn and practice interpersonal relationship skills.
6. Terminate self-damaging behaviors (such as substance abuse, reckless driving, sexual acting out, binge eating, or suicidal behaviors).

__. _____

_____

__. _____

_____

__. _____

_____

SHORT-TERM OBJECTIVES

1. By _____ (enter date), the client is to identify and verbalize the situations that can easily trigger feelings of fear, depression, and anger, noting which emotions and the associated frequency of occurrence _____ (enter frequency in percentage or times per day/week terms for each emotion). (1, 2)

2. By _____ (enter date), the client is to identify and verbalize the negative, distorted cognitions that mediate intense negative emotions, noting which emotions and the associated frequency of occurrence _____ (enter frequency in percentage or times per day/week terms for each emotion). (3, 4)

3. By _____ (enter date), the client is to identify and utilize realistic, positive self-talk to replace distorted negative messages, noting which negative messages and the associated frequency of occurrence _____ (enter frequency in percentage or times per day/week terms of doing so). (5, 6, 7)

THERAPEUTIC INTERVENTIONS

1. Explore the client's situations that trigger feelings of fear, depression, and anger.

2. Assign the client to record a daily journal of feelings along with the circumstances that he/she was reacting to; process the journal material to identify triggers for emotional reactivity.

3. Assist the client in identifying the distorted schemas and related automatic thoughts that mediate his/her anxiety response.

4. Require the client to keep a daily record of self-defeating thoughts (thoughts of hopelessness, helplessness, worthlessness, catastrophizing, negatively predicting the future, etc.); challenge each thought for accuracy, then replace each dysfunctional thought with one that is positive and self-enhancing.

5. Train the client in revising core schema using cognitive restructuring techniques.

6. Reinforce the client's positive, realistic cognitive self-talk that mediates a sense of peace.

7. Assign the client to record instances of successfully using revised, constructive

cognitive patterns; process
and reinforce positive consequences.

4. By ____ (enter date), the
client is to list at least
(enter number) negative
consequences to self and
others of self-defeating impulsive behaviors. (8)

5. By ____ (enter date), the
client is to start utilizing
cognitive methods to control
impulsive behavior ____
(enter frequency in percentage or times per day/week
terms of doing so).
(9, 10, 11)

8. Assign the client to list the
destructive consequences to
self and others of his/her
impulsive behavior.

9. Teach the client mediational and self-control
strategies (e.g., "stop, look,
listen, and think") to delay
gratification and inhibit impulses.

10. Assign the client to record
instances of successfully implementing "stop, look, listen, and think" to control
reactive impulses; process
and reinforce the successes.

11. Teach the client cognitive
methods (thought stoppage,
thought substitution, re-
framing, etc.) for gaining
and improving control over
impulsive actions; encourage implementation in daily
life.

6. By ____ (enter date), the
client is to start to record
and report instances of
using relaxation techniques
to manage intense feelings
and control impulsive reactive behavior at a frequency
of ____ (enter frequency in
percentage or times per
day/week terms of doing so).
(12, 13)

12. Using techniques such as
progressive relaxation, self-
hypnosis, or biofeedback,
teach the client how to relax
completely; then encourage
the client to relax whenever
he/she feels uncomfortable.

13. Ask the client to record instances of using relaxation
techniques to cope with
stress rather than reacting
with anger; reinforce

7. By ____ (enter date), the client is to implement assertiveness and be able to identify and describe the consequences ____ (enter frequency in percentage or times per day/week terms of doing so) of the time. (14, 15, 16)

8. By ____ (enter date), the client is to start to implement the use of "I messages" to communicate feelings without aggression ____ (enter frequency in percentage or times per day/week terms of doing so) of the time. (17, 18)

9. By ____ (enter date), the client is to identify and start to verbalize the impact that childhood experiences of abuse, neglect, or abandonment have upon current feelings and relationships. (19, 20, 21)

successful implementation of this coping skill.

14. Use role playing, modeling, and behavioral rehearsal to teach the client assertiveness (versus passivity or aggressiveness).

15. Refer the client to an assertiveness training group.

16. Review the client's implementation of assertiveness and his/her feelings about it as well as the consequences of it; reinforce success and redirect for failure.

17. Use modeling, role playing, and behavioral rehearsal to teach the client the use of "I messages" to communicate feelings directly (i.e., I feel . . . When you . . . I would prefer it if you . . .).

18. Reinforce the client's reported use of "I messages" in place of aggressiveness or possessiveness when feeling threatened.

19. Explore instances of abuse, neglect, or emotional/physical abandonment in the client's childhood; process the feelings associated with these experiences.

20. Point out to the client the destructive effect of overcontrol of others and angry resentment when others pull back from relationships. Encourage separation of helpless, desperate feelings of

the past from current relationships.

21. Reinforce the client's insight into the effect of childhood experiences of neglect or abuse on current urges to react with rage or possessiveness.

10. By ____ (enter date), the client is to list and start to implement coping strategies to deal with fear of abandonment ____ (enter frequency in percentage or times per day/week terms of doing so) of the time. (22)

22. Teach the client to use coping strategies (e.g., delay of reaction, "stop, look, listen, and plan," relaxation and deep breathing techniques, "I messages," expanded social network versus few intense relationships) to deal with fear of abandonment; process his/her implementation of these strategies in daily life.

11. By ____ (enter date), the client is to start to initiate enjoyable activities that can be done alone ____ (enter frequency in percentage or times per day/week terms of doing so) of the time. (6, 23, 24)

6. Reinforce the client's positive, realistic cognitive self-talk that mediates a sense of peace.

23. Explore the client's automatic thoughts associated with being alone.

24. Encourage the client to break his/her pattern of avoiding being alone by initiating activities without a companion (e.g., starting a hobby; doing exercise; attending lectures, concerts, movies; reading a book; taking a class).

12. By ____ (enter date), the client is to cooperate with a referral to a physician to evaluate the need for psychotropic medication. (25)

25. Refer the client to a physician to evaluate his/her need for a psychotropic medication to stabilize mood.

13. By ____ (enter date), the client is to take medication as prescribed and report ____ (enter period of time, e.g., weekly) as to effectiveness and side effects. (26)

14. By ____ (enter date), the client is to start to verbalize the intense feelings that motivate self-mutilating behavior and how those feelings are relieved by such behavior. (19, 21, 27, 28)

15. By ____ (enter date), the client is to verbalize a promise to contact the therapist or some other emergency helpline if a serious urge toward self-harm arises 100 percent of the time of such occurrences. (29, 30, 31, 32)

26. Monitor and evaluate the client's psychotropic medication prescription compliance, effectiveness, and side effects.

19. Explore instances of abuse, neglect, or emotional/physical abandonment in the client's childhood; process the feelings associated with these experiences.

21. Reinforce the client's insight into the effect of childhood experiences of neglect or abuse on current urges to react with rage or possessiveness.

27. Probe the nature and history of the client's self-mutilating behavior.

28. Interpret the client's self-mutilation as an expression of the rage and helplessness that could not be expressed as a child victim of emotional abandonment or abuse.

29. Assess the client's suicidal gestures as to triggers, frequency, seriousness, secondary gain, and onset.

30. Elicit a promise (as part of a self-mutilation and suicide prevention contract) from the client that he/she will initiate contact with the therapist or a helpline if the suicidal urge becomes strong and before any self-injurious behavior.

16. By ____ (enter date), the client is to list negative consequences of judging people rigidly and harshly. (33, 34)

17. By ____ (enter date), the client is to start to verbalize weaknesses or faults of those who have been previously judged to be perfect and strengths or assets of those people who have previously been judged to be evil, worthless, and deceitful. (35, 36)

___. _____
_____

___. _____
_____

___. _____
_____

31. Provide the client with an emergency helpline telephone number that is available 24 hours a day.

32. Encourage the client to express his/her feelings directly using assertive "I messages" rather than indirectly through self-mutilating behavior.

33. Assist the client in examining his/her style of evaluating people, especially in regard to his/her dichotomous thinking.

34. Teach the client the alienating consequences of judging people harshly and impulsively.

35. Challenge the client in understanding how dichotomous thinking leads to feelings of interpersonal mistrust.

36. Use role reversal and modeling to assist the client in seeing positive and negative qualities in all people.

___. _____
_____

___. _____
_____

___. _____
_____

DIAGNOSTIC SUGGESTIONS

Axis I: 300.4   Dysthymic Disorder
296.3x   Major Depressive Disorder, Recurrent

_____   _____

_____   _____

Axis II: 301.83   Borderline Personality Disorder
301.9   Personality Disorder NOS
799.9   Diagnosis Deferred
V71.09   No Diagnosis

_____   _____

_____   _____

Appendix B

BIBLIOTHERAPY SUGGESTIONS

ANGER MANAGEMENT

Ellis, A. (1977). *Anger: How to Live With and Without It.* Secaucus, NJ: Citadel Press.

Lerner, H. (1985). *The Dance of Anger: A Woman's Guide to Changing the Patterns of Intimate Relationships.* New York: Harper Perennial.

McKay, M., Rogers, P., and McKay, J. (1989). *When Anger Hurts.* Oakland, CA: New Harbinger.

Rosellini, G., and Worden, M. (1986). *Of Course You're Angry.* San Francisco: Harper Hazelden.

Rubin, T. I. (1969). *The Angry Book.* New York: Macmillan.

Smedes, L. (1991). *Forgive and Forget: Healing the Hurts We Don't Deserve.* San Francisco: Harper.

Tavris, C. (1989). *Anger: The Misunderstood Emotion.* New York: Touchstone Books.

Weisinger, H. (1985). *Dr. Weisinger's Anger Work Out Book.* New York: Quill.

ANTISOCIAL BEHAVIOR

Carnes, P. (1983). *Out of the Shadows: Understanding Sexual Addictions.* Minneapolis, MN: CompCare.

Katherine, A. (1993). *Boundaries: Where You End and I Begin.* New York: Fireside Pub.

Pittman, F. (1998). *Grow Up!* New York: Golden Books.

Williams, R., and Williams, V. (1993). *Anger Kills.* New York: Time Books.

ANXIETY

Benson, H. (1975). *The Relaxation Response.* New York: William Morrow.

Burns, D. (1993). *Ten Days to Self-Esteem!* New York: William Morrow.

Davis, M., Eshelman, E., and McKay, M. (1988). *The Relaxation and Stress Reduction Workbook.* Oakland, CA: New Harbinger.

Hauck, P. (1975). *Overcoming Worry and Fear.* Philadelphia: Westminster Press.

Jeffers, S. (1987). *Feel the Fear and Do It Anyway.* San Diego, CA: Harcourt Brace Jovanovich.

Marks, I. (1980). *Living with Fear: Understanding and Coping with Anxiety.* New York: McGraw-Hill.

ATTENTION DEFICIT DISORDER (ADD)—ADULT

Hallowell, E., and Raty, J. (1994). *Driven to Distraction.* New York: Simon & Schuster.

Kelly, K., and Ramundo, P. (1994). *You Mean I'm Not Lazy, Stupid, or Crazy?!* Cincinnati, OH: Tyrell and Jerem Press.

Nadeau, K. (1996). *Adventures in Fast Forward.* New York: Brunner/Mazel.

Quinn, D., and Stern, J. (1991). *Putting on the Brakes.* New York: Magination Press.

Weis, Lynn. (1994). *The Attention Deficit Disorder in Adults Workbook.* Dallas, TX: Taylor Publishing.

Wender, P. (1987). *The Hyperactive Child, Adolescent, and Adult.* New York: Oxford.

BORDERLINE PERSONALITY

Cudney, M., and Handy, R. (1993). *Self-Defeating Behaviors.* San Francisco: HarperCollins.

Katherine, A. (1993). *Boundaries: Where You End and I Begin.* New York: Fireside Pub.

Peurito, R. (1997). *Overcoming Anxiety.* New York: Henry Holt.

CHEMICAL DEPENDENCE

Alcoholics Anonymous. (1975). *Living Sober.* New York: A.A. World Service.

Alcoholics Anonymous. (1976). *Alcoholics Anonymous: The Big Book.* New York, A.A. World Service.

Carnes, P. (1989). *A Gentle Path Through the Twelve Steps.* Minneapolis, MN: CompCare.

Drews, T. R. (1980). *Getting Them Sober: A Guide for Those Living with Alcoholism.* South Plainfield, NJ: Bridge Publishing.

Gorski, T., and Miller, M. (1986). *Staying Sober: A Guide to Relapse Prevention.* Independence, MO: Herald House Press.

Gorski, T. (1992). *Staying Sober Workbook.* Independence, MO: Herald House Press.

Johnson, V. (1980). *I'll Quit Tomorrow.* New York: Harper and Row.

Kasl-Davis, C. (1992). *Many Roads, One Journey.* New York: Harper Collins.

Nuckals, C. (1989). *Cocaine: From Dependence to Recovery.* Blue Ridge Summit, PA: TAB Books.

Wilson, B. (1967). *As Bill Sees It.* New York: A.A. World Service.

CHEMICAL DEPENDENCE—RELAPSE

Alcoholics Anonymous. (1975). *Living Sober.* New York: A.A. World Service.

Alcoholics Anonymous. (1976). *Alcoholics Anonymous: The Big Book.* New York: A.A. World Service.

Burns, D. (1993). *Ten Days to Self-Esteem!* New York: William Morrow.

Carnes, P. (1989). *A Gentle Path Through the Twelve Steps.* Minneapolis, MN: CompCare.

Doe, J. (1955). *The Golden Book of Resentments.* Minneapolis, MN: CompCare Publishing.

Drews, T. R. (1980). *Getting Them Sober: A Guide for Those Living with Alcoholism.* South Plainfield, NJ: Bridge Publishing.

Gorski, T., and Miller, M. (1986). *Staying Sober: A Guide to Relapse Prevention.* Independence, MO: Herald House Press.

Gorski, T. (1989–1992). *The Staying Sober Workbook.* Independence, MO: Herald House Press.

Johnson, V. (1980). *I'll Quit Tomorrow.* New York: Harper and Row.

Kasl-Davis, C. (1992). *Many Roads, One Journey.* New York: HarperCollins.

Larson, E. (1985). *Stage II Recovery: Life Beyond Addiction.* San Francisco: Harper and Row.

Nuckals, C. (1989). *Cocaine: From Dependence to Recovery.* Blue Ridge Summit, PA: TAB Books.

Wilson, B. (1967). *As Bill Sees It.* New York: A.A. World Service.

CHILDHOOD TRAUMAS

Black, C. (1980). *It Will Never Happen to Me.* Denver, CO: MAC Publishing.

Bradshaw, J. (1990). *Homecoming.* New York: Bantam Books.

Gil, E. (1984). *Outgrowing the Pain: A Book for and About Adults Abused as Children.* New York: Dell Publishing.

Kushner, H. (1981). *When Bad Things Happen to Good People.* New York: Schocken Books.

Pittman, F. (1998). *Grow Up!* New York: Golden Books.

Powell, J. (1969). *Why I'm Afraid to Tell You Who I Am.* Allen, TX: Argus Communications.

Smedes, L. (1991). *Forgive and Forget: Healing the Hurts We Don't Deserve.* San Francisco: Harper.

Whitfield, C. (1987). *Healing the Child Within.* Deerfield Beach, FL: Health Communications, Inc.

Whitfield, C. (1990). *A Gift to Myself.* Deerfield Beach, FL: Health Communications, Inc.

CHRONIC PAIN

Benson, H. (1975). *The Relaxation Response.* New York: William Morrow.

Benson, H. (1979). *The Mind / Body Effect.* New York: Simon & Schuster.

Burns, D. (1980). *Feeling Good: The New Mood Therapy.* New York: Signet.

Burns, D. (1989). *The Feeling Good Handbook.* New York: Blume.

Burns, D. (1993). *Ten Days to Self-Esteem.* New York: William Morrow.

Caudill, M. (1995). *Managing Pain Before It Manages You.* New York: Guilford.

Duckro, P., Richardson, W., and Marshall, J. (1995). *Taking Control of Your Headaches.* New York: Guilford.

Fields, H. (1987). *Pain.* New York: McGraw-Hill.

Hunter, M. (1996). *Making Peace with Chronic Pain.* New York: Brunner/ Mazel.

LeShan, L. (1984). *How to Meditate.* New York: Bantam Books.

Morris, D. (1991). *The Culture of Pain.* Berkeley, University of California Press.

Siegel, B. (1989). *Peace, Love, & Healing.* New York: Harper and Row.

COGNITIVE DEFICITS

Ellis, A., and Harper, R. (1974). *A New Guide to Rational Living.* Hollywood, CA: Wilshire Books.

DEPENDENCY

Alberti, R., and Emmons, M. (1990). *Your Perfect Right.* San Luis Obispo, CA: Impact.

Beattie, M. (1987). *Codependent No More: How to Stop Controlling Others and Start Caring for Yourself.* San Francisco: Harper.

Drews, T. R. (1980). *Getting Them Sober: A Guide for Those Living with Alcoholism.* South Plainfield, NJ: Bridge Publishing.

Evans, P. (1992). *The Verbally Abusive Relationship.* Holbrook, MA: Bob Adams, Inc.

Helmfelt, R., Minirth, F., and Meier, P. (1985). *Love Is a Choice.* Nashville, TN: Nelson.

Katherine, A. (1993). *Boundaries: Where You End and I Begin.* New York: Fireside Pub.

Norwood, R. (1985). *Women Who Love Too Much.* Los Angeles: Archer.

Pittman, F. (1998). *Grow Up!* New York: Golden Books.

Smith, M. (1985). *When I Say No, I Feel Guilty.* New York: Bantam Books.

Walker, L. (1979). *The Battered Woman.* New York: Harper & Row.

Whitfield, C. (1990). *A Gift to Myself.* Deerfield Beach, FL: Health Communications, Inc.

Whitfield, C. (1993). *Boundaries and Relationships: Knowing, Protecting, and Enjoying the Self.* Deerfield Beach, FL: Health Communications, Inc.

DEPRESSION

Burns, D. (1980). *Feeling Good: The New Mood Therapy.* New York: Signet.

Burns, D. (1989). *The Feeling Good Handbook.* New York: Blume.

Butler, P. (1991). *Talking to Yourself: Learning the Language of Self-Affirmation.* New York: Stein and Day.

Dyer, W. (1974). *Your Erroneous Zones.* New York: Funk & Wagnalls.

Frankl, V. (1959). *Man's Search for Meaning.* New York: Simon & Schuster.

Geisel, T. (1990). *Oh, The Places You'll Go.* New York: Random House.

Hallinan, P. K. (1976). *One Day at a Time.* Minneapolis, MN: CompCare.

Hazelden Staff. (1991). *Each Day a New Beginning.* Center City, MN: Hazelden.

Helmstetter, S. (1986). *What to Say When You Talk to Yourself.* New York: Fine Communications.

Knauth, P. (1977). *A Season in Hell.* New York: Pocket Books.

Leith, L. (1998). *Exercising Your Way to Better Mental Health.* Morgantown, WV: Fitness Information Technology.

Styron, W. (1990). *Darkness Visible.* New York: Random House.

Zonnebelt-Smeenge, S., and DeVries, R. (1998). *Getting to the Other Side of Grief: Overcoming the Loss of a Spouse.* Grand Rapids, MI: Baker.

DISSOCIATION

Grateful Members of Emotional Health Anonymous. (1982). *The Twelve Steps for Everyone . . . Who Really Wants Them.* Minneapolis, MN: CompCare.

EATING DISORDER

Fairburn, C. (1995). *Overcoming Binge Eating.* New York: Guilford.

Hirschmann, J., and Munter, C. (1988). *Overcoming Overeating.* New York: Ballentine Books.

Hollis, J. (1985). *Fat is a Family Affair.* New York: Harper & Row.

Rodin, J. (1993). *Body Traps.* New York: William Morrow.

Sacker, I., and Zimmer, M. (1987). *Dying to Be Thin.* New York: Warner Books.

Siegel, M., Brisman, J., and Weinshel, M. (1997). *Surviving an Eating Disorder.* San Francisco: HarperCollins.

EDUCATIONAL DEFICITS

de Boro, E. (1982). *de Boro's Thinking Course.* New York: Facts of Life Publishing.

Sandstrom, R. (1990). *The Ultimate Memory Book.* Granada, CA: Stepping Stones Books.

FAMILY CONFLICT

Black, C. (1980). *It Will Never Happen to Me.* Denver, CO: MAC Publishing.

Bloomfield, H., and Felder, L. (1983). *Making Peace with Your Parents.* New York: Random House.

Bradshaw, J. (1988). *On the Family.* Deerfield Beach, FL: Health Communications, Inc.

Cline, F., and Fay, J. (1990). *Parenting with Love and Logic.* Colorado Springs, CO: Navpress.

Faber, A., and Mazlish, E. (1987). *Siblings Without Rivalry.* New York: Norton.

Fassler, D., Lash, M., and Ivers, S. (1988). *Changing Families.* Burlington, VT: Waterfront Books.

Ginott, H. (1969). *Between Parent and Child.* New York: Macmillan.

Ginott, H. (1969). *Between Parent and Teenager.* New York: Macmillan.

Glenn, S., and Nelsen, J. (1989). *Raising Self-Reliant Children in a Self-Indulgent World.* Rocklin, CA: Prima.

Phelan, T. (1995). *1-2-3 Magic.* Glen Ellyn, IL: Child Management, Inc.

Steinberg, L., and Levine, A. (1990). *You and Your Adolescent: A Parents' Guide for Ages 10–20.* New York: Harper Perennial.

FEMALE SEXUAL DYSFUNCTION

Barbach, L. (1982). *For Each Other: Sharing Sexual Intimacy.* New York: Doubleday.

Comfort, A. (1991). *The New Joy of Sex.* New York: Crown.

Heiman, J., and LoPiccolo, J. (1988). *Becoming Orgasmic: A Sexual Growth Program for Women.* New York: Prentice-Hall.

Kaplan, H. S. (1975). *The Illustrated Manual of Sex Therapy.* New York: Quadrangle, The New York Times Book Co.

McCarthy, B., and McCarthy, E. (1984). *Sexual Awareness.* New York: Carroll & Graf.

Penner, C., and Penner, C. (1981). *The Gift of Sex.* Waco, TX: Word.

Valins, L. (1992). *When a Woman's Body Says No to Sex: Understanding and Overcoming Vaginismus.* New York: Penguin.

Zibergeld, B. (1992). *The New Male Sexuality.* New York: Bantam.

FINANCIAL STRESS

Abentrod, S. (1996). *10 Minute Guide to Beating Debt.* New York: Macmillan.

Burkett, L. (1989). *Debt Free Living.* Chicago: Moody Press.

Loungo, T. (1997). *10 Minute Guide to Household Budgeting.* New York: Macmillan.

Ramsey, D. (1997). *Financial Peace.* New York: Penguin Books.

GRIEF/LOSS UNRESOLVED

Colgrove, M. (1991). *How to Survive the Loss of a Love.* Los Angeles: Prelude Press.

Kushner, H. (1981). *When Bad Things Happen to Good People.* New York: Schocken Books.

Lewis, C. S. (1961). *A Grief Observed.* New York: The Seabury Press.

Rando, T. (1991). *How to Go on Living When Someone You Love Dies.* New York: Bantam.

Schiff, N. (1977). *The Bereaved Parent.* New York: Crown Publications.

Smedes, L. (1982). *How Can It Be All Right When Everything Is All Wrong?* San Francisco: Harper.

Smedes, L. (1991). *Forgive and Forget: Healing the Hurts We Don't Deserve.* San Francisco: Harper.

Westberg, G. (1962). *Good Grief.* Philadelphia: Augsburg Fortress Press.

Wolterstorff, N. (1987). *Lament for a Son.* Grand Rapids, MI: Eerdmans.

Zonnebelt-Smeenge, S., and DeVries, R. (1998). *Getting to the Other Side of Grief: Overcoming the Loss of a Spouse.* Grand Rapids, MI: Baker.

IMPULSE CONTROL DISORDER

Helmstetter, S. (1986). *What to Say When You Talk to Yourself.* New York: Fine Communications.

Kelly, K., and Ramundo, P. (1994). *You Mean I'm Not Lazy, Stupid or Crazy?! A Self-Help Book for Adults with Attention Deficit Disorder.* Cincinnati, OH: Tyrell & Jerem Press.

Wander, P. (1987). *The Hyperactive Child, Adolescent, and Adult.* New York: Oxford.

INTIMATE RELATIONSHIP CONFLICTS

Abrams-Spring, J. (1996). *After the Affair.* New York: Harper Collins.

Bach, G., and Wyden, P. (1976). *The Intimate Enemy: How to Fight Fair in Love and Marriage.* New York: Avon Books.

Colgrove, M., Bloomfield, H., and McWililams, P. (1991). *How to Survive the Loss of a Love.* Los Angeles: Prelude Press.

Fisher, B. (1981). *Rebuilding: When Your Relationship Ends.* San Luis Obispo, CA: Impact.

Fromm, E. (1956). *The Art of Loving.* New York: Harper & Row.

Gorski, T. (1993). *Getting Love Right: Learning the Choices of Healthy Intimacy.* New York: Simon & Schuster.

Gray, J. (1993). *Men and Women and Relationships: Making Peace with the Opposite Sex.* Hillsboro, OR: Beyond Words.

Gray, J. (1992). *Men Are From Mars, Women Are From Venus.* New York: Harper Collins.

Harley, W. (1994). *His Needs, Her Needs, Building an Affair-Proof Marriage*. Grand Rapids, MI: Revell.

Hendrix, H. (1988). *Getting the Love You Want*. New York: Henry Holt.

Lerner, H. (1989). *The Dance of Intimacy: A Woman's Guide to Courageous Acts of Change in Key Relationships*. New York: Harper Perennial.

Lindbergh, A. (1955). *A Gift from the Sea*. New York: Pantheon.

Markman, H., Stanley S., and Blumberg, S. (1994). *Fighting for Your Marriage*. San Francisco: Jossey-Bass.

Schnarch, D. (1997). *Passionate Marriage*. New York: Norton.

LEGAL CONFLICTS

Carnes, P. (1983). *Out of the Shadows: Understanding Sexual Addictions*. Minneapolis, MN: CompCare.

Williams, R., and Williams, V. (1993). *Anger Kills*. New York: Time Books.

LOW SELF-ESTEEM

Branden, N. (1994). *The Six Pillars of Self-Esteem*. New York: Bantam Books.

Burns, D. (1993). *Ten Days to Self-Esteem!* New York: William Morrow.

Helmstetter, S. (1986). *What to Say When You Talk to Yourself.* New York: Fine Communications.

McKay, M., and Fanning, P. (1987). *Self-Esteem*. Oakland, CA: New Harbinger.

Zimbardo, P. (1987). *Shyness: What It Is and What to Do About It*. Reading, MA: Addison-Wesley.

MALE SEXUAL DYSFUNCTION

Comfort, A. (1991). *The New Joy of Sex*. New York: Crown.

Kaplan, H. S. (1975). *The Illustrated Manual of Sex Therapy*. New York: Quadrangle, The New York Times Book Co.

McCarthy, B., and McCarthy, E. (1981). *Sexual Awareness*. New York: Carroll & Graf.

Penner, C., and Penner, C. (1981). *The Gift of Sex*. Waco, TX: Word.

Zilbergeld, B. (1992). *The New Male Sexuality*. New York: Bantam.

MANIA OR HYPOMANIA

Grateful Members of Emotional Health Anonymous. (1987). *The Twelve Steps for Everyone . . . Who Really Wants Them*. Minneapolis, MN: CompCare.

MEDICAL ISSUES

Friedman, M., and Ulmer, P. (1984). *Treating Type A Behavior and Your Heart.* New York: Alfred A. Knopf.

OBSESSIVE-COMPULSIVE DISORDER (OCD)

Burns, D. (1993). *Ten Days to Self-Esteem!* New York: William Morrow.
Foa, E., and Wilson, R. (1991). *S.T.O.P. Obsessing: How to Overcome Your Obsessions and Compulsions.* New York: Bantam Books.
Levenkron, S. (1991). *Obsessive-Compulsive Disorders.* New York: Warner Books.

PARANOID IDEATION

Burns, D. (1989). *The Feeling Good Handbook.* New York: Plume.
Cudney, M., and Hard, R. (1991). *Self-Defeating Behaviors.* San Francisco: Harper Collins.
Ross, J. (1994). *Triumph Over Fear.* New York: Bantam Books.

PARENTING

Cline, F., and Fay, J. (1990). *Parenting with Love and Logic.* Colorado Springs, CO: Navpress.
Dobson, J. (2000). *Preparing for Adolescence: How to Survive the Coming Years of Change.* New York: Regal Press.
Edwards, C. D. (1999). *How to Handle a Hard to Handle Kid.* Minneapolis, MN: Free Spirit Publishing.
Faber, A., and Mazlish, E. (1982). *How to Talk So Kids Will Listen and Listen So Kids Will Talk.* New York: Avon.
Ginott, H. (1969). *Between Parent and Teenager.* New York. Macmillan.
Gordon, T. (2000). *Parent Effectiveness Training.* New York: Three Rivers Press.
Greene, R. (1998). *The Explosive Child.* New York: HarperCollins.
Greenspan, S. (1995). *The Challenging Child.* Reading, MA: Perseus Books.
Ilg, F., Ames, L., and Baker, S. (1992). *Child Behavior: The Classic Childcare Manual from the Gesell Institute of Human Development.* New York: Harper Perennial.
Phelan, T. (1995). *1-2-3 Magic: Training Your Preschoolers and Preteens to Do What You Want.* Glen Ellyn, IL: Child Management, Inc.
Renshaw-Joslin, K. (1994). *Positive Parenting from A to Z.* New York: Fawcett Books.
Tracy, F. (1994). *Grounded for Life: Stop Blowing Your Fuse and Start Communicating.* Seattle, WA: Parenting Press.

Turecki, S., and Tonner, L. (1988). *The Difficult Child.* New York: Bantam Books.
Wolf, A. (1992). *Get Out of My Life but First Could You Drive Me and Cheryl to the Mall?: A Parent's Guide to the New Teenager.* New York: Noonday Press.

PHASE OF LIFE PROBLEMS

Alberti, R., and Emmons, M. (2001). *Your Perfect Right: Assertiveness and Equality in Your Life and Relationships.* San Luis Obispo, CA: Impact Publishers, Inc.
Black, J., and Enns, G. (1998). *Better Boundaries: Owning and Treasuring Your Life.* Oakland, CA: New Harbinger Pub.
Bower, S., and Bower, G. (1991). *Asserting Yourself: A Practical Guide for Positive Change.* Cambridge, MA: Perseus Publishing.
Katherine, A. (1993). *Boundaries: Where You End and I Begin.* New York: Fireside Pub.
Paterson, R. (2000). *The Assertiveness Workbook: How to Express Your Ideas and Stand Up for Yourself at Work and in Relationships.* Oakland, CA: New Harbinger Pub.
Simon, S. (1993). *In Search of Values: 31 Strategies for Finding Out What Really Matters Most to You.* New York: Warner Books.
Simon, S., Howe, L., and Kirschenbaum, H. (1995). *Values Clarification.* New York: Warner Books.
Smith, M. (1975). *When I Say No, I Feel Guilty.* New York: Bantam.
Whitfield, C. (1993). *Boundaries and Relationships: Knowing, Protecting, and Enjoying the Self.* Deerfield Beach, FL: Health Communications.

PHOBIA-PANIC/AGORAPHOBIA

Gold, M. (1988). *The Good News About Panic, Anxiety, and Phobias.* New York: Villard/Random House.
Marks, I. (1980). *Living with Fear: Understanding and Coping with Anxiety.* New York: McGraw-Hill.
Swede, S., and Jaffe, S. (1987). *The Panic Attack Recovery Book.* New York: New American Library.
Wilson, R. (1986). *Don't Panic: Taking Control of Anxiety Attacks.* New York: Harper & Row.

POSTTRAUMATIC STRESS DISORDER (PTSD)

Frankel, V. (1959). *Man's Search for Meaning.* Boston: Beacon Press.
Jeffers, S. (1987). *Feel the Fear and Do It Anyway.* New York: Random House.
Leith, L. (1998). *Exercising Your Way to Better Mental Health.* Morgantown, WV: Fitness Information Technology.

Matsakis, A. (1992). *I Can't Get Over It: A Handbook for Trauma Survivors.* Oakland, CA: New Harbinger.

Simon, S., and Simon, S. (1990). *Forgiving: How to Make Peace with Your Past and Get On with Your Life.* New York: Warner Books.

PSYCHOTICISM

Torrey, M. D., and Fuller, E. (1988). *Surviving Schizophrenia: A Family Manual.* New York: Harper & Row.

SEXUAL ABUSE

Bass, E., and Davis, L. (1988). *The Courage to Heal: A Guide for Women Survivors of Child Sexual Abuse.* San Francisco: HarperCollins.

Bradshaw, J. (1988). *Healing the Shame That Binds You.* Deerfield Beach, FL: Health Communications, Inc.

Burns, D. (1993). *Ten Days to Self-Esteem!* New York: William Morrow.

Davis, L. (1990). *The Courage to Heal Workbook: For Men & Women Survivors of Child Sexual Abuse.* San Francisco: HarperCollins.

Forward, S., and Buck, C. (1978). *Betrayal of Innocence: Incest and Its Devastation.* New York: Penguin Books.

Fossum, M. A., and Mason, M. J. (1986). *Facing Shame: Families in Recovery.* New York: Norton.

Gil, E. (1984). *Outgrowing the Pain: A Book for and About Adults Abused as Children.* New York: Dell Publishing.

Kaufman, G. (1992). *Shame: The Power of Caring.* Rochester, VT: Schenkman Books.

Simon, S., and Simon, S. (1990). *Forgiving: How to Make Peace with Your Past and Get On with Your Life.* New York: Warner Books.

Smedes, L. (1991). *Forgive and Forget: Healing the Hurts We Don't Deserve.* San Francisco: Harper.

SEXUAL IDENTITY CONFUSION

Beam, J. (1986). *In the Life: A Black Gay Anthology.* Boston: Alyson Publications.

Eichberg, R. (1991). *Coming Out: An Act of Love.* New York: Penguin.

Katz, J. (1996). *The Invention of Heterosexuality.* New York: Plume.

Marcus, E. (1993). *Is It a Choice? Answers to 300 of the Most Frequently Asked Questions About Gays and Lesbians.* San Francisco: Harper.

Signorile, M. (1996). *Outing Yourself: How to Come Out as Lesbian or Gay to Your Family, Friends, and Coworkers.* New York: Fireside Books.

SLEEP DISTURBANCE

Dotto, L. (1990). *Losing Sleep: How Your Sleeping Habits Affect Your Life.* New York: William Morrow.

Hewish, J. (1985). *Relaxation.* Chicago: NTC Publishing Group.

Leith, L. (1998). *Exercising Your Way to Better Mental Health.* Morgantown, WV: Fitness Information Technology.

SOCIAL DISCOMFORT

Bradshaw, J. (1988). *Healing the Shame That Binds You.* Deerfield Beach, FL: Health Communications, Inc.

Burns, D. (1985). *Intimate Connections: The New Clinically Tested Program for Overcoming Loneliness.* New York: William Morrow.

Burns, D. (1993). *Ten Days to Self-Esteem!* New York: William Morrow.

Burns, D. (1989). *The Feeling Good Handbook.* New York: William Morrow.

Dyer, W. (1978). *Pulling Your Own Strings.* New York: T. Crowell.

Fossum, M. A., and Mason, M. J. (1986). *Facing Shame: Families in Recovery.* New York. Norton.

Harris, T. (1996). *I'm OK You're OK.* New York: Avon.

James, M., and Jongeward, D. (1971). *Born to Win.* Reading, MA: Addison-Wesley, Inc.

Nouwen, H. (1975). *Reaching Out.* New York: Doubleday.

Zimbardo, P. (1987). *Shyness: What It Is and What to Do About It.* Reading, MA: Addison-Wesley.

SOMATIZATION

Benson, H. (1980). *The Mind-Body Effect.* New York: Simon & Schuster.

Grateful Members of Emotional Health Anonymous. (1987). *The Twelve Steps for Everyone . . . Who Really Wants Them.* Minneapolis, MN: CompCare.

SPIRITUAL CONFUSION

Armstrong, K. (1993). *A History of God.* New York: Alfred A. Knopf.

Augustine, St. (1949). *The Confessions of St. Augustine.* New York: Random House.

Cleaver, E. (1992). *The Soul on Fire.* Grand Rapids, MI: Zondervan.

Foster, R. (1988). *Celebration of Discipline.* San Francisco: Harper.

Helmfelt, R., and Fowler, R. (1990). *Serenity: A Companion for 12 Step Recovery.* Nashville, TN: Nelson.

Keen, S. (1994). *Hymns to an Unknown God.* New York: Bantam Books.

Lewis, C. S. (1955). *Surprised by Joy.* New York: Harcourt Brace & Co.

Merton, T. (1948). *The Seven Storey Mountain.* New York: Harcourt Brace.

Miles, J. (1995). *God: A Biography.* New York: Alfred A. Knopf.

Moore, T. (1992). *The Care of the Soul.* New York: Harper Collins.

Norris, K. (1996). *The Cloister Walk.* New York: Riverhead Books.

Peck, M. S. (1978). *The Road Less Traveled.* New York: Simon & Schuster.

Peck, M. S. (1993). *Further Along the Road Less Traveled.* New York: Simon & Schuster.

Presnall, L. (1959). *Search for Serenity: and How to Achieve It.* Salt Lake City, UT: V.A.F. Publishing.

SUICIDAL IDEATION

Butler, P. (1991). *Talking to Yourself: Learning the Language of Self-Affirmation.* New York: Stein and Day.

Hutschnecker, A. (1951). *The Will to Live.* New York: Cornerstone Library.

Seligman, M. (1990). *Learned Optimism: The Skill to Conquer Life's Obstacles, Large and Small.* New York: Pocket Books.

TYPE A BEHAVIOR

Friedman, M., and Ulmer, P. (1984). *Treating Type A Behavior and Your Heart.* New York: Alfred A. Knopf.

Glasser, W. (1976). *Positive Addiction.* San Francisco: HarperCollins.

Peck, M. S. (1978). *The Road Less Traveled.* New York: Simon & Schuster.

Peck, M. S. (1993). *Further Along the Road Less Traveled.* New York: Simon & Schuster.

Pirsig, R. (1974). *Zen and the Art of Motorcycle Maintenance.* New York: William Morrow.

Robinson, B. (1993). *Overdoing It.* Deerfield Beach, FL: Health Communications, Inc.

VOCATIONAL STRESS

Bolles, R. (1992). *What Color Is Your Parachute?* Berkeley, CA: Ten-Speed Press.

Charland, R. (1993). *Career Shifting: Starting Over in a Changing Economy.* Holbrook, MA: Bob Adams.

Jandt, F. (1985). *Win-Win Negotiating: Turning Conflict into Agreement.* New York: John Wiley & Sons, Inc.

Weiss, R. (1990). *Staying the Course: The Emotional and Social Lives of Men Who Do Well at Work.* New York: Free Press.

Appendix C

INDEX OF *DSM-IV-TR*™ CODES ASSOCIATED WITH PRESENTING PROBLEMS

Academic Problem   **V62.3**
   Educational Deficits

Acute Stress Disorder   **308.3**
   Posttraumatic Stress Disorder
      (PTSD)

Adjustment Disorder   **309.xx**
   Posttraumatic Stress
      Disorder (PTSD)

Adjustment Disorder
With Anxiety   **309.24**
   Anxiety
   Intimate Relationship Conflicts
   Medical Issues
   Phase of Life Problems
   Sexual Identity Confusion—Adult
   Vocational Stress

Adjustment Disorder
With Depressed Mood   **309.0**
   Depression
   Grief/Loss Unresolved
   Intimate Relationship Conflicts
   Medical Issues
   Phase of Life Problems
   Sexual Identity Confusion—Adult
   Vocational Stress

Adjustment Disorder
With Disturbance of Conduct   **309.3**
   Antisocial Behavior

   Grief/Loss Unresolved
   Legal Conflicts
   Medical Issues
   Parenting

Adjustment Disorder
With Mixed Anxiety
and Depressed Mood   **309.28**
   Medical Issues
   Phase of Life Problems
   Sexual Identity Confusion—Adult

Adjustment Disorder With
Mixed Disturbance of
Emotions and Conduct   **309.4**
   Medical Issues
   Parenting

Adult Antisocial Behavior   **V71.01**
   Chemical Dependence
   Legal Conflicts

Agoraphobia Without
History of Panic Disorder   **300.22**
   Phobia-Panic/Agoraphobia

Alcohol Abuse   **305.00**
   Attention-Deficit Disorder
      (ADD)—Adult
   Chemical Dependence
   Chemical Dependence—Relapse
   Posttraumatic Stress Disorder
      (PTSD)

Alcohol Dependence   **303.90**
  Antisocial Behavior
  Attention-Deficit Disorder (ADD)—
    Adult
  Chemical Dependence
  Chemical Dependence—Relapse
  Cognitive Deficits
  Family Conflict
  Legal Conflicts
  Obsessive-Compulsive Disorder
    (OCD)
  Posttraumatic Stress Disorder
    (PTSD)
  Sexual Abuse
  Vocational Stress

Alcohol-Induced Persisting
Amnestic Disorder   **291.1**
  Chemical Dependence
  Chemical Dependence—Relapse
  Cognitive Deficits

Alcohol-Induced Persisting
Dementia   **291.2**
  Chemical Dependence
  Cognitive Deficits

Amnestic Disorder Due to
Axis III Disorder   **294.0**
  Cognitive Deficits

Amnestic Disorder NOS   **294.8**
  Cognitive Deficits

Anorexia Nervosa   **307.1**
  Eating Disorder

Antisocial Personality
Disorder   **301.7**
  Antisocial Behavior
  Chemical Dependence
  Chemical Dependence—Relapse
  Childhood Traumas
  Family Conflict
  Financial Stress
  Impulse Control Disorder
  Legal Conflicts
  Parenting
  Vocational Stress

Anxiety Disorder NOS   **300.00**
  Anxiety

  Family Conflict
  Intimate Relationship Conflicts
  Medical Issues
  Obsessive-Compulsive Disorder
    (OCD)
  Sexual Identity Confusion—Adult
  Spiritual Confusion

Attention-Deficit/Hyperactivity
Disorder, Combined Type   **314.01**
  Parenting

Attention-Deficit/Hyperactivity
Disorder NOS   **314.9**
  Attention-Deficit Disorder (ADD)—
    Adult

Attention-Deficit/Hyperactivity
Disorder, Predominantly
Hyperactive-Impulsive
Type   **314.01**
  Attention-Deficit Disorder (ADD)—
    Adult

Attention-Deficit/Hyperactivity
Disorder, Predominantly
Inattentive Type   **314.00**
  Attention-Deficit Disorder (ADD)—
    Adult

Avoidant Personality
Disorder   **301.82**
  Dependency
  Obsessive-Compulsive Disorder
    (OCD)
  Sexual Abuse
  Sexual Identity Confusion—Adult
  Social Discomfort

Bereavement   **V62.82**
  Depression
  Grief/Loss Unresolved

Bipolar Disorder NOS   **296.80**
  Mania or Hypomania

Bipolar I Disorder   **296.xx**
  Attention-Deficit Disorder (ADD)—
    Adult
  Depression
  Low Self-Esteem
  Mania or Hypomania

Schizophrenia   295.xx
    Psychoticism

Schizophrenia, Paranoid
Type   295.30
    Paranoid Ideation
    Psychoticism

Schizophreniform Disorder   295.40
    Psychoticism

Schizotypal Personality
Disorder   310.22
    Paranoid Ideation
    Social Discomfort

Sedative, Hypnotic, or
Anxiolytic Dependence   304.10
    Chemical Dependence
    Chronic Pain
    Obsessive-Compulsive Disorder
      (OCD)

Sexual Abuse of Adult
(*if focus of clinical attention*
***is on the victim*)**   995.83
    Posttraumatic Stress Disorder
      (PTSD)
    Sexual Abuse

Sexual Abuse of Child   V61.21
    Parenting

Sexual Abuse of Child
(*if focus of clinical attention*
***is on the victim*)**   995.53
    Childhood Traumas
    Female Sexual Dysfunction
    Male Sexual Dysfunction
    Posttraumatic Stress Disorder
      (PTSD)
    Sexual Abuse

Sexual Aversion Disorder   302.79
    Female Sexual Dysfunction
    Male Sexual Dysfunction

Sexual Disorder NOS   302.9
    Sexual Identity Confusion—Adult

Sexual Dysfunction NOS   302.70
    Chronic Pain
    Female Sexual Dysfunction
    Male Sexual Dysfunction

Sleep Terror Disorder   307.46
    Sleep Disturbance

Sleepwalking Disorder   307.46
    Sleep Disturbance

Social Phobia   300.23
    Low Self-Esteem
    Paranoid Ideation
    Social Discomfort

Somatization Disorder   300.81
    Chronic Pain
    Somatization

Specific Phobia   300.29
    Phobia-Panic/Agoraphobia

Trichotillomania   312.39
    Impulse Control Disorder

Undifferentiated Somatoform
Disorder   300.81
    Somatization

Vaginismus (Not Due to a
Medical Condition)   306.51
    Female Sexual Dysfunction